Christian
SPIRITUALITY

D0796567

Christian
SPIRITUALITY
An Introduction

ALISTER E. McGRATH

Blackwell
Publishing

© 1999 by Alister E. McGrath

350 Main Street, Malden, MA 02148-5020, USA
108 Cowley Road, Oxford OX4 1JF, UK
550 Swanston Street, Carlton, Victoria 3053, Australia

The right of Alister E. McGrath to be identified as the Author of this Work has been
asserted in accordance with the UK Copyright, Designs, and Patents Act 1988.

All rights reserved. No part of this publication may be reproduced, stored in a
retrieval system, or transmitted, in any form or by any means, electronic, mechanical,
photocopying, recording or otherwise, except as permitted by the UK Copyright,
Designs, and Patents Act 1988, without the prior permission of the publisher.

First published 1999 by Blackwell Publishing Ltd
Reprinted 2000 (twice), 2001, 2002, 2003, 2004

Library of Congress Cataloging-in-Publication Data

McGrath, Alister E., 1953–
    Christian spirituality: an introduction / Alister E. McGrath.
        p.cm
    Includes bibliographical references and index.
    ISBN 0–631–21280–9 (alk. paper) — ISBN 0–631–21281–7 (pbk. : alk. paper)
    1. Spirituality. I. Title.
    BV4501.2.M2357 1999
    248—dc21   98-33147
                                                        CIP

A catalogue record for this title is available from the British Library.

Set in 10 on 12.5 pt Galliard
by Best-set Typesetter Ltd, Hong Kong
Printed and bound in the United Kingdom
by MPG Books Ltd, Bodmin, Cornwall

For further information on
Blackwell Publishing, visit our website:
http://www.blackwellpublishing.com

CONTENTS

CONTENTS

CONTENTS

ACKNOWLEDGEMENTS

The author and publishers would like to thank the following for permission to reproduce material in this book:

Saint Augustine, *Confessions,* translated by Henry Chadwick. Oxford: Oxford University Press, 1991; copyright © Henry Chadwick 1991, reproduced by permission of Oxford University Press.

The Prayers and Meditations of St Anselm, translated by Benedicta Ward, Penguin Classics, 1973; copyright © Benedicta Ward, 1973, reproduced by permission of Penguin Books.

Revelations of Divine Love, Julian of Norwich, translated by Clifton Wolters, Penguin Classics, 1966; copyright © Clifton Wolters 1966, reproduced by permission of Penguin Books.

How to Use this Book

This book is an introduction to Christian spirituality, probably one of the most fascinating subjects anyone can study. It assumes little knowledge of the subject, apart from a basic familiarity with some aspects of Christianity, and aims to explain as much as possible. By the end of this book, you should be able to move on to more advanced studies of the subject, including detailed study of some of the classic primary texts of Christian spirituality. It will enable to you get far more than you otherwise might out of lectures on the subject, and encourage you to take the subject further.

This book is subtitled: "An Introduction." Those two words need to be noted carefully, as they indicate the restrictions under which the work operates. Like all introductions to any subject, this book has its limits. There is not enough space to go into some subjects in the detail and depth that they deserve. Many issues that clearly ought to be discussed have had to be omitted, due to lack of space. At times, complex issues have been simplified somewhat, with the needs of those beginning the study of the subject in mind. These issues merit much deeper analysis than is possible within the limited space of this work. Unless a much larger work were to be written, there is little that can be done to remedy these weaknesses. The work attempts to remedy them by identifying suitable works for further study, to allow you to develop your thinking about any matter that interests you. The work aims simply to introduce you to its subject, and then to allow you to pass on to more advanced, specialized, detailed, and stimulating works. You will be able to make much better use of these, and gain far much more from them, if you have worked through the material provided in this introduction.

Most introductions to Christian spirituality take the form of historical surveys, which set out the main approaches to the subject that have evolved down the ages.

Although there is some historical material in the text, this approach has generally been avoided as too didactic and not sufficiently engaging. This book aims to equip you to engage with the great spiritual riches of the Christian tradition, and it does so by introducing you to some of the great themes and texts of that tradition and encouraging and enabling you to engage with it. The climax of this work is its final chapter, which sets out ways of getting the most out of reading classic texts. The work adopts an approach which is designed to encourage and assist the *active engagement* (rather than just passive reading) of classic texts. Although only a small selection of texts are treated in this manner, the general approach can be transferred to any text you wish to study.

In addition to these texts in the final chapter, the work makes extensive use of primary sources at other points. These are intended to encourage you to read and explore primary sources. These texts are sourced, so that you can consider following them through in greater detail at a later stage. A wide range of resources are used in this work, including Catholic, Orthodox, Protestant, and evangelical writers. The aim is to offer an overview of Christian spirituality which reflects its rich diversity, yet at the same time identifies some of its common themes. The work does not advocate any one specific form of Christian spirituality, but aims to enable its readers to gain a firm understanding and appreciation of the many traditions represented within its ample scope.

I must acknowledge the help of many others during the long process of planning and writing. This book had its origins in a series of lectures given in 1990 at Drew University, Madison, New Jersey, on "Reformation Spirituality," which gave me the opportunity to wrestle with the origins and styles of the new forms of spirituality which came into being in the sixteenth century. My thinking on how the subject could best be taught was stimulated by my experience of teaching Christian spirituality at the annual six-week summer school organized by the Centre for Medieval and Renaissance Studies at Oxford over the period 1992–8. I owe an enormous debt to the hundreds of students attending those weekly seminars who helped me evaluate a range of approaches to the subject, and identify suitable texts for engagement. I am also deeply grateful to many colleagues at Oxford, particularly Carolyn Headley, and elsewhere for invaluable discussions on the nature and scope of Christian spirituality, and particularly the difficulties encountered in teaching the subject.

I also gratefully acknowledge the kindness of librarians at the Bodleian Library, the Taylorian Institute, and several colleges of Oxford University in tracing rare primary and secondary sources. Blackwell Publishers have been all that a good publisher should have been, and more, both in terms of encouraging this author and arranging for generous market-testing of the work. Both the publisher and the author welcome comments on this work, which will be invaluable in revising it for future editions.

Alister McGrath
Oxford, September 1998

1

INTRODUCTION

There has been a remarkable growth in interest in the general area of spirituality in recent years. A resurgent cynicism concerning the value of material possessions has led to much greater attention being paid to the spiritual dimensions of life. A growing body of evidence suggests that personal spirituality has a positive therapeutic effect on individuals, pointing to an increasing recognition of the importance of spirituality to human fulfillment and well-being. Alongside a gradual general decline in appeal of institutionalized forms of religion in western culture, there has been a clear rise in popular interest in spirituality, including the various forms of Christian spirituality. This work aims to serve as an introduction to these specifically Christian forms of spirituality.

In this brief opening chapter, we shall explore something of what is understood by the term "spirituality" in general, before moving on to consider what is meant by the more specific term "Christian spirituality." This introductory chapter is intended simply to clarify some of the terms used in the discussion of Christian spirituality, before moving on to engage with the subject in more detail in the following chapters. To stress the introductory nature of this chapter, we shall adopt a "work-book" approach. This has the merit of encouraging engagement with the material, and will be used more extensively in the final chapter.

Defining "Spirituality"

The word "spirituality" draws on the Hebrew word *ruach* – a rich term usually translated as "spirit," yet which includes a range of meanings including "spirit," yet extending to "breath" and "wind." To talk about "the spirit" is to discuss what gives life and animation to someone. "Spirituality" is thus about the life of faith – what drives and motivates it, and what people find helpful in sustaining and developing it. It is about that which animates the life of believers, and urges them on to deepen and perfect what has at present only been begun.

Spirituality is the outworking in real life of a person's religious faith – what a person *does* with what they believe. It is not just about ideas, although the basic ideas of the Christian faith are important to Christian spirituality. It is about the way in which the Christian life is conceived and lived out. It is about the full apprehension of the reality of God. We could summarize much of this by saying that Christian spirituality is reflection on the whole Christian enterprise of achieving and sustaining a relationship with God, which includes both public worship and private devotion, and the results of these in actual Christian life.

A Basic Definition of "Spirituality"

Spirituality concerns the quest for a fulfilled and authentic religious life, involving the bringing together of the ideas distinctive of that religion and the whole experience of living on the basis of and within the scope of that religion.

A Basic Definition of "Christian Spirituality"

Christian spirituality concerns the quest for a fulfilled and authentic Christian existence, involving the bringing together of the fundamental ideas of Christianity and the whole experience of living on the basis of and within the scope of the Christian faith.

The term "spirituality" has gained wide acceptance in the recent past as the preferred way of referring to aspects of the devotional practices of a religion, and especially the interior individual experiences of believers. It is often contrasted with a purely academic, objective or detached approach to a religion, which is seen as merely identifying and listing the key beliefs and practices of a religion, rather than dealing with the manner in which individual adherents of the religion experience and practise their faith. The term is resistant to precise definition, partly due to the variety of senses in which the term is used, and partly due to controversy within the community of scholars specializing in the field over the manner in which the term ought to be used. The definition provided above is an attempt to help students to get a broad idea of the nature and scope of the subject, and should not be regarded as the only way of defining it.

Defining "Christian Spirituality"

Having examined the word "spirituality," we may now move on and consider the more precise term "Christian spirituality," which has already been used in a loose sense. For Christianity, spirituality concerns the living out of the encounter with Jesus

Christ. The term "Christian spirituality" refers to the way in which the Christian life is understood and the explicitly devotional practices which have been developed to foster and sustain that relationship with Christ. Christian spirituality may be thus understood as the way in which Christian individuals or groups aim to deepen their experience of God, or to "practise the presence of God," to use a phrase especially associated with Brother Lawrence (c.1614–91).

It is helpful to think of Christianity as having three main elements.

1   *A set of beliefs.* Although there are differences between Christians on a number of doctrinal matters, it is relatively easy to show that a common core of beliefs lies behind the different versions of Christianity. These are set out in the Creeds of Christianity, which are accepted as statements of faith by all the main Christian churches. These beliefs have a significant impact on the way in which Christians live.

2   *A set of values.* Christianity is a strongly ethical faith. This does not, however, mean that Christianity is about a set of rules, in which Christians mechanically conform to a set of instructions. Rather, it is about a set of values which arises from being redeemed, such as loving other people and a willingness to deny oneself. These values are strongly linked with the character of Jesus of Nazareth, who is regarded by Christians as both the basis of the life of faith and the supreme example of a life lived in close fellowship with God. A spirit-filled life would thus be expected to reflect and embody Christian values.

3   *A way of life.* Being a Christian is not just about beliefs and values; it is about real life, in which those ideas and values are expressed and embodied in a definite way of living. The everyday life of believers is affected in certain ways by their faith. At its most obvious, this is reflected in going to a church or other form of Christian community which meets for prayer and worship. There are enormous variations in the ways in which Christianity expresses itself, reflecting differences of climate, geography, culture, tradition, and theology. Part of this way of life is the general area which has come to be known as "spirituality," and which is the subject of this book.

At this point, you will find it helpful to look at some working definitions of spirituality offered by respected authors in this area. You will find it helpful to read each

---

Some Working Definitions of "Spirituality"

Spirituality is a lived experience, the effort to apply relevant elements in the deposit of Christian faith to the guidance of men and women towards their spiritual growth, the progressive development of their persons which flowers into a proportionately increased insight and joy.
George Ganss, "Introduction" to *Ignatius of Loyola*, p. 61.

Spirituality has to do with our experiencing of God and with the transformation of our consciousness and our lives as outcomes of that experience.
Richard O'Brien, *Catholicism*, p. 1058.

> Spirituality refers to a *lived* experience and a disciplined life of prayer and action, but it cannot be conceived apart from the specific theological beliefs that are ingredients in the forms of life that manifest authentic Christian faith.
> **Don E. Saliers, "Spirituality," p. 460.**
>
> [Spirituality] is a useful term to describe how, individually and collectively, we personally appropriate the traditional Christian beliefs about God, humanity and the world, and express them in terms of our basic attitudes, life-style and activity.
> **Philip Sheldrake, *Images of Holiness* p. 2.**
>
> Whatever else may be affirmed about a spirituality which has a biblical precedent and style, spiritual maturity or spiritual fulfillment necessarily involves the *whole* person – body, mind and soul, place, relationships – in connection with the whole of creation throughout the era of time. Biblical spirituality encompasses the whole person in the totality of existence in the world, not some fragment or scrap or incident of a person.
> **William Stringfellow, *Politics of Spirituality*, p. 22.**
>
> [Spirituality] is the self-transcending character of all human persons, and everything that pertains to it, including, most importantly, the ways in which that perhaps infinitely malleable character is realized concretely in everyday life situations.
> **Richard Woods, *Christian Spirituality*, p. 9.**

definition twice, and reflect on the main points the author is attempting to convey. At this point, you should pause, and write down the points which seem to be important to these writers as they attempt to define or describe "spirituality." You may find that you disagree with some of the points which they make, but the points are helpful in clarifying the general nature of spirituality. Ask yourself what particular point each author is concerned to emphasize, and how this helps gain an understanding of the nature of spirituality.

Now look at each of the bulleted points below. Each states a theme of importance to spirituality. How do these brief statements help us understand what spirituality is? And in what ways do they help us clarify the distinction between spirituality and Christian doctrine?

- Knowing God, not just knowing about God.
- Experiencing God to the full.
- Transformation of existence on the basis of the Christian faith.
- Attaining Christian authenticity in life and thought.

You may find it helpful to relate these to the working definitions which we have just been considering.

Now consider the following words of an American Protestant professor of theology, explaining to his readers why he chose to spend three months in a Trappist monastery, high up in the Rockies. He regarded himself as an atheist; someone who knew about what theologians were saying, but had no personal experience of God. Read his words, and then turn to the questions that follow.

I am a theologian – I spend my life reading, teaching, thinking, writing about God. But I must be honest – *I have never experienced God*, not really. I am embarrassed by piety; I am ill at ease with those who thrive on God-talk; I have no awareness of what one might mean by the "presence of God."

Look again at the bulleted points set out earlier. Which of these does this passage best illustrate? And how does it relate to the definitions of spirituality which were set out earlier?

Now note how the passage clearly supposes that it is possible to be a theologian without any experience of God. What does this suggest about the relation between theology and spirituality? And what does it suggest about the place of spirituality in theological education?

We shall be exploring these issues in greater depth later in this work; at this early stage, it is important just to be aware of them. We now turn to clarify the vocabulary used in relation to spirituality, before beginning a detailed engagement with its themes in the following chapter.

Clarifying Terms: Mysticism and Spirituality

We need to consider a term which has been used extensively in the past to designate the general area of spirituality – "mysticism." Although this word continues to be used, especially within Catholic and Orthodox circles, it is gradually being displaced by the term "spirituality." In this section, we shall explore how the term "mysticism" came to be used in this context, and the reasons why it is gradually being superseded in general use.

The use of the word "mystical" to refer to the spiritual (as opposed to purely academic) dimension of theology can be traced back to the treatise *On Mystical Theology*, written in the early sixth century by Dionysius the Areopagite. The modern terms "spirituality" and "mysticism" both trace their origins back to seventeenth-century France, and specifically in the rather elitist circles of salon society associated with Madame de Guyon. The French terms *spiritualité* and *mysticisme* were both used to refer to direct interior knowledge of the divine or supernatural, and were apparently treated as more or less synonymous at the time. Since then, both terms have been brought back into circulation.

Some degree of confusion has arisen over their precise meaning, with some writers suggesting that the two are just different ways of speaking about an authentic personal relationship with God, while others suggest that mysticism is to be seen as a special type of spirituality which places particular emphasis on a direct personal experience of God. The present work avoids the use of the term "mysticism," believing that it has become unhelpful and confusing to those beginning the study of spirituality. The term "spirituality" is thus used in preference to many terms which are encountered in older writings, including "mystical theology," "spiritual theology," and "mysticism."

The term "mysticism" (and related terms such as "mystical" and "mystic") means very different things to different people. This can be confusing and unhelpful, especially in discussions of Christian spirituality. The three senses of the word are identified below.

1   Mysticism is an approach to the Christian faith which places particular emphasis upon the relational, spiritual, or experiential aspects of the faith, as opposed to the more cognitive or intellectual aspects, which are traditionally assigned to the field of theology. The Protestant reformer John Calvin (1509–64), who is noted for his theological precision, had no difficulty in using the term *unio mystica* ("mystical union") to refer to the relationship between Christ and the individual believer, but understands this to refer to being united with Christ and sharing in his life and benefits. Some writers therefore contrast "mystical theology" (which deals with the existential or relational aspects of Christian thought) with "dogmatic theology," which focuses on the distinctive ideas of the Christian faith. On the basis of this understanding of the term, a "mystic" or "mystical writer" is a Christian who deals primarily with the experiencing of God and with the transformation of the religious consciousness. In the present study, the term "spiritual writer" is used as equivalent to "mystic," and "spirituality" to refer to "mystical theology" in the specific sense of the terms, noted above.

2   In everyday language, mysticism is an approach to spiritual issues, found in religious and non-religious contexts, which stresses inner experience and correspondingly marginalizes or rejects any use of cognitive approaches to spirituality. In this sense of the word, mysticism denotes potentially irrational and anti-intellectual approaches to experience, often regarding apparent contradiction as a virtue. "Mysticism," on this understanding of the word, would mean "concerned with esoteric teachings, enhanced psychological awareness, or exotic sensory experience."

3   Mysticism is used to refer to certain specific schools of Christian spirituality, including the "English mystics" of the fourteenth century (such as Richard Rolle and Walter Hilton) and the "German mystics" of the later Middle Ages (such as Meister Eckhart and Johannes Tauler). Although this usage has become widespread, it is somewhat misleading. First, the writers in question do not use this term to refer to themselves; second, the term implies that their outlook is defined by "mysticism" as defined in sense (2) above, which is often a misrepresentation of their concerns and emphases. Given the widespread use of the term to refer to these medieval schools of spirituality, it is probably impossible to reverse the trend. However, its drawbacks need to be noted and taken into account.

The difficulty in using the term "mysticism" to refer to what is now more widely known as "spirituality" is that the term has so many unhelpful associations and misleading overtones that its continued use is problematic. For this reason, the terms "spirituality" and "spiritual writer" are now to be preferred, and have passed into general use within Christian discussion of the subject. The present work adopts and endorses this convention.

This brief introduction to the discipline of Christian spirituality has raised the question of the various types of spirituality which can be identified. In the following chapter, we shall explore the diversity of Christian spiritualities in more detail.

FOR FURTHER READING

The following are useful introductions to the field of Christian spirituality. Although drawn from a wide variety of perspectives, they illuminate many of the themes of this introductory chapter.

Lawrence S. Cunningham and Keith J. Egan, *Christian Spirituality: Themes from the Tradition*. New York: Paulist, 1996.

Michael Downey (ed.), *The New Dictionary of Christian Spirituality*. Collegeville, MN: Liturgical Press, 1993.

George Ganss, *Ignatius of Loyola: Exercises and Selected Works*. New York: Paulist, 1991.

Bradley C. Holt, *Thirsty for God: A Brief History of Christian Spirituality*. Minneapolis: Augsburg, 1993.

Cheslyn Jones, Geoffrey Wainwright and Edward Yarnold (eds), *The Study of Spirituality*. London: SPCK, 1986.

Richard McBrien, *Catholicism*, new edn. San Francisco: HarperCollins, 1994.

John Macquarrie, *Paths in Spirituality*, 2nd edn. Harrisburg: Morehouse, 1992.

William Reiser, *Looking for a God to Pray To: Christian Spirituality in Transition*. New York: Paulist, 1994.

Don E. Saliers, "Spirituality," in D. Musser and J. Price (eds), *A New Handbook of Christian Theology*. Nashville: Abingdon, 1992.

Philip Sheldrake, *Images of Holiness: Explorations in Contemporary Spirituality*. Notre Dame, IN: Ave Maria, 1988.

William Stringfellow, *The Politics of Spirituality*. Philadelphia: Westminster Press, 1984.

Dennis E. Tamburello, *Union with Christ: John Calvin and the Mysticism of St. Bernard*. St Louis, KY: Westminster John Knox Press, 1994.

Rowan Williams, *The Wound of Knowledge: Christian Spirituality from the New Testament to St John of the Cross*. London: DLT, 1991.

Richard Woods, *Christian Spirituality: God's Presence through the Ages*. Allen, TX: Christian Classics, 1996.

2

TYPES OF CHRISTIAN SPIRITUALITY

The use of the term "Christian spirituality" might seem to suggest that there is a single, well-defined entity of this name. In fact, Christianity is a complex and diverse religion. Although there is widely agreed to be a "core" of Christian beliefs, summarized in widely-accepted documents such as the Apostles' Creed, there is a significant degree of divergence within Christianity over the interpretation of some foundational beliefs, and especially the forms of church order and life which are appropriate for Christians. In addition, individual characteristics on the part of Christians lead to divergences in spiritual preferences. Given the wide variety of spiritualities which are encountered in Christian history, it clearly makes sense to attempt to gain some sense of the types which are to be found.

One factor of major importance is the basic beliefs of the individual or community. Theology has a profound impact upon spirituality. The importance of this issue is such that it demands that two chapters of this work have been devoted to exploring its contours (see chapters 3 and 4). However, the following factors are also of major importance in shaping spirituality.

1   *Personal issues.* Individual Christians have different backgrounds, personalities, locations on sociological maps, in addition to having slightly different "takes" on the major themes of the Christian faith. The issue of personality is thus of considerable importance in relation to spirituality.

2   *Denominational considerations.* Different Christian communities have significantly different understandings of the nature of the Christian life, and are often linked with theological emphases or teachings which distinguish them from other

such groupings. It is therefore of importance to gain at least a basic understanding of the different types of Christianity present in the modern world.

3 *Attitudes to the World, Culture, and History.* Some forms of spirituality are strongly world-renouncing, arguing that Christian authenticity demands withdrawal from the everyday world; others argue that authentic Christianity can only be found by engaging with the world. It is important to appreciate that these distinctions cut across denominational boundaries. For example, some forms of Protestantism are strongly world-affirming, where others seek to renounce the world, especially its attitudes to power and economics. Being a Protestant (or belonging to any other denomination, for that matter) does not automatically entail a positive or negative attitude to the world.

The present chapter will explore these three general factors, after which we shall move on to a more sustained engagement with the complex and important issue of theological foundations for spirituality.

Spirituality, Theology, and Personality

Christian spirituality can be thought of as the attempt to bring into contact and correlate a set of theological beliefs on the one hand with a very specific set of personal and institutional factors on the other. In making this assertion, I am not arguing for the priority of either theology or experience; some begin from theology, and attempt to correlate this with their personal experience; others find that their experience raises questions and issues which require to be informed by theological reflection. The point is that it is this *process of correlation* which is of central importance within spirituality. Spirituality is not something that is deduced totally from theological presuppositions, nor is it something which is inferred totally from our experience. It arises from a creative and dynamic synthesis of faith and life, forged in the crucible of the desire to live out the Christian faith authentically, responsibly, effectively, and fully.

We could perhaps explore this process in terms of the concept of "the fusion of horizons," which is so characteristic a theme in the writings of the noted German philosopher Hans-Georg Gadamer (1900–) in relation to the issue of textual interpretation and application. Gadamer argues that there is a need to allow the "horizon" of the text and the "horizon" of the individual's situation to be correlated. In the same manner, there is a need for the "horizon" of the individual's world of experience to be brought into relation with the themes of Christian theology.

It will therefore be clear that a substantial range of "spiritualities" is to be expected, reflecting a set of differing (though clearly related) theological assumptions on the one hand, and the remarkable variety of personal and institutional circumstances which have existed throughout Christian history on the other. We may illustrate this point by considering some of the variables on each side of the process of correlation.

Theological variables

The term "Christian theology" refers to a set of ideas which are recognizably grounded in the Christian tradition, having its origins in the Bible and maintained and developed in the process of reflection, interpretation and transmission within the community of faith. Although there are certain themes which are found within all recognizably Christian theologies (such as the idea that Jesus Christ is the final self-revelation of God), there are important variations between different types of Christian theology. Some examples of such differences will illustrate the potential for diversity within spirituality.

1   A significantly different attitude to Mary, the "mother of God," is to be found within different Christian traditions. Broadly speaking, the Catholic and Orthodox traditions place considerable emphasis upon the role of Mary, whereas Protestants do not. One clear consequence of this divergence is the virtual absence of any form of Marian devotion within Protestantism.
2   A wide range of viewpoints can be identified within Christianity concerning the nature and significance of the sacraments. Some Christians regard the sacraments as signs of God's grace, helpful reminders of something that they already know about. Others see them as signs of the real presence of God within the world, and a powerful affirmation of the divine presence within the created order. Once more, this has potential implications for spirituality – not simply in terms of the role which the sacraments play in personal devotion, but also in terms of how God is understood to be present and active in the world.
3   One of the most noticable features of Christian history is that groups and individuals who may share a common theological foundation chose to place their emphasis on different aspects of that theology. Thus some Christians place considerable emphasis on the saving work of Christ, where others prefer to think of the doctrine of the incarnation (which we shall explore more fully later: see p. 54) as having supreme importance. The same set of theological beliefs might be affirmed, yet with differing understandings concerning which of those beliefs is of supreme importance.

We shall be exploring some further aspects of the interaction of theology and spirituality later in this work.

Historical variables

Although this work has avoided the purely historical approach to spirituality which characterizes so many introductions to the subject, this does not mean that history is of no importance to the study of spirituality. History determines one's personal location, and the options which are available. A simple consideration will make this point clear. Most western Christians are well used to the idea of reading their Bibles, either through membership of a study group, for personal devotion, or following a passage as it is read out in church. Yet this is a possibility which depends upon two specific historical circumstances:

1 The widespread availability of Bibles;
2 The ability to read.

If we were to travel back in time to western Europe a millennium earlier, neither of these circumstances would have applied. Bibles were simply not widely available (in that the technology of printing was still centuries away). And literacy was at a very low level. It is thus perhaps little cause for surprise that biblically-focused forms of spirituality were largely found within monasteries, where copyists provided the texts of biblical books (often beautifully illustrated), and levels of literacy were vastly superior to those found in society as a whole.

An understanding of the historical situation of a spiritual writer is essential to grasping her importance. History defines one's horizons, by limiting the resources available. The present book does not focus on the history of spirituality; nevertheless, you are strongly encouraged to read about this if you intend to take the study of spirituality further. It is essential to appreciate that the historical situation of both the writer and reader plays a major role in relation to the personal spiritual value which the reader finds in the a text. We shall explore this matter again in the final chapter of this work, as we consider how to engage with classic texts from the past.

Personal variables

As we noted above, the personal situation of the individual or group is also of considerable importance in relation to spirituality. Factors which affect the type of spirituality which an individual finds most helpful include issues which could be described as aesthetic, psychological, and sociological. Examples of these factors include the following.

1 There is widespread disagreement over what constitutes "beauty" in art, architecture, music, and the spoken or written word. Many Christians believe passionately that the most appropriate response to the beauty of God is to worship and praise God using the most beautiful language, music, and architecture possible. Yet there is no agreement as to exactly what these forms should be. Thus some find that spirituality is assisted by Baroque architecture and church music; others prefer the simplicity of open-air worship with simple folk tunes. Issues of personal taste play a major role in spirituality, and cannot be predetermined by theological considerations.
2 Some individuals are very "verbal" in their thinking, and prefer to think of God conceptually. Others (possibly the majority) find that they need images or mental pictures to help them in both their thinking and devotion. For the former, spirituality might be best assisted by good sermons and helpful books. For the latter, however, good images are of central importance to spirituality. For example, the use of illuminated images in "Books of Hours" or works of religious art in churches does not simply reflect an interest in beautification. It represents a response to the recognition that many people require images or "visual aids" for the purposes of devotion and reflection. Once more, an issue which is more

psychological than theological can be seen to have a major potential impact on the area of spirituality.

3   The situations in which individuals find themselves vary enormously. For example, the situations faced by a monk in medieval France, an upper-class widow in eighteenth-century England, and a wealthy financier in 1980s New York are radically different. Each situation is limited in different manners, and offers different opportunities for practising the Christain faith.

Alongside these aesthetic and other such considerations must be set the great issues of gender, class, and race. It must be pointed out that these factors interconnect, making it extremely problematic to isolate them as determinative individually. In what follows, we shall simply note some of the points which need to be borne in mind.

1   Issues of gender are of considerable importance to spirituality, even though there continues to be debate over the nature and extent of the differences between the genders. At one level, this is reflected in the language used to conceive and refer to God: for example, Julian of Norwich (c.1342 – after 1416) makes extensive use of language of motherhood when speaking of Christ. At another, it is reflected in differing conceptions of sin, which are held to reflect gender differences – for example, the suggestion that the predominantly male sin is that of pride, whereas its female equivalent is that of low self-esteem. One of the results of the feminist movement in recent years has been the recovery of women spiritual writers, especially of the Middle Ages.

2   Issues of race must also be noted, particularly within multicultural contexts (such as North America) in which race and cultural identity are often closely linked. Traditions of spirituality have emerged within Black holiness churches which are quite distinct from those found elsewhere in Protestant Christianity. Similarly, Asian Christians (particularly those having their origins in China or Korea) often incorporate elements deriving from their native culture into their approaches to spirituality.

3   Issues of class must also be noted, not least in that class is often linked with matters of taste and the issue of literacy. Forms of spirituality which are strongly populist often adopt the cultural standards of the groups to which they are directed. These are reflected in the music and literature which are used to sustain contemplation, as well as the forms of art used to encourage meditation and reflection. Thus nineteenth-century American revivalism made extensive use of techniques normally associated with popular theater in its worship.

Even on the basis of this very brief analysis, it will be clear that differences in personal temperament and social milieu will inevitably have implications for spirituality. Even if each person were to share identical theological beliefs and emphases, differences in personal temperament and social context would lead to a multiplicity of spiritualities. It could reasonably be argued that there are as many spiritualities as there are Christians, in that each Christian attempts to respond to the Christian faith in terms of her specific (and unique) circumstances.

It will thus be clear that excellent reasons can be given for speaking of both "Christian spirituality" on the one hand, and "Christian spiritualities" on the other. An analogous situation exists in the related discipline of Christian theology, in which shared core assumptions nevertheless lead to a variety of "theologies." The present work has chosen to speak primarily in terms of "Christian spirituality," in that all such forms of spirituality ultimately flow from the life, death, and resurrection of Jesus Christ. Nevertheless, the use of the term in the singular is most emphatically not intended to imply that the discipline is monolithic.

Denominational Considerations

Earlier, we noted the importance of having a working definition of Christian spirituality (p. 2), which identified some of the central points at issues without being over-precise about their interpretation. The working definition offered took the form as detailed in the box below.

Basic Definition of "Christian Spirituality"

Christian spirituality concerns the quest for a fulfilled and authentic Christian existence, involving the bringing together of the fundamental ideas of Christianity and the whole experience of living on the basis of and within the scope of the Christian faith.

The basic definition of "Christian spirituality" allows a fundamental distinction to be made between the idea of "spirituality" in general, and the specific forms of spirituality associated with Christianity. However, the definition itself points to another issue of fundamental importance: *there are different types of Christianity*, thus leading to different types of spiritualities. There is no difficulty in speaking of "catholic spirituality," "Orthodox spirituality," "Lutheran spirituality," "evangelical spirituality," or "charismatic spirituality." All of these are types of Christian spirituality, whose differences partly reflect prior differences between the types of Christianity in question. It will therefore be clear that it is essential to explore the different types of Christianity which are encountered, both in history and in the present day, and to note their distinctive features and the differences which exist between them. We thus turn to look at some denominational differences within Christianity, and explore their potential relevance for spirituality.

One point of particular importance concerns the vocabulary used to refer to the general area of spirituality. For example, by the end of the seventeenth century, Catholicism had developed a relatively sophisticated terminology to deal with this general area, including distinctions between "mystical theology" and "ascetical theology," which had no direct counterpart in Protestant thought. Older Protestant writers tended to use terms such as "piety" or "godliness" to refer to what is now generally designated as "spirituality." Protestant writers appear to have adopted the term "spirituality" in the second half of the twentieth century. With the progression of time, there has been a degree of convergence of vocabularies across denominational boundaries, so that the terminology a writer uses is no longer a reliable guide to the denominational tradition to which the writer belongs.

Pressure on space means that it is not possible to do more than indicate some of the ways in which denominational issues impact on spirituality. What follows must be regarded as little more than an indication of the potential importance of denominational issues, rather than a detailed listing of those issues and an analysis of their relevance. It should, however, be noted that these differences are not as rigidly defined as they might have been a century ago, and there is considerable evidence that a process of erosion of denominational distinctives is under way within western Christianity. In part, this erosion reflects growing contacts between the denomination, and a concern to defend shared Christian beliefs against what is often seen as an increasingly secular society. The suggestions for further reading at the end of this chapter will be of use in providing considerably more detailed coverage of the denominational issues treated so briefly in this section, and should be consulted by those wishing to take this matter further.

It should also be noted that it is virtually impossible to convey the distinctive characteristics of the various styles of Christianity in writing. The reader who wants to understand Anglicanism, Orthodoxy, Catholicism, or any other form of Christianity will need to experience its regular worship and prayer life, and get to know those who have chosen to adopt this form of Christianity. Outsider perspectives have limited value; to understand any form of Christianity, you will need to get involved in it.

Catholicism

Catholicism (still sometimes referred to as "Roman Catholicism" by some) is at present by far the largest form of Christianity in the world. It has a particularly strong presence in western and central Europe. Several European nations – such as Ireland, Italy, and Poland – have a strong sense of national identity which is closely linked with the Catholic church. As a result of the colonial expansion of Spain and Portugal in the sixteenth century, and Belgium and France in the nineteenth, there are particularly strong Catholic communities in North America, South America, southern Africa, and the Philippines. Parts of southern India, particularly the region of Goa, are also strongly Catholic. The former Portugese colony of East Timor, annexed by Indonesia in the 1980s, remains a stronghold of Catholicism in a largely Islamic region of southeast Asia.

The distinctive ethos of Catholicism is difficult to summarize, on account of the complexity of the movement. However, the following points are of particular importance in relation to spirituality.

- The church is generally seen as a visible divine institution, whose structures are grounded in divine reality. Although this view of the church was modified slightly by Vatican II, it remains of importance for modern Catholicism. Lying behind this is a strongly corporate conception of the Christian life and of authority within the church, contrasting sharply with the individualism which has become characteristic of modern western culture during the twentieth century.

- Catholicism is strongly liturgical. In other words, the forms of worship used by the church are fixed and laid down centrally, reflecting the conviction that the way in which the church prays and worships is inextricably linked to what the church believes (a point sometimes made using the Latin slogan *lex orandi, lex credendi*, which can be translated as "the way you pray determines the way you believe"). The liturgy is seen as a public statement of the beliefs and values of the church, and a means by which continuity with the apostolic tradition is maintained. Until the Second Vatican Council, the language of the liturgy was Latin; the use of native languages is now permitted, although considerable care is taken to ensure that vernacular translations accurately reflect the sense of the original Latin versions of the liturgy. This point is of particular importance in relation to spirituality, in that it draws attention to the importance of the church community in relation to spiritual growth and development.

- Catholicism is strongly sacramental, placing considerable emphasis on the "sacramental economy" (that is, the view that the benefits of Christ, which result from his death and resurrection, are communicated to the church through the sacraments). The Catholic church recognizes seven sacraments (whereas Protestants recognize only two). In terms of the regular liturgical life of the church, the most importance sacrament is the Mass, which is understood to make present the body and blood of Christ. Once more, this is of considerable importance to spirituality, in that it affirms the importance of sacraments to catholic spirituality. For example, consider the following definition of "spirituality" from a leading catholic writer.

A Catholic Definition of Spirituality

"Spirituality" refers to the unfolding, day by day, of that fundamental decision to become or remain a Christian which we make at baptism, repeat at confirmation, and renew each time we receive the eucharist.
William Reiser, SJ, *Looking for a God to Pray To,* **p. 2.**

Note how this understanding of spirituality interlocks the sacraments in the process of spiritual growth and development.

- Catholicism places an emphasis on the role of the saints in general, and the Virgin Mary in particular. The saints and Mary are understood to act as intercessors for both the living and the dead. The doctrine of the immaculate conception of Mary states that Mary was conceived without her sharing in the common human condition of original sin, thus providing a theological formalization for the high place of Mary in Catholic life and devotion. Nevertheless, Catholic writers are careful to draw attention to the distinction between the *veneration* due to Mary (which is honorific), and the *worship* which is due to God and to Jesus Christ as the Son of God. Once more, this is of major importance in relation to spirituality, and serves to distinguish Catholic forms of spirituality from their Protestant equivalents. For example, one of the most notable features of popular Catholic spirituality is the use of the Rosary – a series of 150 prayers, including "Hail Mary" – which are counted off using a string of beads as a counter. Popular Catholic spirituality also makes extensive use of the cult of the saints – for example, in the novena, a series of nine days of prayer in which the aid of a specific patron saint is invoked for some particular intention. Many Catholics find it helpful to adopt a particular patron saint in their personal devotions.

Anyone wishing to gain a fuller understanding of the fundamental beliefs and practices of Catholicism is strongly recommended to study the 1994 *Catechism of the Catholic Church*, which sets out clearly and at length the basics of the Catholic faith. We shall be considering some aspects of Catholic spirituality throughout the course of this work; our attention now turns to Orthodoxy.

Orthodoxy

Orthodoxy, whether in its Greek or Russian forms, represents a form of Christianity which retains a strong degree of continuity with the early Greek church, and traces its liturgy and doctrines directly back to the early church. Orthodoxy is numerically strongest in eastern Europe, particularly in Russia and Greece, where it has had a major influence in shaping a sense of national identity. However, it has also established a major presence in North America and Australia through emigration. The Australian city of Melbourne, for example, is home to one of the largest Greek Orthodox communities in the world.

Any attempt to describe the distinctive ethos of Orthodoxy would include the following elements.

- A strong sense of historical continuity with the early church. Orthodoxy is thus strongly orientated towards the idea of *paradosis* ("tradition"), particularly the writings of the Greek fathers. Writers such as Gregory of Nyssa, Maximus the Confessor, and the writer who adopted the pseudonym "Dionysius the Areopagite" are of particular importance in this respect. Tradition is seen as a living entity, which remains essentially unchanged while being capable of meeting the new challenges of each succeeding age. Orthodox spirituality thus stresses the importance of the tradition as a resource for the present, and particularly values the writings of such leading patristic writers as Gregory of Nyssa, Gregory of Nazianzus, and John of Damascus.
- Theologically distinctive ideas of importance for spirituality include an insistence that the Holy Spirit proceeds from the Father alone (rather than, as in western churches, from the Father and the Son), and particularly the understanding of salvation as "deification." "God became human, in order that humans might become God." This theological refrain may be discerned as underlying much of the soteriological reflections of the eastern Christian tradition, both during the patristic period and in the modern Greek and Russian Orthodox theological

traditions. As the citation suggests, there is an especially strong link between the doctrine of the incarnation and this understanding of salvation. For Athanasius, salvation consists in the human participation in the being of God. The divine Logos is imparted to humanity through the incarnation. On the basis of the assumption of a universal human nature, Athanasius concluded that the Logos did not merely assume the specific human existence of Jesus Christ, but human nature in general. As a consequence, all human beings are able to share in the deification which results from the incarnation. Human nature was created with the object of sharing in the being of God; through the descent of the Logos, this capacity is finally realized. This understanding of the nature of salvation has important implications for spirituality, as will become clear elsewhere in this work.

- The Orthodox use of icons – that is, pictures of Jesus Christ, Mary or some other religious figure – is of particular importance for our study. The strong emphasis on the incarnation of the Son of God is understood to have consequences for prayer and spirituality. Icons are "windows of perception," through which the believer may catch a glimpse of the divine reality (see p. 61).
- The Orthodox tradition places considerable importance on the repetitive use of the "Jesus Prayer" – that is, the prayer which takes the form: "Lord Jesus Christ, Son of God, have mercy on me." Although this prayer originally had associations with hesychasm, it has found wide acceptance outside this movement.
- Monasteries continue to play a critically important role in the articulation and defense of the Orthodox ethos, and especially its distinctive forms of spirituality. Perhaps the most important monastic center remains Mount Athos, a peninsula stretching into the Aegean Sea. Most bishops are drawn from monasteries.

Protestantism

The term "Protestantism" is widely used to refer to those churches which trace their historical origins back to the European Reformation of the sixteenth century. The term is potentially misleading, in that most Protestant churches stress their historical and theological continuity with the early church. A number of traditions stemming from the Reformation – especially Anglicanism – are to be regarded as "broad churches," which include sections more sympathetic to Catholicism (such as Anglo-Catholicism), as well as sections more sympathetic to the Reformation (such as evangelicalism).

The term "denomination" is often used to refer to specific Protestant churches, such as Lutheranism or Methodism. A number of trends have developed within Protestant denominations in recent times, of which two are of particular importance. Evangelicalism is now a major influence within most mainline Protestant denominations in the English-speaking west, although its influence has been, until relatively recently, significantly less noticable in continental Europe. A number of independent churches have now sprung up with a distinctively evangelical ethos, especially in South America and southern Africa. The charismatic movement has also been of significance in the life of many mainline Protestant churches, and its influence has also been felt within Catholicism. A number of specifically charismatic denominations (such as the Assemblies of God) are now of growing importance in global Protestantism.

- Protestantism has often been described as the "religion of the Bible." There is much truth in this statement (although it is not quite as straightforward as might at first be thought). One of the most important features of the Reformation was its emphasis on the importance of the public and private reading of the Bible. This is perhaps seen most clearly in traditional Protestant preaching, which often takes the form of biblical-based cycles of sermons, or in the traditional evangelical "quiet time," in which a period of time is set aside for the reading of the Bible and prayer based upon that reading.
- A cluster of characteristic Catholic beliefs are rejected, or treated as strictly optional private beliefs for individuals rather than the official teaching of the denomination. These include: purgatory; the intercession of the saints; and any form of devotion to the Virgin Mary. Many of these rejected beliefs have considerable implications for spirituality.
- Until the Second Vatican Council (1962–5), the liturgy of the Catholic church was required to be read in Latin. This contrasted with the views of the reformers, who argued that all forms of public worship had to be in a language which the common people could understand.

Readers interested in following up on some of these historical and theological points are recommended to read works that deal with the history and theology of the Reformation, which will provide considerably more detailed explanations of these points, as well as expanding on them.

In recent years, evangelicalism has become of increasing importance within Protestantism. It is therefore of importance to understand something of the nature of this movement, and its distinctive approach to spirituality. Although some new Protestant denominations have been formed which are explicitly evangelical in orientation, the general pattern which has emerged is that evangelicalism is a movement within the mainline denominations. Hence evangelicals within the Reformed churches retain much of the ethos of those churches (including its church structures), while supplementing these with at least some of the characteristics of evangelicalism, noted below. Similarly, evangelicals within Anglicanism adopt many of the characteristics of the latter (such as the episcopal system of church government, and the use of a fixed liturgy), while retaining an evangelical ethos within this church.

The four main distinctive features of the evangelical ethos are the following.

- Evangelicalism is strongly biblical in its emphasis. This is especially evident in the styles of preaching found within the movement. This emphasis is carried over into other aspects of evangelical life, including the importance attached to small Bible study groups within the life of the church, and to the regular reading of the Bible in personal devotion (see p. 82). The evangelical emphasis upon the reading of the Bible has had a major impact in shaping evangelical spirituality, which often focuses on personal and corporate Bible study. It is interesting to note that similar emphases can be discerned within Franciscan and Benedictine writings and practices of the Middle Ages.

- Evangelicalism places a particular emphasis on the cross of Jesus. Although Jesus is of central importance to evangelicalism, its emphasis has tended to fall upon the saving death of Jesus on the cross. This is especially reflected in evangelical hymns and songs. The implications of this emphasis for spirituality will be clear; many forms of evangelicalism have developed forms of spirituality which take the form of extended meditation on the death of Christ on the cross.
- Evangelicalism stresses the need for personal conversion. Considerable emphasis is placed on the dangers of "nominalism," meaning by this "a purely formal or external acceptance of Christian teachings, without any personal transformation in consequence." Evangelical preaching often stresses the need for Christians to be "born again" (see John 3:1–16).
- Evangelical churches and individual evangelicals have a deep commitment to evangelism – that is, to converting others to the Christian faith. Billy Graham (1918–), noted for his global evangelistic ministry, is a good example of a twentieth-century evangelical who has become well known on account of this emphasis. It should be noted that the words "evangelicalism" and "evangelism" are often confused, on account of their similar spelling. The former refers to a movement; the latter to an activity – but an activity which is especially associated with this specific movement.

Thus far, we have considered some of the elements which distinguish the different Christian denominations, and which have implications for their distinctive spiritualities. But there are also some more general factors which are not specific to any denomination which shape spiritualities. In what follows, we shall explore the attitudes to the world and human culture. It must be stressed that the different attitudes outlined can be found within all major denominations, resulting in a complex interaction between these general factors and more specifically denominational or theological issues.

Attitudes to the World, Culture, and History

As we have noted, spirituality is about Christian life and experience. Inevitably, this raises questions about attitudes to the world, culture, and history. One helpful way of understanding the different types of spirituality which are to be found within Christianity has been developed by the Methodist writer Geoffrey Wainwright. In 1951, the Harvard theologian H. Richard Niebuhr published a major study entitled *Christ and Culture*, in which he identified five major ways in which Christianity related to culture in general. The five categories which he proposed gained wide acceptance, and became very influential in Christian discussion of social ethics. In his major essay "Types of Spirituality," Wainwright suggests that the five categories set out by Niebuhr could be used equally well to analyze the types of spirituality within Christianity. In what follows, we shall set out the five main types, following Wainwright's analysis.

1 Christ against culture

According to this approach, the world is to be seen as a hostile environment for Christian belief and practice. The values of the Kingdom of God stand in contrast to those of the world. This type of spirituality was of considerable importance in the first few centuries of Christian history, when Christianity was viewed with intense distrust and suspicion by the secular authorities, and on occasion actively persecuted. Once the Roman emperor Constantine was converted to Christianity, however, a very different situation resulted. Christianity rapidly became the official religion of the Roman Empire. In the eyes of many, this resulted in a compromise with secular values. Bishops began to imitate the dress and customs of secular rulers – for example, by wearing purple robes (a symbol of wealth and power).

This led to many Christians believing that some authentically Christian ideals were becoming compromised. The rise of the monastic movement is widely seen as a revolt against the easy accommodation which began to emerge between church and state, with the result that it began to become difficult to tell them apart. The monasteries saw themselves as centers of authentic Christainity, insulated from the temptations of power and wealth, in which the true Christian vision could be pursued. Many works of monastic spirituality spoke of the cultivation of "contempt for the world," meaning a studied rejection of the temptations offered by the world, which were seen as an obstacle to salvation and personal spiritual growth. Withdrawal from the world was the only guaranteed means of ensuring one's salvation.

Although the Protestant Reformation rejected the monastic ideal, the dual themes of the renunciation of the world and the hostility of the world for authentic Christianity was taken up and developed by the more radical wing of the movement. Anabaptist writers stressed the need to form alternative Christian communities, often in rural areas. Anabaptist writers refused to have anything to do with secular power or authority, rejecting the use of force. A tension can be discerned at this point between radical writers and the mainline reformers (such as Luther and Calvin), who encouraged a more positive and interactive approach to society and culture. Similar attitudes can be found within North American fundamentalist circles today.

It will therefore be clear that the "Christ against Culture" approach to spirituality remains significant today. Much the same can be said about the diametrically opposed trend, which Niebuhr designates "the Christ of culture," to which we now turn.

2 The Christ of culture

Once the Roman empire accepted Christianity as its official religion, the way was opened to the possibility of a strongly positive understanding of the relationship of Christian faith and secular culture. It must be stressed that this approach would have been an impossibility in the early period of Christian history, when the church was strongly opposed by the secular authorities. The acceptance of the church as the official religion of the Roman Empire brought with it certain privileges. Its bishops were now seen as persons of importance, who took to wearing Roman symbols of rank as indications of their new social status. It also brought about the rise of what is often referred to as the "imperial theology" – that is, an approach to theology and spirituality which sees Rome as the new Jerusalem, playing a divinely-ordained role in the government of the world.

The "imperial theology" was especially associated with Eusebius of Caesarea. This theology saw the Roman Empire as the climax of God's redemptive purposes. As we have noted, with the conversion of the Roman emperor Constantine in the fourth century, a new era in Christian history had dawned. Some Christian writers, most notably Eusebius of Caesarea (*c*.260–*c*.340), portrayed Constantine as an instrument chosen by God for the conversion of the empire. Eusebius' "Rome-theology" appears to have had a deep impact upon Christian thinking in this crucial period, not least in rendering Rome virtually immune from reflective criticism on the part of Christian writers.

Indeed, so intimate was the connection which came to be presupposed between empire and gospel that the sack of Rome (410) endangered the future of western Christianity. The fall of Rome raised a series of potentially difficult questions for the imperial theology. Why had Rome been sacked? Augustine of Hippo (354–430) addressed such questions in *The City of God*, partly to discredit a "theology of history" which had become influential in Christian circles, and to liberate Christianity from this straitjacket which had been imposed upon it. *The City of God* topples Rome from its position in Eusebius' theology of history. No longer is Rome portrayed as God's chosen instrument for the salvation of the world, and the preservation of the gospel.

Similar uncritically positive understandings of the relation between Christianity and culture can be illustrated from other periods in Christian history. An excellent example can be provided from the Middle Ages, which witnessed a reaction on the part of "secular clergy" (that is, clergy who worked in the world) against monastic withdrawal from the world. Philip of Harvengt (died 1183), reacting against the monastic rejection of the world (which he here terms "Babylon"), wrote that:

> It is as safe as it is easy to run away from the middle of Babylon; it is much more important (and difficult) to be crowned victor in the center of Babylon. Monastic perfection, then, although commendable for its merit, is to be considered both lower and easier than its clerical equivalent.

A further example of a world-affirming approach can be found in nineteenth-century German liberal Protestantism, which tended to amalgamate German culture with Christian ideals. Liberal Protestantism was inspired by the vision of a humanity which was ascending upwards into new realms of progress and prosperity. The doctrine of evolution gave new vitality to this belief, which was nurtured by strong evidence of cultural stability in western Europe in the late nineteenth century. Religion came increasingly to be seen as relating to the spiritual needs of modern humanity, and giving ethical guidance to society. The strongly ethical dimension of liberal Protestantism is especially evident in the writings of Albrecht Benjamin Ritschl (1822–89).

For Ritschl, the idea of the "kingdom of God" was of central importance. Ritschl tended to think of this as a static realm of ethical values, which would undergird the development of German society at this point in its history. History, it was argued, was in the process of being divinely guided toward perfection. Civilization is seen as part of this process of evolution. In the course of human history, a number of individuals appear who are recognized as being the bearers of special divine insights. One such individual was Jesus. By following his example and sharing in his inner life, other human beings are able to develop. The movement showed enormous and unbounded optimism in human ability and potential. Religion and culture were, it was argued, virtually identical. Later critics of the movement (including Niebuhr himself) dubbed it "culture Protestantism," on account of their belief that it was too heavily dependent upon accepted cultural norms. Many critics would argue that this kind of approach to culture paved the way for the rise of Nazism in the 1930s, in that it encouraged the identification of German culture and Christian faith.

Where the "Christ against culture" model suggests that the Christian life is lived in constant hostility with the world, and stresses the costliness of faith and the importance of martyrdom, the "Christ of culture" approach implies that Christian authenticity is to be found by affirmation of, and even immersion in, the culture of the day. Wainwright dismisses both these approaches as "crippingly deficient," and instead urges his readers to adopt one of the three remaining approaches, which we shall now consider.

3   Christ above culture

The third approach to be discussed is related to the second, but recognizes the need to appreciate that culture is far from perfect. Indeed, it could be argued that this third model is grounded in the recognition that culture is neither perfect nor evil, but is something which can be elevated and transformed through the Christian faith. Wainwright argues that this approach "emphasizes the positive elements in human nature and culture, while recognizing that even these need to be purified and lifted." The famous maxim of St Thomas Aquinas (c.1225–74) can be seen as underlying this approach: "Grace does not abolish nature, but perfects it."

Wainwright argues that this approach to spirituality is often linked to an emphasis upon the incarnation (see p. 54), associated with the Athanasian slogan "God became human, in order that humans might become God." This statement exemplifies the kind of ideas associated with the "Christ above culture" approach. For example, this approach would hold that Christ, by taking upon himself human nature, elevates something which is already good to a higher plane. The approach thus affirms the goodness of the world without any kind of perfectionist delusions. Creation is good, but still needs improvement. Human nature is good, but it is open to further elevation. Human culture is good, but it is capable of transformation through the impact of the gospel. This elevation is seen as something which happens in the present: thus human nature has already been elevated through the incarnation. It allows us to distinguish this approach from the fifth and final model we shall consider, in which the transformation in question is seen in future, rather than in present, terms.

4 Christ and culture in paradox

The fourth approach, according to Wainwright, is also to be regarded as more "central" than the "Christ against culture" or the "Christ of culture" models. Just as the "Christ over culture" can be regarded as a central model which leans towards the "Christ of culture" approach, the fourth model can be seen as a central approach with "Christ against culture" tendencies. This approach does not regard the world and human culture as fundamentally evil; nevertheless, it argues that the Christian must expect to struggle in the attempt to lead an authentic Christian life.

Niebuhr saw the sixteenth-century German reformer Martin Luther (1483–1546) as an excellent representative of this understanding of the relation of Christianity and culture, and Wainwright suggests that this is also true of Luther's spirituality. On the one hand, Luther stresses that the proper place of Christian believers is in the world, in which they are meant to live and bear witness; on the other, he argues that the world has the potential to corrupt believers, who must therefore be on their guard against such influence. For Luther, the Christian life is characterized by what he terms *Anfechtung,* a German word which could be translated as "temptation," but which denotes far more than this. Prayer, for Luther, is a struggle with God, just as faith is a constant struggle against unbelief.

According to this model, the Christian community must expect to live in a degree of tension with the world. Luther set out this tension in terms of his doctrine of the "two kingdoms" – the "kingdom of the world" and the "kingdom of God." These two very different realms of authority coexist and overlap, with the result that Christians experience the tension of living in one kingdom, yet trying to obey the authority of another. The standards of God do not always find acceptance within the world; indeed, at points the world dismisses the ideas and ideals of the Christian church as stupidity and folly. The "paradox" model of spirituality identifies this tension, and encourages Christians to learn to live with it. It cannot be eliminated, as it arises from the very essence of the Christian faith itself.

This does not mean that at each and every point the church will find itself in tension with the world; at points, there will be sharing of ideas and values. At others, however, tension is inevitable, and a struggle will result. Wainwright points to Dietrich Bonhoeffer as an excellent example of this kind of spirituality – someone who was caught up in the tension between his faith and culture, and who maintained his integrity despite the complexity of the situations which he faced.

5 Christ the transformer of culture

The fifth model which Wainwright sets out bears a degree of resemblance to the third. The approach rests upon a positive understanding of creation, which is seen as something that is in itself good yet which requires transformation. This transformation, however, is not seen as a present reality, but as a future hope. Wainwright places the founders of Methodism, John and Charles Wesley (1703–91 and 1707–88 respectively), in this category, partly on account of their emphasis upon personal conversion, which stresses the need for the transformation of the individual.

Wainwright suggests that this transformationist approach to spirituality is likely to be strongly sacramental in character. He illustrates this aspect of the matter by pointing out that the sacrament of baptism is linked with the imagery of death and rebirth, indicating both the necessity and possibility of the radical transformation of human nature.

The five models developed by Wainwright are helpful in mapping out some broad positions. But they are not exhaustive, and at points several appear to overlap.

It is now appropriate to explore the way in which theology relates to spirituality. In view of the importance of this issue, we shall explore it in some detail.

FOR FURTHER READING

Robert A. Baker (ed.), *A Baptist Source Book*. Nashville, TN: Broadman, 1966.

Henry Bett, *The Spirit of Methodism*. London: Epworth Press, 1937.

Emory S. Bucke, *The History of American Methodism*. New York: Abingdon, 1964.

Ian Bunting (ed.), *Celebrating the Anglican Way*. London: Hodder & Stoughton, 1996.

Rupert E. Davies, *Methodism*. London: Epworth Press, 1976.

Werner Elert, *The Structure of Lutheranism*. St Louis, MO: Concordia, 1962.

Timothy George and David S. Dockery, *Baptist Theologians*. Nashville, TN: Broadman, 1990.

Urban T. Holmes, *A History of Christian Spirituality*. New York: Seabury Press, 1981.

Bradley C. Holt, *Thirsty for God: A Brief History of Christian Spirituality*. Minneapolis: Augsburg, 1993.

John H. Leith, *Introduction to the Reformed Tradition*. Atlanta, GA: John Knox Press, 1981.

H. Leon McBeth, *The Baptist Heritage*. Nashville, TN: Broadman, 1987.

Richard McBrien, *Catholicism*, new edn. San Francisco: HarperCollins, 1994.

Alister E. McGrath, *Evangelicalism and the Future of Christianity*. Downers Grove, IL: InterVarsity Press, 1995.

Alister E. McGrath (ed.), *The SPCK Handbook of Anglican Theologians*. London: SPCK, 1998.

Elsie Anne McKee and Brian G. Armstrong, *Probing the Reformed Tradition*. Louisville, KY: Westminster/John Knox Press, 1989.

Donald K. McKim (ed.), *Major Themes in the Reformed Tradition*. Grand Rapids, MI: Eerdmans, 1992.

John Meyendorff, *The Orthodox Church*, 3rd edn. Crestwood, NY: St Vladimir's Seminary Press, 1981.

Philip Sheldrake, *Spirituality and History: Questions of Interpretation and Method*. London: SPCK, 1995.

Stephen W. Sykes and John Booty (eds), *The Study of Anglicanism*. London: SPCK, 1988.

Geoffrey Wainwright, "Types of Spirituality," in C. Jones, G. Wainwright and E. Yarnold (eds), *The Study of Spirituality*. London: SPCK, 1986, 592–605.

3

Theological Foundations for Spirituality: Basic Issues

The term "spirituality" has been widely used in recent years to refer to the reaction against purely materialist ways of viewing the world. The growing recognition of the importance of the interior world of personal experience has resulted in considerable interest in the concept of spirituality. Yet not all spirituality can be regarded as "Christian." The use of the adjective "Christian" indicates that Christian beliefs interact with spirituality, fostering and encouraging certain approaches to the spiritual life and rejecting or criticizing others. It is therefore of considerable importance to explore the way in which Christian ideas impact upon spirituality.

The term "theology" is widely used to refer to the body of Christian beliefs, and the discipline of study which centers upon them. Theology is a discipline of convictions, an attempt to survey and correlate the matrix of Christian beliefs. Perhaps the simplest way of characterizing the relation between theology and spirituality is to suggest that the former is about the theory, and the latter the practice, of the Christian life. Like all simplifications, it has the potential to mislead. For example, there are continuing debates within the disciplines over the precise meanings of "theology" and "spirituality," with the result that any understanding of the relation between the two disciplines is dependent upon prior agreement as to exactly how each is to be understood. Many writers, for example, would argue that theology, rightly understood, embraces spirituality. After all, did not Evagrius Ponticus (346–99) argue that theology was all about prayer? Might not theology therefore be thought of as the application of Christianity to the mind, and spirituality the application of Christianity to the heart?

In the present chapter, we shall be exploring some of the general ways, both positive and negative, in which theology and spirituality interact. Before doing this, we shall explore how the discipline of "theology" came to emerge.

The Nature of Theology

The term "theology" is widely used to refer to systematic reflection on the intellectual content of the Christian faith. The word can be broken down into two constituent elements, based on the Greek word *theos* ("god") and *logos* ("word" or "discourse"). Theology could thus be said to be "discourse about God," in much the same way as biology is "discourse about life" (Greek: *bios*), or pharmacology is "discourse about drugs" (Greek: *pharmaka*). There is evidence that, at an early stage in the development of the Christian tradition, the term "theology" was used to refer specifically to Christian teachings about God (rather, than, for example, its teachings about the person and work of Jesus Christ, the nature of the church, and so forth.) However, the term has since developed the more general sense of "systematic analysis of the nature of the Christian faith," including – but not limited to – the Christian understanding of God. A number of technical terms are used to refer to specific areas of theology; some of these are listed below.

Technical Terms Relating to Areas of Theology

anthropology	the understanding of human nature
Christology	the person of Jesus Christ
ecclesiology	the doctrine of the church
eschatology	the last things
hamartiology	the doctrine of sin
soteriology	the doctrine of salvation

The discipline of "Christian theology" is to be rigorously distinguished from "religious studies." "Christian theology" deals with the specific teachings of the Christian faith; "religious studies" is used to designate a more general approach to religion and religious issues, often on the basis of the assumption that "religion" is a genuinely universal concept. One of the reasons for making this point is that Christian spirituality rests on the basis of assumptions which, as we shall see, are not universal to all religions. For example, the concepts of "incarnation" and "resurrection" are specific to the Christian faith, and have major implications for the shaping of the Christian worldview and outlook. (Some scholars have argued that echoes of these ideas may be found in other religions, especially Hinduism; the parallels are, however, rather less than persuasive.)

A major development which has implications for the relation of Christian theology and spirituality may be traced back to the eighteenth century, but has become increasingly importance in the last hundred years. Most of the great theologians of the Christian faith prior to the eighteenth century were themselves concerned for spirituality. Athanasius (*c*.296–373), Augustine of Hippo (354–430), Anselm of Canterbury (*c*.1033–1109), Thomas Aquinas (*c*.1225–74), Martin Luther (1483–1546), and Roberto Bellarmine (1542–1621) – to name but a few examples – were theologians who saw no tension between the intellectual exploration of the Christian faith and its practical outworking in spirituality, preaching, ministry, and pastoral care.

In more recent times, theology has come to be viewed as a professional academic discipline, set apart from the life of the church. The Enlightenment held that any form of religious commitment was an obstacle to objectivity, and thus cultivated the idea of religious neutrality in theology. This is now widely regarded as incorrect; nevertheless, the Enlightenment paradigm has had considerable influence within western academic circles. The outcome of this is that "theology" has often been conceived as the academic study of religious concepts, with no connection with Christian life as a whole. This paradigm has been disastrous for the right understanding of the relation of theology and spirituality, as it deliberately eliminated such a connection in the first place. Happily, the widespread rejection of the Enlightenment paradigm in the West is now opening the way to a re-establishment of the original link between theology and spirituality – a development which can only be welcomed.

The Relationship of Theology and Spirituality

Many writers in the field of spirituality argue that there is a serious tension between the disciplines of "theology" and "spirituality." There can be no doubt that this is the case if theology is defined in highly abstract terms – such as "the study of Christian concepts or doctrines." Yet it needs to be realized that, partly in response to pressures within western academic culture in general, the western understanding of "theology" has undergone a shift in the last two centuries which inevitably leads to precisely this tension emerging. It is thus important to appreciate that the tension is thus not primarily between *theology* and spirituality, but *between modern western concepts of theology* and spirituality.

In his important study (1983) *Theologia: The Fragmentation and Unity of Theological Education*, the noted American writer Edward Farley (1929–) points to a series of developments in theological education which have led to the loss of a defining theological vision characterized by the coinherence of piety and intellect. Farley argues that the term *theologia* has lost its original meaning, which he defines as "sapiential and personal knowledge of divine self-disclosure" leading to "wisdom or discerning judgement indispensable for human living." Theology used to be – and, in Farley's view, still ought to be! – "not just objective science, but a personal knowledge of God and the things of God."

This is an important point, as it indicates that the term "theology" has suffered a serious and detrimental shift in meaning in the last century. Properly understood, theology embraces, informs and sustains spirituality. It is easy to argue for a gulf having opened up between theology and spirituality in the last century or so – but this must be seen in the light of cultural assumptions, especially within the western academy, which have forced theology to see itself as an academically-neutral subject, not involving commitment on the part of its teachers or students, which is primarily concerned with information about abstract ideas. This is not how theology was understood in earlier generations. It is perfectly proper to point out that Christian theology cannot remain faithful to its subject matter if it regards itself as purely propositional or cognitive in nature. The Christian encounter with God is transformative. As John Calvin (1509–64) pointed out, to know God is to be changed by God; true knowledge of God leads to worship, as the believer is caught up in a transforming and renewing encounter with the living God. To know God is to be changed by God. The idea of a purely "objective" or "disinterested" knowledge of God is thus precluded. For someone to speak objectively about "knowing God" is as realistic as the lover speaking dispassionately of the beloved. The Danish philosopher Søren Kierkegaard (1813–55) argued that to know the truth is to be *known by the truth*. "Truth is something which affects our inner being, as we become involved in an appropriation process of the most passionate inwardness."

Theology, in this classic sense of the term, is a "heartfelt knowledge of divine things" (Farley), something which affects the heart and the mind. It relates to both *fides quae creditur* and *fides qua creditur*, the objective content of faith, and the subjective act of trusting. But all this has changed, not on account of any fundamental difficulties with this classic conception of theology, but on account of the increasing professionalization and specialization of theological educators. The study of theology has become little more than the mastery of discrete bodies of data. It has something you simply know about – where it should be something relational, something that is *known*, that shapes your life, provides a reason to live, and gives direction to ministry.

It is thus little wonder that so many seminaries report a burgeoning interest in spirituality on the part of their students, when they have been starved of the experiential and reflective dimensions of theology by the unwarranted intrusion of the academic attitude towards the subject just noted. The idea of theology as a purely academic subject forces issues of personal spiritual formation and Christian living – originally, it must be stressed, part of the idea of "theology" – out on a limb. The time has come to welcome them back, and to do so by both rediscovering what theology is meant to be all about, and ensuring that the close link between theology and spirituality is preserved.

In what follows, we shall explore some of the positive and negative aspects of the relation between theology and spirituality.

Positive aspects of the relationship

For the purposes of this analysis, let us assume that theology can be thought of simply as the systematic analysis of the basic teachings of the Christian faith. What relevance might this have for spirituality?

The most important role of theology is to establish a framework within which spirituality is to be set. Christianity cannot really be thought of as a vague and muddled set of attitudes or values. At its heart is a series of quite specific beliefs. An excellent example of this is provided by the doctrine of human nature and destiny, often referred to as "anthropology." A central theme of all Christian thinking about human nature is that its true nature and destiny can only be understood and fulfilled through a relationship with God. A more secular approach might well stress the autonomy of human nature, and regard God as something of an irrelevance to human fulfillment and identity. We shall be exploring this issue in more detail later in this work (see pp. 41–7); at this point, however, we may note that Christian spirituality is grounded in the belief that human fulfillment can only be fully achieved through a deepened relationship with God.

It is thus no accident that "Creeds" play a major role within Christianity, as they give a quite definite shape to what Christians believe about God and human nature, to mention only two major themes for spirituality. A classic distinction within Christianity relates to the meaning of the word "faith." This can be understood in two different, though clearly related, senses: "faith as trust in God" and "what is actually believed." (These two senses are often referred to by the Latin slogans *fides qua creditur* and *fides quae creditur*, respectively.) Faith can thus be understood to have both volitional and intellectual elements.

We can explore this point a little further by considering the Apostles' Creed, perhaps one of the best-known of the Christian Creeds. This opens with the assertion "I believe in God." At one level, this could be taken simply as an assertion that I believe that God exists. However, as the creed progresses, it becomes clear that the Creed is affirming certain quite definite things about God and Jesus Christ, which give Christianity its shape and substance. The Apostles' Creed is widely used in the western church as a succinct summary of the leading themes of the Christian faith. During the twentieth century, the Apostles' Creed has become widely accepted by most churches, eastern and western, as a binding statement of Christian faith despite the fact that its statements concerning the "descent into hell" and the "communion of saints" (here printed within brackets) are not found in eastern versions of the work. In a later section of this chapter, we shall explore the relevance of some of these articles of the creed for spirituality.

The basic point being made here is that theology has a major effect on the way in which Christian people live and behave. Theological differences between different

---

The Apostles' Creed

1 I believe in God, the Father almighty, creator of the heavens and earth;
2 and in Jesus Christ, his only Son, our Lord;
3 who was conceived by the Holy Spirit and born of the Virgin Mary;
4 suffered under Pontius Pilate, was crucified, dead and buried;
   [he descended to hell;]
5 on the third day he was raised from the dead;
6 he ascended into the heavens, and sits at the right hand of God the Father almighty;
7 from where he will come to judge the living and the dead.
8 I believe in the Holy Spirit;
9 in the holy catholic church;
   [the communion of saints;]
10 the forgiveness of sins;
11 the resurrection of the flesh;
12 and eternal life.

types of Christians also lie behind some significant differences between styles of Christian spirituality, as we shall see during the course of this volume. To illustrate the importance of theology for spirituality, we may consider two beliefs, one of which is Christian, and the other not.

1 The world was created by God.
2 The world was created by an evil and demonic force, opposed to God.

The first of these is a classic Christian belief; the second represents a form of Gnosticism (see p. 36), which became influential in the second century. To understand the importance of theology to spirituality, we need to ask this question: what difference would accepting one of these beliefs make to the way we live?

The first belief encourages us to affirm and explore the natural world as a way of finding out more about God. If God made the world, God's "signature" (so to speak) may be found within the created order. Thomas Aquinas puts this point as follows:

> Meditation on [God's] works enables us, at least to some extent, to admire and reflect on God's wisdom . . . We are thus able to infer God's wisdom from reflection upon God's works . . . This consideration of God's works leads to an admiration of God's sublime power, and consequently inspires reverence for God in human hearts . . . This consideration also incites human souls to the love of God's goodness . . . If the goodness, beauty and wonder of creatures are so delightful to the human mind, the fountainhead of God's own goodness (compared with the trickles of goodness found in creatures) will draw excited human minds entirely to itself.

Something of the torrent of God's beauty can thus be known in the rivulets of the beauty of the creation. Furthermore, the creation is not to be worshipped *as God*, but is to be honored *as God's*. Immediately, we can see the foundations of a Christian approach to ecology emerging. If the world belongs to God, and not to us, then our responsibility is that of stewardship – we are to tend and care for something which belongs to God. We do not have the right to exploit it, because it is not ours.

The second belief, in marked contrast, leads to the idea that involvement in the world leads us away from God. It encourages the idea that the material order is evil, so that those who study it or care for it are rebelling against God or deliberately affirming forces which are opposed to God. Salvation is thus likely to be achieved only by withdrawing from the world, in order to avoid becoming contaminated by its evil influence. As the study of Christian history makes clear, precisely these attitudes can be discerned within some forms of Gnosticism in the second century, and also some variants of Christianity during the Middle Ages which were influenced by such ideas.

It will thus be clear that theology impacts on attitudes to the world, and the manner in which people live. Yet it must be noted that the traffic between theology and spirituality is not one-way. The way in which Christians worship and pray has a major impact on Christian theology. The nature of this interaction is sometimes expressed in the Latin tag *lex orandi, lex credendi* (a loose translation of which is "the way you pray affects the way you believe"; or, more precisely, "the law of prayer is the law of faith"). This became especially clear during the Arian controversy of the fourth century, which we shall consider in more detail presently (pp. 55–8). Here, the fact that Christians worshipped Jesus Christ and prayed to him were seen as factors which had to be accommodated within the Christian understanding of the identity and significance of Jesus.

Theology, then, rightly understood (and this qualification is of considerable importance), has a positive relation to spirituality. For Thomas Aquinas, theology had its origins in God, spoke of God, and led to God. In a later section of this work, we shall explore further aspects of the positive interaction of theology and spirituality, with specific reference to seven areas of Christian doctrine. However, it is important to appreciate that this relationship is not always harmonious. Sometimes the tension arises through the intrusion of western ideas about detachment and neutrality into theology; sometimes it comes about as a result of an impatience with the limits of theology. In what follows, we shall explore the potentially negative aspects of this interaction.

Negative aspects of the relationship

As we suggested earlier, western Christian theology has often taken the form of explicitly academic reflection on the content of the Christian faith. In other words, it is about knowledge, reflection and speculation. Particularly within the modern western academic context, this can lead to two serious difficulties.

1   Theology becomes so concerned with intellectual intricacies that it loses sight of the relational aspects of the Christian faith.
2   The western academic demand that scholarship should be detached and disinterested leads to a weakening of the link between theology and prayer.

Each of these difficulties has been recognized for some considerable time. We shall illustrate each of them from the rich tradition of Christian spirituality.

First, we consider the danger that theology will become so absorbed in abstract ideas that it loses touch with the living reality of God. This point was made particularly clearly during the fifteenth century by Thomas à Kempis (c.1380–1471). During the Middle Ages, the theology of the Trinity became the subject of considerable theological speculation, occasionally leading to the Trinity being seen as little more than a mathematical puzzle or logical riddle. Thomas vigorously opposed this trend, seeing the proper role of theology as leading to love for God, contrition, and a changed life. In his *Imitation of Christ*, Thomas sets out a strongly anti-speculative approach to the Christian faith, which rests firmly on the need to obey Christ rather than indulge in flights of intellectual fancy. Speculation concerning the Trinity is singled out as a case of such speculation, which he urges his readers to avoid.

> What good does it do you if you dispute loftily about the Trinity, but lack humility and therefore displease the Trinity? It is not lofty words that make you righteous or holy or dear to God, but a virtuous life. I would much rather experience contrition than be able

> to give a definition of it. If you knew the whole of the Bible by heart, along with all the definitions of the philosophers, what good would this be without grace and love? "Vanity of vanities, and all is vanity" (Ecclesiastes 1 : 2) – except, that is, loving God and serving him alone. For this is supreme wisdom: to draw nearer to the heavenly kingdom through contempt for the world. . . . Naturally, everyone wants knowledge. But what use is that knowledge without the fear of God? A humble peasant who serves God is much more pleasing to him than an arrogant academic who neglects his own soul to consider the course of the stars . . . If I were to possess all the knowledge in the world, and yet lacked love, what good would this be in the sight of God, who will judge me by what I have done? So restrain an extravagant longing for knowledge, which leads to considerable anxiety and deception. Learned people always want their wisdom to be noticed and recognized. But there are many things, knowledge of which leads to little or no benefit to the soul. In fact, people are foolish if they concern themselves with anything other than those things which lead to their salvation.

Notice the manner in which Thomas stresses the limits on knowledge and its benefits. Knowledge is not necessarily a good thing; it can be a distraction from God, and a temptation to become arrogant.

The second danger (which we noted earlier) concerns the way in which western academia has come to regard detachment as essential to academic integrity. All academic disciplines – such as theology, philosophy, and history – are to be studied without any precommitment on the part of students. Often, this approach is characterized as "objective," meaning that the filtering out of any precommitments on the part of students will allow them to get a much more accurate and unbiased understanding of the subject. Yet Christian spirituality is widely regarded as presupposing exactly some such commitment to the Christian faith! There is thus a tension between spirituality and a detached approach to theology. However, this is not the only approach to theology; monasteries and seminaries foster a sense of commitment to the Christian faith on the part of their students, and thus create an ideal intellectual environment for the development of spirituality.

The point about the negative implications for spirituality of a "detached" approach to theology has been made by many western spiritual writers, who are critical of the trend towards fostering "neutral" attitudes toward theology in the academic work. We shall note two writers who express criticisms of this trend, and argue for the integration of theology and contemplation.

Our first example is Thomas Merton (1915–68), a Trappist monk who has had a major influence on modern western spirituality. Merton affirms that there is a close link between the two disciplines, which must be affirmed and recognized for the mutual good of each.

> Contemplation, far from being opposed to theology, is in fact the normal perfection of theology. We must not separate intellectual study of divinely revealed truth and contemplative experience of that truth as if they could never have anything to do with one another. On the contary, they are simply two aspects of the same thing. Dogmatic and mystical theology, or theology and "spirituality," are not to be set in mutually exclusive categories, as if mysticism were for saintly women and theological study were for practical but, alas, unsaintly men. This fallacious division perhaps explains much that is actu-

ally lacking in both theology and spirituality. But the two belong together. Unless they are united there is no fervour, no life and no spiritual value in theology; no substance, no meaning and no sure orientation in the contemplative life.

Note how Merton forges a link between the two disciplines, and indicates that their artificial separation is to their mutual impoverishment. You may find it helpful to try to summarize in your own words the danger that Merton identifies in studying or pursuing either theology or spirituality on its own, without reference to the other discipline.

A second example of a writer who opposes this trend, and notes its serious implications, is the noted evangelical theologian James I. Packer (1927–), who comments thus on the positive relation between spirituality and theology.

> I question the adequacy of conceptualizing the subject-matter of systematic theology as simply revealed truths about God, and I challenge the assumption that has usually accompanied this form of statement, that the material, like other scientific data, is best studied in cool and clinical detachment. Detachment from what, you ask? Why, from the relational activity of trusting, loving, worshipping, obeying, serving and glorifying God: the activity that results from realizing that one is actually in God's presence, actually being addressed by him, every time one opens the Bible or reflects on any divine truth whatsoever. This . . . proceeds as if doctrinal study would only be muddled by introducing devotional concerns; it drives a wedge between . . . knowing true notions about God and knowing the true God himself.

Notice how Packer is critical of conceiving theology in purely informational terms; rightly understood, it is relational. You will find it helpful to summarize Packer's concerns about the pursuit of neutrality in theology in your own words. You might like to ask how the relationship between theology and worship illustrates this general point.

It will thus be clear that the understanding of the relation between theology and spirituality rests, in part, on how theology is to be understood. The new interest in spirituality suggests that the understandings of theology which have emerged in the recent past are viewed as deficient by some, not least on account of their apparent lack of connection with the life of faith.

In order to understand this matter properly, in the next chapter we shall explore the spiritual dimensions of seven leading themes of Christian theology, noting the vital connections between the two disciplines.

FOR FURTHER READING

The specific issue of the interaction of theology and spirituality can be explored from the following:

Louis Bouyer, *Introduction to Spirituality*. London: Darton, Longman and Todd, 1963.
J. de Guibert, *The Theology of the Spiritual Life*. New York: Sheed & Ward, 1953.
Bradley Hanson, "Theological Approaches to Spirituality: A Lutheran Approach," *Christian Spirituality Bulletin*, Spring 1994, 5–8.

Andrew Louth, *Discerning the Mystery: An Essay on the Nature of Theology*, Oxford: Oxford University Press, 1983.

Robin Maas and Gabriel O'Donnell, "An Introduction to Spiritual Theology: The Theory that undergirds our Practice," in R. Maas and G. O'Donnell (eds), *Spiritual Traditions for the Contemporary Church*. Nashville, TN: Abingdon, 1990, 11–21.

Eugene Megyer, "Theological Trends: Spiritual Theology Today," *The Way* 21 (1981), 55–67.

James I. Packer, "An Introduction to Systematic Spirituality," *Crux* 26 No. 1 (March 1990), 2–8.

Wolfhart Pannenberg, *Christian Spirituality and Sacramental Community*. Philadelphia: Westminster Press, 1983.

Sandra Schneiders, "Theology and Spirituality: Strangers, Rivals or Partners?" *Horizons* 13 (1986), 253–74.

Philip Sheldrake, *Spirituality and Theology: Christian Living and the Doctrine of God*. London: Darton, Longman and Todd, 1998.

Terry Tastard, "Theology and Spirituality in the Nineteenth and Twentieth Centuries," in P. Byrne and L. Houlden (eds), *Companion Encyclopaedia of Theology*. London: Routledge, 1995, 594–619.

Geoffrey Wainwright, *Doxology. The Praise of God in Worship, Doctrine and Life*. New York: Oxford University Press, 1980.

Edward Yarnold, "The Theology of Christian Spirituality," in C. Jones, G. Wainwright and E. Yarnold (eds), *The Study of Spirituality*. London: SPCK, 1986, 9–17.

4

THEOLOGICAL
FOUNDATIONS FOR
SPIRITUALITY: CASE
STUDIES

In the previous chapter, we considered some of the general issues concerning the relation of Christian theology and spirituality. Given these considerations, it is clearly of some interest to explore the way in which certain aspects of Christian theology have relevance for spirituality. It must be stressed that what is being offered here is not a comprehensive account of Christian theology. Rather, seven areas of Christian theology which are known to be of considerable significance for spirituality are being studied with a view to illustrating the manner in which theology and spirituality interact. Other aspects of Christian theology (for example, relating to the nature of the church or the function of the sacraments) have important roles in spirituality which are not fully explored in this work.

Each area of theology to be explored will be treated in an identical manner, to make it easier to understand the points at issue. In each case, the section opens with an *explanation* of the doctrine in question. This will include consideration of the biblical foundations of the doctrine, and the manner in which it has been developed within the rich tradition of subsequent Christian theological reflection. This is followed by an exploration of its *application* – that is, the potential relevance of the doctrine for Christian spirituality. The aim of this discussion is to demonstrate the ways in which theology supports, sustains and stimulates Christian spirituality. Finally, an *illustration* is provided of the way in which this theological theme is exploited in Christian spirituality, by focusing on the manner in which it is developed by a single writer. The singling out of individual writers in this manner is not intended to imply that they are superior to others. It must be recalled that many other writers could have been called upon to illustrate the points involved. The selection has been made entirely on the basis of the clarity of their presentation, so that readers who are new to the field will be able to grasp the points being made as simply as possible.

With these points in mind, let us turn to the first major area to be considered – the doctrine of creation.

Creation

Although the idea of "creation" can be found in classic secular philosophy – for example, in the writings of the Greek philosopher Aristotle – it is generally regarded as being a distinctly religious notion. The idea that the world was created is one of the most foundational of religious ideas, which finds different expressions in the various religions of the world. Religions of the ancient near east often take the form of a conflict between a creator deity and the forces of chaos. The dominant form of the doctrine of creation is that associated with Judaism, Christianity, and Islam. In what follows, we shall consider the basic features of this doctrine.

Explanation

The theme of "God as creator" is of major importance within the Old Testament. Attention has often focused on the creation narratives found in the first two chapters of the book of Genesis, with which the Old Testament canon opens. However, it must be appreciated that the theme is deeply embedded in the wisdom and prophetic literature. Job 38:1–42:6 sets out what is unquestionably the most comprehensive understanding of God as creator to be found in the Old Testament, stressing the role of God as creator and sustainer of the world. It is possible to discern two distinct, though related, contexts in which the notion of "God as creator" is encountered: first, in contexts which reflect the praise of God within Israel's worship, both individual and corporate; and secondly, in contexts which stress that the God who created the world is also the God who liberated Israel from bondage, and continues to sustain her in the present.

As we have seen, the doctrine of God as creator has its foundations firmly laid in the Old Testament (e.g., Genesis 1, 2). In the history of theology, the doctrine of God the creator has often been linked with the authority of the Old Testament. The continuing importance of the Old Testament for Christianity is often held to be grounded in the fact that the god of which it speaks is the same god to be revealed in the New Testament. The creator and redeemer god are one and the same. In the case of Gnosticism, which became especially influential during the second century, a vigorous attack was mounted on both the authority of the Old Testament, and the idea that God was creator of the world. We shall explore the importance of this in what follows.

For Gnosticism, in most of its significant forms, a sharp distinction was to be drawn between the God who redeemed humanity from the world, and a somewhat inferior deity (often termed "the demiurge") who created that world in the first place. The Old Testament was regarded by the Gnostics as dealing with this lesser deity, whereas the New Testament was concerned with the redeemer God. As such, belief in God as creator and in the authority of the Old Testament came to be interlinked at an early stage. Of the early writers to deal with this theme, Irenaeus of Lyons (*c*.130–*c*.200) is of particular importance, on account of his vigorous defense of Christianity against its Gnostic critics.

Irenaeus of Lyons (c.130–c.200). Probably a native of Asia Minor, who was elected as bishop of the southern French city of Lyons around 178. He is chiefly noted for his major writing *adversus haereses* ("Against the heresies"), which defended the Christian faith against Gnostic misrepresentations and criticisms.

A distinct debate centred on the question of whether creation was to be regarded as *ex nihilo* – that is to say, out of nothing. In one of his dialogues (*Timaeus*), Plato developed the idea that the world was made out of pre-existent matter, which was fashioned into the present form of the world. This idea was taken up by most Gnostic writers, who were here followed by some Christian theologians of the second century, such as Justin Martyr (*c*.100–*c*.165). These writers affirmed the existence of pre-existent matter, which they understood to have been shaped into the world in the act of creation. In other words, creation was not *ex nihilo*; rather, it was to be seen as an act of construction, on the basis of material which was already to hand, as one might construct an igloo out of snow, or a house from stone. The existence of evil in the world was thus to be explained on the basis of the intractability of this pre-existent matter. God's options in creating the world were limited by the poor quality of the material available. The presence of evil or defects within the world are thus not to be ascribed to God, but to deficiencies in the material from which the world was constructed.

However, the conflict with Gnosticism forced reconsideration of this issue. In part, the idea of creation from pre-existent matter was discredited by its Gnostic associations; in part, it was called into question by an increasingly sophisticated reading of the Old Testament creation narratives. Writers such as Theophilus of Antioch insisted upon the doctrine of creation *ex nihilo*, which may be regarded as gaining the ascendency from the end of the second century onwards. From that point onwards, it became the received doctrine within the church.

A radical dualism between God and creation was thus eliminated, in favor of the view that the truth, goodness, and beauty of God (to use the Platonic triad which so influenced many writers of the period) could be discerned within the natural order, in consequence of that order having been established by God. For example, Origen (*c*.185–*c*.254) argued that it was God's creation of the world which structured the natural order in such a manner that it could be comprehended by the human mind, by conferring upon that order an intrinsic rationality and order which derived from and reflected the divine nature itself.

Three main ways of conceiving the creative action of God became widely established within Christian circles by the end of the fifth century. We shall note them briefly, and identify their relevance to our theme.

1 *Emanation*. This term was widely used by early Christian writers to clarify the relation between God and the world on the one hand, and the divine Logos on the other. Although the term is not used by either Plato or Plotinus, many patristic writers sympathetic to the various forms of Platonism saw it as a convenient and appropriate way of articulating Platonic insights. The image that dominates this approach is that of light or heat radiating from the sun, or a human source such as a fire. This image of creation (hinted at in the Nicene Creed's phrase "light from light") suggests that the creation of the world can be regarded as an overflowing of the creative energy of God. Just as light derives from the sun and reflects its nature, so the created order derives from God, and expresses the divine nature. There is, on the basis of this model, a *natural* or *organic* connection between God and the creation.

However, the model has weaknesses, of which two may be noted. First, the image of a sun radiating light, or a fire radiating heat, implies an involuntary emanation, rather than a conscious decision to create. The Christian tradition has consistently emphasized that the act of creation rests upon a prior decision on the part of God to create, which this model cannot adequately express. This naturally leads on to the second weakness, which relates to the impersonal nature of the model in question. The idea of a personal God, expressing a personality both in the very act of creation and the subsequent creation itself, is difficult to convey by this image. Nevertheless, the model clearly articulates a close connection between creator and creation, leading us to expect that something of the identity and nature of the creator is to be found in the creation. Thus the beauty of God – a theme which was of particular importance in early medieval theology, and has emerged as significant again in the later writings of Hans Urs von Balthasar (1905–88) – would be expected to be reflected in the nature of the creation.

2 *Construction*. Many biblical passages portray God as a master builder, deliberately constructing the world (for example, Psalm 127:1). The imagery is powerful, conveying the ideas of purpose, planning, and a deliberate intention to create. The image is important, in that it draws attention to both the creator and the creation. In addition to bringing out the skill of the creator, it also allows the beauty and ordering of the resulting creation to be appreciated, both for what it is in itself, and for its testimony to the creativity and care of its creator.

However, the image has a deficiency, which relates to a point made earlier concerning Plato's dialogue *Timaeus*. This portrays creation as involving pre-existent matter. Here, creation is understood as giving shape and form to something which is already there – an idea which, we have seen, causes at least a degree of tension with the doctrine of creation *ex nihilo*. The image of God as a builder would seem to imply the assembly of the world from material which is already to hand, which is clearly deficient. Nevertheless, despite this slight difficulty, it can be seen that the model expresses the insight that the character of the creator is, in some manner, expressed in the natural world, just as that of an artist is communicated or embodied in her work. In particular, the notion of "ordering" – that is, the imparting or imposing of a coherence or structure to the material in question – is clearly affirmed by this model. Whatever else the complex notion of "creation" may mean within a

Christian context, it certainly includes the fundamental theme of ordering – a notion which is especially significant in the creation narratives of the Old Testament.

3 *Artistic expression.* Many Christian writers, from various periods in the history of the church, speak of creation as the "handiwork of God," comparing it to a work of art which is both beautiful in itself, as well as expressing the personality of its creator. This model of creation as the "artistic expression" of God as creator is particularly well expressed in the writings of the eighteenth-century North American theologian Jonathan Edwards (1705–58), as we shall see presently.

The image is profoundly helpful, in that it supplements a deficiency of both the two models noted above – namely, their impersonal character. The image of God as artist conveys the idea of personal expression in the creation of something beautiful. Once more, the potential weaknesses need to be noted: for example, the model could easily lead to the idea of creation from pre-existent matter, as in the case of a sculptor with a statue carved from an already existing block of stone. However, the model offers us at least the possibility of thinking about creation from nothing, as with the author who writes a novel, or the composer who creates a melody and harmony. It also encourages us to seek for the self-expression of God in the creation, and gives added theological credibility to the notion of "natural theology" (that is, the idea that something of God may be known through nature). There is also a natural link between the concept of creation as "artistic expression" and the highly significant concept of "beauty," which will feature prominently in any Christian approach to the creation.

Application

The doctrine of creation has a number of major implications for Christian spirituality, of which we shall note two of especial importance. First, the doctrine of creation affirms the goodness of creation; second, it affirms that something of God may be known through the creation. We shall explore each of these in what follows.

The Gnostics argued that the material world was evil, and could only serve to contaminate humanity (see p. 36). The doctrine of creation affirms that the material world was created by God, and in some way reflects God's goodness. This has major implications for Christian spirituality. For example, it affirms that it is not necessary to withdraw from the world in order to secure salvation or to serve God properly. One of the most interesting developments in modern spirituality is the emergence of forms of spirituality which are specifically directed to those working in the marketplace, dedicated to allowing them to live the Christian life to the full while continuing to work outside specifically or explicitly religious contexts (such as monasteries or seminaries). It also affirms that caring for the world – including both the environment and human beings – is of profound spiritual importance, thus offering a major motivation for environmental and welfare work.

The doctrine of creation also offers a major stimulus to the study of nature as a means of learning more about the wisdom and majesty of God. It has often been pointed out that the doctrine of creation offers a major stimulus to the natural sciences. To study the creation is to gain an enhanced appreciation of the wisdom and beauty of the creator. There are few who are not moved by the sight of a glorious sunset, the brilliance of the star-studded night sky, or the immensity of an Alpine landscape. In every case, the sense of wonder evoked by the creation is of spiritual significance, and leads to an increased sense of wonder in the presence of God. This can be seen clearly in the writings of the French renaissance thinker Jean Bodin (1539–96), especially his *Universae naturae theatrum* ("The Theater of the Universe of Nature"):

> We have come into this theater of the world for no other reason than to understand the admirable power, goodness and wisdom of the most excellent creator of all things, to the extent that this is possible, by contemplating the appearance of the universe and all his actions and individual works, and thus to be swept away more ardently in praise of him.

A further area of relevance concerns the specific question of human nature as a creation of God; this will be explored further in the next section of this chapter. We may now illustrate the importance of the doctrine of creation in general for our theme.

Illustration

The theme of the beauty of creation resonates throughout the history of Christian spirituality. Hildegard of Bingen's *Liber divinorum operum* ("book of divine works"), written between 1163 and 1174, addresses this theme at several points. For Hildegard, "God cannot be seen, but can be known through his creation, just as the body of a human being cannot be seen on account of his clothes."

Hildegard of Bingen (1098–1179). Abbess of Rupertsberg, near Bingen. One of the most influential women spiritual writers of the Middle Ages, who is remembered chiefly for her visionary and prophetic writings, particularly the *Scivias*, which contain 26 visions relating to the nature and destiny of the cosmos. She also produced some musical compositions, and two medical treatises.

One of the most important applications of this principle of the beauty of God's creation can be found in the writings of Jonathan Edwards (1703–58), first President of Princeton University, and widely regarded as America's greatest theologian. At several points, Edwards sets out the importance of the fact that the natural world has been created by God for an appreciation of the wonder and glory of God.

> It is very fit and becoming of God who is infinitely wise, so to order things that there should be a voice of His in His works, instructing those that behold him and painting forth and shewing divine mysteries and things more immediately appertaining to Himself and His spiritual kingdom. The works of God are but a kind of voice or language of God to instruct intelligent beings in things pertaining to Himself. And why should we not think that he would teach and instruct by His works in this way as well as in others, viz., by representing divine things by His works and so painting them forth, especially

since we know that God hath so much delighted in this way of instruction. . . . If we look on these shadows of divine things as the voice of God purposely by them teaching us these and those spiritual and divine things, to show of what excellent advantage it will be, how agreeably and clearly it will tend to convey instruction to our minds, and to impress things on the mind and to affect the mind, by that we may, as it were, have God speaking to us. Wherever we are, and whatever we are about, we may see divine things excellently represented and held forth.

Notice how Edwards speaks of good and beautiful things within the natural world as "shadows of divine things." Those "divine things" – such as God's wisdom and beauty – may be difficult for us to grasp and appreciate as abstract ideas. Yet God, for Edwards, has not left us grasping after abstractions; instead, we can see these divine realities expressed and exhibited within the created order, which thus bears witness to its creator.

Jonathan Edwards (1703–58). Widely regarded as the most important American the-ologian to date, noted especially for his metaphysical defense of Christianity in the light of the increasingly influential ideas of the Enlightenment, and his positive statements of traditional Reformed doctrines.

Human Nature and Destiny

It will be clear that an understanding of human nature is central to any form of spir-ituality, whether Christian or not. Is human spiritual fulfillment to be sought with God, or apart from God? Does God assist us in our spiritual development, or are we required to achieve fulfillment through our own unaided merits? These two very basic questions (to which many more might be addded) indicate the importance of an understanding of human nature (including its spiritual capacities) and destiny to Christian spirituality. Within a Christian framework, human nature and destiny are alike to be understood in terms of the creation of humanity by God, and its ultimate intended destiny with God. We may therefore begin by considering the various approaches to this theme within the Christian tradition.

Explanation

A major theme in Christian discussion of human nature is the notion that humanity has been created "in the image of God" (Genesis 1:27). This idea has been the subject of considerable discussion within the Christian tradition of biblical interpre-tation. Some writers, such as Augustine, argue that the "image of God" is to be understood as the human ability to reason, which is fashioned in the likeness of the wisdom of God. Others argue that the idea implies an affinity between humanity and God which forms the basis of a relationship between them. If human beings exist in the "image of God," it follows that a potential for a relationship exists between individual human beings and God. The process of redemption is thus seen as the means by which this image is brought to its fulfillment in a perfect relation with God.

This idea is clearly of relevance to spirituality. If human beings are created with some type of capacity to relate to God, and if it is intended by God that such a relationship should exist and develop, then the question of how a relationship with God can be established and nurtured is of considerable interest. The theme of humanity as created in the image of God can thus be seen as underlying the basic task of Christian spirituality.

But what are the respective roles of God and humanity in spiritual development? Is spiritual growth something which we can achieve by ourselves? Or is it something which needs us to look for assistance from someone or something else?

The Pelagian controversy of the early fifth century can be regarded as a landmark in the debate within the Christian tradition over the relation of the human and divine contributions to spiritual growth. Pelagius, a British monk who settled in Rome in the late fourth century, was convinced of the need for reformation within the church. Noting that many Christians of the period appeared to be somewhat lax in their religious observances, he argued that ability to keep the law of God implied an obligation to keep that law.

The Pelagian controversy centered on Pelagius and Augustine, and is perhaps most conveniently summarized in terms of a number of headings.

1   *Human autonomy.* For Pelagius, humanity had complete freedom, including a freedom to obey the moral law of God. A failure to do so was thus inexcusable. Having ordained what humanity should do, God no longer required to be involved, in that human beings possessed the ability to pursue God's will unaided. Pelagius thus argues that believers are capable of fulfilling the law (such as the Ten Commandments); for that reason, they are under an absolute obligation to do so. For Augustine, human nature was weakened and incapacitated by the ravages of sin, making it impossible for human beings to fulfil the law or do God's will. Knowing what God wanted did not imply an ability to achieve this. For Augustine, fallen humanity depended totally upon the grace of God for its salvation, and could not achieve spiritual growth unaided. Believers are incapable of keeping the law of God unaided; their failure thus points them to the need for God's grace throughout the Christian life, and the importance of prayer as an acknowledgement of the dependence of humanity upon God.

2   *Sin.* Pelagius argued that individual sinful actions were the result of an imperfect understanding of what God required of humanity, or the imitation of sinful actions by others. Human nature was basically good, and therefore not capable of a deliberate rebellion against God. Pelagius thus points out that God graciously provides examples of what constitutes good conduct – for example, in the Ten Commandments or in the example of Jesus Christ. It is then up to believers to bring themselves into line with these examples. For Augustine, humanity was contaminated by original sin, which he likened to some form of congenital illness. Individual sinful human actions were thus the result of an underlying sinful condition, in much the same way as symptoms are the result of an illness. There was no point in attempting

to cure the symptoms (for example, by demanding that believers keep the law perfectly) when the real problem lay deeper. For Augustine, salvation must involve an inner transformation of human nature; merely offering external guidance or instruction will not alter the situation.

In the end, the Council of Carthage (418) settled the argument more or less in Augustine's favor, ruling that human beings depended on God for their salvation, which could not be achieved by human effort alone. The basic position, developed by Augustine and endorsed by the Council, can be summarized in Augustine's slogan "God operates without us, and cooperates with us." This is to be understood that God brings about our conversion without any cooperation on our part; thereafter, however, there is some form of cooperation between God and the believer as the process of Christian living gets under way. Within this Augustinian perspective, spirituality thus relates to the development of the Christian spiritual life, which is to be seen as some form of collaboration between God and the believer. For Augustine, this does not imply an *equal* collaboration, as if God and the believer performed equally arduous roles. Augustine's position is that God performs the major and more difficult part in the process of renewal and regeneration; nevertheless, the believer contributes in a small but real manner to this process.

These same issues have been debated constantly since the fifth century. In view of their importance, we shall look at the positions of Pelagius and Augustine in a little more detail, focusing on some primary texts. In a letter written to the Roman noblewoman Demetrias in the early fifth century, Pelagius argued that God knew human abilities, and that a divine command implied both a human ability and obligation.

> [Instead of regarding God's commands as a privilege] . . . we cry out at God and say, "This is too hard! This is too difficult! We cannot do it! We are only human, and hindered by the weakness of the flesh!" What blind madness! What blatant presumption! By doing this, we accuse the God of knowledge of a twofold ignorance – ignorance of God's own creation and of God's own commands. It would be as if, forgetting the weakness of humanity – God's own creation – God had laid upon us commands which we were unable to bear. And at the same time – may God forgive us! – we ascribe to the righteous One unrighteousness, and cruelty to the Holy One; first, by complaining that God has commanded the impossible, second, by imagining that some will be condemned by God for what they could not help; so that – the blasphemy of it! – God is thought of as seeking our punishment rather than our salvation. . . . No one knows the extent of our strength better than the God who gave us that strength. . . . God has not willed to command anything impossible, for God is righteous; and will not condemn anyone for what they could not help, for God is holy.

Note how Pelagius insists that God's commands are made on the basis of a perfect understanding of the human situation. Human nature is such that it is capable of achieving the good which God intends without any form of divine intervention or assistance. Augustine responded with a very different understanding of the situation. Human nature is fallen, and as a result cannot achieve the goals which God originally intended for it.

Human nature was certainly originally created blameless and without any fault; but the human nature by which each one of us is now born of Adam requires a physician, because it is not healthy. All the good things, which it has by its conception, life, senses, and mind, it has from God, its creator and maker. But the weakness which darkens and disables these good natural qualities, as a result of which that nature needs enlightenment and healing, did not come from the blameless maker but from original sin, which was committed by free will. For this reason our guilty nature is liable to a just penalty. For if we are now a new creature in Christ, we were still children of wrath by nature, like everyone else. But God, who is rich in mercy, on account of the great love with which He loved us, even when we were dead through our sins, raised us up to life with Christ, by whose grace we are saved. But this grace of Christ, without which neither infants nor grown persons can be saved, is not bestowed as a reward for merits, but is given freely (*gratis*), which is why it is called grace (*gratia*).

Augustine thus places considerable emphasis upon the gift-character of grace. Grace is something undeserved and even intrinsically undeservable. It is something which reflects the sheer graciousness and liberality of God, rather than the intrinsic goodness and value of human nature.

Three major positions may be noted within the Christian tradition concerning the relation of human and divine action in spiritual development.

1 *Spiritual development is primarily a human achievement.* This view was associated to some extent with Pelagius, and also finds support within Orthodox Christianity. Interestingly, it was given a cautious welcome by John Wesley (1703–91), who felt that Pelagius was right in his emphasis on the need for Christian perfection, a notion which finds some degree of support in Wesley's doctrine of "entire sanctification."

2 *Spiritual development results from human action in cooperation with the grace of God.* This view is found in the later Augustine, and is summarized in his famous maxim: "God operates without us, and cooperates with us." This expresses the idea that conversion is a work of God, but that the Christian life itself takes the form of a collaboration (though not necessarily an *equal* collaboration) between the believer and God.

3 *Spiritual development results from the grace of God acting upon an essentially passive human nature.* This view can be found in a number of Reformed writers, who place particular emphasis on the role of divine grace in the Christian life.

From this brief analysis, it will be clear that a number of different understandings of the capacity of human nature are to be found in modern Christianity. Each has significantly different implications for Christian spirituality. The first of the three positions set out above finds support within Greek Orthodoxy, yet is regarded with suspicion by many within western Christianity. The second and third positions are more typical of western Christianity. In what follows, we shall explore their application to spirituality.

Application

We have already noted how the idea of being created "in the image of God" has profound implications for any Christian understanding of human nature and destiny. Humanity has been made *by God and for God*; its true goal lies in the fulfillment of its relationship with God. Augustine's famous statement can be regarded as an excellent summary of this point: "You have made us for yourself, and our heart is restless until it finds its rest in you." This is perhaps one of the clearest points of tension between a Christian spirituality and one of its secular counterparts. For Christianity, it is impossible to frame an understanding of human origins, development, or destiny without reference to God.

The significance of this point is best appreciated when set against the backdrop of the growing recognition within western medical research of the importance of personal spirituality in relation to health. A growing body of experimental evidence suggests a strong positive correlation between personal spirituality and a positive therapeutic outcome. A growing number of North American medical schools now include courses on "medicine and spirituality," addressing the spiritual aspects of healing. The Christian understanding of human nature strongly affirms that it is impossible to be truly human – that is, to be what God intended humanity to be – without considering the relation of humanity to God as its creator and redeemer. This is an area of considerable practical importance, and it is to be expected that exploration of the interface between spirituality and healthcare will be continued in the foreseeable future.

The question of human nature is also of importance within Christian spirituality itself, considered in isolation from other disciplines. An understanding of the capacities of human nature is presupposed or required by the question: "what can we do to deepen our sense of the presence of God?", or: "How can I draw nearer to God?" The questions involve engaging with the question of whether spiritual development is something that we do, or something that God does to us – or, of course, something that is achieved in partnership.

As we have noted, the majority opinion within Christian theology has been that humanity cannot cause or create God's grace, but that individual believers may benefit from that grace in various ways. The vocabulary which came to be used extensively following the theological renaissance of the twelfth century was that of "disposing oneself towards grace." This way of phrasing the matter made two important statements:

1 That God's grace was not in any way caused by human actions;
2 That believers could benefit from grace by behaving in certain ways – such as being penitent, or turning to God in prayer and humility.

Two main analogies were used to make this point clear. Alan of Lille (died 1202/3) argued that penitence on the part of someone was the means by which that person received grace. However, the penitence itself could not strictly be seen as the cause of grace, but merely the occasion or means by which it was received.

> Penitence is indeed a necessary cause [of grace], in that unless someone is penitent, God will not forgive that person's sins. It is like the sun, which illuminates a house when a shutter is opened. The opening of that shutter is not the efficient cause of that illumination, in that the sun itself is the efficient cause of that illumation. However, it is nevertheless its occasion.

The point that Alan of Lille is making can be summarized like this. The sun is always radiating its illumination. Nevertheless, for that light to enter into and illuminate a room in the house, a shutter must be opened. The opening of that shutter does not cause the sun to shine, in that this is already happening. Rather, the opening of the shutter is the means by which that light enters and illuminates the house. The removal of an obstacle to illumination thus serves a real role in the lighting up of that dark room. In the same way, human beings can remove obstacles to God's grace, so that they may develop and progress in the spiritual life.

A related analogy was developed by late medieval preachers, including Johann Geiler of Keisersberg, who was cathedral preacher at Strasbourg from 1478 to 1510. Geiler uses the analogy of a man sailing a boat. He can do nothing to cause the wind to blow; that lies outside his control. However, he can do certain things which allow him to take advantage of the wind when it does blow – such as unfurl the sail, or turn the sail directly into the wind. In the same way, Geiler argues, believers cannot cause God's grace; they can nevertheless dispose themselves in such a way as to make the most of it, in terms of spiritual growth and personal development. Believers must therefore expect to actively contribute towards their sanctification and renewal, while recognizing that their ultimate source and cause lies in God.

Both these analogies presuppose that believers are in a position to actively contribute to their spiritual growth, even though the grace of God must be acknowledged to play a major role. While this is widely regarded to be the majority position, it is important to appreciate that other positions exist, particularly within the Reformed tradition of Protestantism, which traces its origins back to John Calvin (1509–64). The Puritan school of spirituality provides an excellent example of an approach which places particular emphasis on the transforming role of the Holy Spirit, and we shall consider this in more detail later (see p. 96).

Illustration

It is widely agreed that Jean-Pierre de Caussade (1675–1751) offers one of the finest explorations of the interaction of the divine and human roles in spirituality. In his *Self-Abandonment to Divine Providence*, de Caussade spoke of a "dynamic surrender to the will and way of God." The phrase "dynamic surrender" points to the complexity of the interaction of the divine and the human in spiritual growth; on the one hand, it is necessary to unreservedly surrender to divine providence, allowing God to take the upper hand; on the other hand, that very act of surrender is itself an act of human will. This surrender to the divine providence is thus seen as an active decision on the part of the human will to submit itself to God, who will then bring about the good that God wills for the believer. The believer must actively discern the will of God, and then gladly submit to it.

If it is the duty of the moment to read something, the book will achieve this mysterious purpose in the depths of the heart. If the divine will abandons reading for an act of contemplation, that duty brings regeneration in the depths of our heart – whereas reading would be harmful and useless. If the divine will should reject contemplation to hear confessions and so forth (especially if this takes a long time!), then that very duty will establish Jesus Christ in the depths of our heart – whereas all the sweetness of contemplation would only destroy him . . . We must surrender and abandon ourselves to his divine will in perfect confidence. This divine will is infinitely wise, powerful and benevolent towards those who completely and unreservedly place their hope in it, and who love and seek it alone, and who believe with an unshakeable faith and confidence that what it effects in us at each moment is indeed the best.

The Trinity

The doctrine of the Trinity is one of the most distinctive Christian teachings. It also one of the most difficult doctrines to understand. In what follows, we shall attempt to present an outline sketch of the main features of this teaching, focusing on the factors which led to its historical development in the early church.

Explanation

The basic theme of the Christian doctrine of the Trinity is that of the richness of God, and the inability of human language or imagery to capture fully the wonder of God. Even this very simple statement of the role of the Trinity will indicate its importance for Christian spirituality. At one level, the doctrine is notoriously difficult to comprehend, particularly in its statements concerning "three persons and one substance." However, as Augustine of Hippo once pointed out, "if you can comprehend it, it is not God." The doctrine can thus be seen as a safeguard against simplistic or reductionist approaches to God, which inevitably end up by robbing God of mystery, majesty, and glory.

It should be noted that the doctrine is not explicitly taught in the New Testament, although there are two passages which are certainly open to an explicitly Trinitarian interpretation: Matthew 28:19 and 2 Corinthians 13:14. Both these verses have become deeply rooted in the Christian consciousness, the former on account of its baptismal associations, and the latter through the common use of the formula in Christian prayer and devotion. Yet these two verses, taken together or in isolation, can hardly be thought of as constituting a doctrine of the Trinity.

The biblical foundations of this doctrine are not, however, to be found solely in these two verses, but in the pervasive pattern of divine activity to which the New Testament bears witness. The Father is revealed in Christ through the Spirit. There is the closest of connections between the Father, Son, and Spirit in the New Testament writings. Time after time, New Testament passages link together these three elements as part of a greater whole. The totality of God's saving presence and power can only, it would seem, be expressed by involving all three elements (for example, see 1 Corinthians 12:4–6; 2 Corinthians 1:21–2; Galatians 4:6; Ephesians 2:20–22; 2 Thessalonians 2:13–14; Titus 3:4–6; 1 Peter 1:2).

The same Trinitarian structure can be seen in the Old Testament. Three major "personifications" of God can be discerned within its pages, which naturally lead on to the Christian doctrine of the Trinity. These are:

1   *Wisdom*. This personification of God is especially evident in the Wisdom literature, such as Proverbs, Job, and Ecclesiasticus. The attribute of divine wisdom is here treated as if it were a person (hence the idea of "personification"), with an existence apart from, yet dependent upon, God. Wisdom (who is always treated as female, incidentally) is portrayed as active in creation, fashioning the world in her imprint (see Proverbs 1:20–3; 9:1–6; Job 28; Ecclesiasticus 24).

2   *The Word of God*. Here, the idea of God's speech or discourse is treated as an entity with an existence independent of God, yet originating with him. The Word of God is portrayed as going forth into the world to confront men and women with the will and purpose of God, bringing guidance, judgment and salvation (see Psalm 119:89; Psalm 147:15–20; Isaiah 55:10–11).

3   *The Spirit of God*. The Old Testament uses the phrase "the spirit of God" to refer to God's presence and power within his creation. The spirit is portrayed as being present in the expected Messiah (Isaiah 42:1–3), and as being the agent of a new creation which will arise when the old order has finally passed away (Ezekiel 36:26; 37:1–14).

These three "hypostatizations" of God (to use a Greek word in place of the English "personification") do not amount to a doctrine of the Trinity in the strict sense of the term. Rather, they point to a pattern of divine activity and presence in and through creation, in which God is both immanent and transcendent. A purely unitarian conception of God proved inadequate to contain this dynamic understanding of God. And it is this pattern of divine activity which is expressed in the doctrine of the Trinity.

The doctrine of the Trinity can be regarded as the outcome of a process of sustained and critical reflection on the pattern of divine activity revealed in Scripture, and continued in Christian experience. This is not to say that Scripture contains a doctrine of the Trinity; rather, Scripture bears witness to a God who demands to be understood in a Trinitarian manner.

The development of the doctrine of the Trinity is organically related to the evolution of the Christian understanding of the identity and significance of Jesus, especially in relation to the doctrine of the incarnation. It became increasingly clear that there was a consensus to the effect that Jesus was "of the same substance" (Greek: *homoousios*) as God, rather than just "of similar substance" (Greek: *homoiousios*). But if Jesus was God, in any meaningful sense of the word, what did this imply about God? If Jesus was God, were there now two Gods? Or was a radical reconsideration of the nature of God appropriate? Historically, it is possible to argue that the doctrine of the Trinity is closely linked with the development of the doctrine of the divinity of Christ. The more emphatic the church became that Christ was God, the more it came under pressure to clarify how Christ related to God. Although there were some early Christian writers who hoped to be able to operate with a simple concept of God, this became increasingly problematical as the richness and profundity of the Christian understanding of God was explored and articulated. The recognition of the full divinity of Christ can be seen as a landmark on the road to the doctrine of the Trinity.

The starting point for Christian reflections on the Trinity is, as we have seen, the New Testament witness to the presence and activity of God in Christ and through the Spirit. For Irenaeus of Lyons (*c*.130–*c*.200), the whole process of salvation, from its beginning to its end, bore witness to the action of Father, Son, and Holy Spirit. Irenaeus made use of a term which features prominently in future discussion of the Trinity: "the economy of salvation." That word "economy" needs clarification. The Greek word *oikonomia* basically means "the way in which one's affairs are ordered" (the relation to the modern sense of the word will thus be clear). For Irenaeus, the "economy of salvation" means "the way in which God has ordered the salvation of humanity in history."

At the time, Irenaeus was under considerable pressure from Gnostic critics, who argued that the creator god was quite distinct from (and inferior to!) the redeemer god. An excellent representative of this opposition is to be found in Marcion (died *c*.160), who held that the Old Testament god is a creator god, and totally different from the redeemer god of the New Testament. As a result, the Old Testament should be shunned by Christians, who should concentrate their attention upon the New Testament. Irenaeus vigorously rejected this idea. He insisted that the entire process of salvation, from the first moment of creation to the last moment of history, was the work of the one and the same God. There was a single economy of salvation, in which the one God – who was both creator and redeemer – was at work to redeem his creation.

In his *Demonstration of the Preaching of the Apostles*, Irenaeus insisted upon the distinct yet related roles of Father, Son, and Spirit within the economy of salvation. He affirmed his faith in:

> God the Father uncreated, who is uncontained, invisible; one God, creator of the universe . . . and the Word of God, the Son of God, our Lord Jesus Christ, who . . . in the fullness of time, to gather all things to himself, became a human among humans, to . . . destroy death, bring life, and achieve fellowship between God and humanity . . . And the Holy Spirit . . . was poured out in a new way on our humanity to make us new throughout the world in the sight of God.

This passage brings out clearly the idea of an economic Trinity – that is to say, an understanding of the nature of the Godhead in which each of the three persons is responsible for an aspect of the economy of salvation. Far from being a rather pointless piece of theological speculation, the doctrine of the Trinity is grounded directly in the complex human experience of redemption in Christ, and is concerned with the explanation of this experience.

By the second half of the fourth century, the debate concerning the relation of the Father and Son gave every indication of having been settled. The recognition that Father and Son were "of one being" settled the Arian controversy, and established a consensus within the church over the divinity of the Son. But further theological construction was necessary. What was the relation of the Spirit to the Father? and to the Son? There was a growing consensus that the Spirit could not be omitted from the Godhead. Writers such as Basil of Caesarea (c.330–79) and Gregory of Nazianzus (329–89) defended the divinity of the Spirit in such persuasive terms that the foundation was laid for the final element of Trinitarian theology to be put in its place. The divinity and co-equality of Father, Son, and Spirit had been agreed; it now remained to develop Trinitarian models to allow this understanding of the Godhead to be visualized.

In general, eastern theology tended to emphasize the distinct individuality of the three persons, and safeguard their unity by stressing the fact that both the Son and the Spirit derived from the Father. The relation between the persons is grounded in what those persons *are*. Thus the relation of the Son to the Father is defined in terms of "being begotten" and "sonship." Augustine moves away from this approach, preferring to treat the persons in *relational* terms. The western approach was thus more marked by its tendency to begin from the unity of God, especially in the work of revelation and redemption, and to interpret the relation of the three persons in terms of their mutual fellowship.

The eastern approach might seem to suggest that the Trinity consists of three independent agents, doing quite different things. This possibility was excluded by two later developments, which are usually referred to by the terms "mutual interpenetration (*perichoresis*)" and "appropriation." Although these ideas find their full development at a later stage in the development of the doctrine, they are unquestionably hinted at in both Irenaeus and Tertullian (c.160–c.225), and find more substantial expression in the writings of Gregory of Nyssa (c.330–c.395). We may usefully consider both these ideas at this stage.

1   *Perichoresis.* This Greek term, which is often found in either its Latin (*circumincessio*) or English ("mutual interpenetration") forms, came into general use in the sixth century. It refers to the manner in which the three persons of the Trinity relate to one another. The concept of *perichoresis* allows the individuality of the persons to be maintained, while insisting that each person shares in the life of the other two. An image often used to express this idea is that of "a community of being," in which each person, while maintaining its distinctive identity, penetrates the others and is penetrated by them.

2   *Appropriation.* The modalist heresy argued that God could be considered as existing in different "modes of being" at different points in the economy of salvation, so that, at one point, God existed as Father and created the world; at another God existed as Son and redeemed it. The doctrine of appropriation insists that the works of the Trinity are a unity; every person of the Trinity is involved in every outward action of the Godhead. Thus Father, Son, and Spirit are all involved in the work of creation, which is not to be viewed as the work of the Father alone. For example, Augustine of Hippo pointed out that the Genesis creation account speaks of God, the Word, and the Spirit (Genesis 1:1–3), thus indicating that all three

persons of the Trinity were present and active at this decisive moment in salvation history.

Yet it is appropriate to think of creation as the work of the Father. Despite the fact that all three persons of the Trinity are implicated in creation, it is properly seen as the distinctive action of the Father. Similarly, the entire Trinity is involved in the work of redemption. It is, however, appropriate to speak of redemption as being the distinctive work of the Son.

Taken together, the doctrines of *perichoresis* and appropriation allow us to think of the Godhead as a "community of being," in which all is shared, united, and mutually exchanged. Father, Son, and Spirit are not three isolated and diverging compartments of a Godhead, like three subsidiary components of an international corporation. Rather, they are differentiations within the Godhead, which become evident within the economy of salvation and the human experience of redemption and grace. The doctrine of the Trinity affirms that beneath the surface of the complexities of the history of salvation and our experience of God lies one God, and one God only.

One of the most significant events in the early history of the church was agreement throughout the Roman Empire, both east and west, concerning the Nicene Creed. This document was intended to bring doctrinal stability to the church in a period of considerable importance in its history. Part of that agreed text referred to the Holy Spirit "proceeding from the Father." By the ninth century, however, the western church routinely altered this phrase, speaking of the Holy Spirit "proceeding from the Father *and from the Son*" (my emphasis). The Latin term *filioque* ("and from the Son") has since come to refer to this addition, now widely accepted within the western churches, and the theology which it expresses. This idea of a "double procession" of the Holy Spirit was a source of intensive irritation to Greek Christians. Not only did it raise serious theological difficulties for them; it also involved tampering with the supposedly inviolable text of the creeds. Many scholars see this bad feeling as contributing to the split between the eastern and western churches, which took place around 1054. Although this is a significant debate, with continuing relevance for ecumenical discussions, it is not of decisive importance for our purposes, and we shall therefore not pursue it further.

Application

The doctrine of the Trinity serves as the foundation for a number of major themes in Christian spirituality. In that the Trinity can be seen as a statement of a specifically *Christian* approach to and understanding of God, it is to be expected that it will feature prominently in many writings on Christian spirituality. The following themes are of particular importance.

1   Christian understandings of worship and prayer are often constructed around a trinitarian framework. For example, Christians often speak of "worshipping God through Christ in the Spirit." Thus Basil of Caesarea, in his treatise *On the Holy Spirit*, argues that all of God's activity in creation, redemption and sanctification takes place

"through the Son" and "in the Spirit." This has interesting implications for spirituality, particularly in relation to prayer. From a trinitarian perspective, prayer is not to be seen as a purely human activity, but as the Holy Spirit moving and prompting the believer to turn to God. In the New Testament, we find clear statements to the effect that it is the Holy Spirit to enables us to pray "Abba, Father" (Romans 8:15–16).

2   The doctrine of the Trinity gathers together the richness of the complex Christian understanding of God, to yield a vision of God to which the only appropriate response is adoration and devotion. The doctrine knits together into a coherent whole the Christian doctrines of creation, redemption, and sanctification. By doing so, it sets before us a vision of a God who created the world, and whose glory can be seen reflected in the wonders of the natural order; a God who redeemed the world, whose love can be seen in the tender face of Christ; and a God who is present now in the lives of believers. In this sense, the doctrine can be said to "preserve the mystery" of God, in the sense of ensuring that the Christian understanding of God is not impoverished through reductionism or rationalism. The Brazilian liberation theologian Leonardo Boff (1938–) makes this point as follows:

> Seeing mystery in this perspective enables us to understand how it provokes reverence, the only possible attitude to what is supreme and final in our lives. Instead of strangling reason, it invites expansion of the mind and heart. It is not a mystery that leaves us dumb and terrified, but one that leaves us happy, singing and giving thanks. It is not a wall placed in front of us, but a doorway through which we go to the infinity of God. Mystery is like a cliff: we may not be able to scale it, but we can stand at the foot of it, touch it, praise its beauty. So it is with the mystery of the Trinity.

3   Many writers note how the doctrine of the Trinity models a perfect community of equals, united by a bond of love. This approach is particularly associated with the notion of *perichoresis* (see p. 50). The love of God for the creation reflects a mutual love within the Godhead itself. Richard of St Victor is an excellent example of a medieval writer who explores the implications of the mutual love of the persons within the Godhead for both theology and spirituality. More recently, the coequality of the persons of the Trinity has been seen as the basis for social action, particularly in relation to models of equality in society. Writers such as Leonardo Boff have developed these themes with particular reference to the Latin American context.

Illustration

As we noted earlier, one of the major themes linked with the doctrine of the Trinity is the affirmation of the immensity of the Christian vision of God. This theme has been developed in innumerable works of spirituality, but is developed with particular force in a work of Celtic spirituality – the ancient Irish hymn generally known as "St Patrick's Breastplate," traditionally ascribed to the fifth-century figure of St Patrick, patron saint of Ireland. In this hymn, the believer is constantly reminded of the richness and the depth of the Christian understanding of God, and that it is this God who has been bonded to the believer through faith.

> I bind unto myself today
> The strong name of the Trinity,
> By invocation of the same,
> The Three in One, and One in Three.

The hymn then moves on to survey the vast panorama of the works of God in history. It affirms that the God who believers have made their own through faith is the same God who brought the Earth into being. The God whose presence and power undergirds the world of nature is the same God whose presence and power is channeled into individual existences:

> I bind unto myself today
> The virtues of the star-lit heaven,
> The glorious sun's life-giving ray,
> The whiteness of the moon at even,
> The flashing of the lightning free,
> The whirling wind's tempestuous shocks,
> The stable earth, the deep salt sea,
> Around the old eternal rocks.

Attention then turns to the work of God in redemption. The same God who created the world – the Earth, the sea, the sun, moon, and stars – acted in Jesus Christ to redeem humanity. In the history of Jesus Christ, from his incarnation to his second coming, God may be seen as acting to redeem humanity.

> I bind this day to me for ever,
> By power of faith, Christ's incarnation;
> His baptism in Jordan river;
> His death on Cross for my salvation;
> His bursting from the spicèd tomb;
> His riding up the heavenly way;
> His coming at the day of doom;
> I bind unto myself today.

Believers are thus invited to reflect upon the history of Jesus Christ: his incarnation, baptism, death, resurrection, ascension, and final coming on the last day. And all these, Patrick affirms, are the action of the same God who created the world.

Finally, the hymn affirms that the God who called the universe into being and redeemed humanity through the great sequence of events which is the history of Jesus Christ is also the God who remains with believers, strengthening and supporting them here and now.

> I bind unto myself today
> The power of God to hold and lead,
> His eye to watch, his might to stay,
> His ear to hearken to my need.

> The wisdom of my God to teach,
> His hand to guide, his shield to ward;
> The word of God to give me speech,
> His heavenly host to be my guard.

Incarnation

The doctrine of the incarnation is one of the most distinctive of Christian doctrines, and requires some explanation. Classical Christianity affirms that the only way of doing full justice to Jesus Christ is to recognize that he is both divine and human. This central Christian doctrine is generally referred to as "the doctrine of the incarnation," which focuses on the fact that God chose to enter into our world in Jesus Christ. (The word "incarnation" comes from the Latin, and means "being in the flesh.") Before considering the importance of this doctrine for spirituality, we shall take a little time to explore it further.

Explanation

This theme of God entering into our world in Christ is set out clearly in the opening section of John's gospel (John 1:1–18), which culminates in the statement that "The Word became flesh, and dwelt among us, and we saw his glory – the glory, such as belongs to the only-begotten of the Father, full of grace and truth" (John 1:14). The related phrase "the doctrine of the two natures" is also used to refer to the affirmation of the divinity and humanity of Jesus Christ.

Look at the verse in the New Testament which is generally regarded as the classic statement of the doctrine of the incarnation: "the Word became flesh, and dwelt among us" (John 1:14). The *Word* (the term used for one who is living, imperishable, creative, and divine) *became* (entered into human history) *flesh* (the term used for what is creaturely, perishable, finite, mortal, and human). The idea of "incarnation" simply means God taking on human flesh, undergoing a voluntary process of humiliation to enter into human history and take on the entire experience of existence as a human being. A famous Christmas carol – *Hark the Herald Angels Sing!*, which dates back to the eighteenth century in its original form – states this point succinctly:

> Veiled in flesh the Godhead see,
> Hail the incarnate Deity!
> Pleased as man with man to dwell,
> Jesus our Emmanuel!

The full force of this idea and its meaning for Christian spirituality will become clear in the following section.

The patristic period saw considerable attention being paid to the doctrine of the person of Christ, an area of theology which is widely referred to as "Christology." The task confronting the writers of this period was basically the development of a unified Christological scheme, which would bring together and integrate the various

Christological hints and statements, images, and models found within the New Testament, including the statement that "the Word became flesh" (John 1.14). That task proved complex, and focused on the manner in which Jesus Christ could be said to be "divine" and "human" without implying that he was in reality two persons, or that his divinity was more "real" than his humanity (or vice versa). The New Testament was seen as affirming both the divinity and the humanity of Christ, making the development of models which accommodated these insights of critical importance. In view of its importance for Christian theology and spirituality, we shall consider its main stages of development in what follows.

The first period of the development of Christology centered on the question of the divinity of Jesus. That Jesus was human appeared to be something of a truism to most early patristic writers. What required explanation about Jesus concerned the manner in which he differed from, rather than the ways in which he was similar to, other human beings.

Two early viewpoints were quickly rejected as heretical. *Ebionitism*, the practice of a primarily Jewish sect which flourished in the early first centuries of the Christian era, regarded Jesus as an ordinary human being, the human son of Mary and Joseph. This reduced Christology was regarded as totally inadequate by its opponents, and soon passed into oblivion. More significant was the diametrically opposed view, which came to be known as *Docetism*, from the Greek verb *"dokein"* (to seem or appear). This approach – which is probably best regarded as a tendency within theology rather than a definite theological position – argued that Christ was totally divine, and that his humanity was merely an appearance. The sufferings of Christ are thus treated as apparent rather than real. Docetism held a particular attraction for the Gnostic writers of the second century, during which period it reached its zenith. By this time, however, other viewpoints were in the process of emerging, which would eventually eclipse this tendency. The second-century writer Justin Martyr (*c*.100–*c*.165) represents one such viewpoint, generally known as a "logos-Christology" (from the Greek term *logos*, "word").

It is, however, in the writings of Origen (*c*.185–*c*.254) that the Logos-Christology appears to find its fullest development. It must be made clear that Origen's Christology is complex, and that its interpretation at points is highly problematical. What follows is a simplification of his approach. In the incarnation, the human soul of Christ is united with the Logos. On account of the closeness of this union, Christ's human soul comes to share in the properties of the Logos. Nevertheless, Origen insists that the Logos must be regarded as subordinate to the Father. Although both the Logos and Father are co-eternal, the Logos is subordinate to the Father.

One controversy of especial importance to the formation of the definitive Christian statement of the identity of Jesus broke out in the fourth century, and is known as the "Arian controversy." This controversy, which focused on the teaching of Arius (*c*.250–*c*.336), remains a landmark in the development of classical Christology, and therefore needs to be considered in detail. Arius emphasizes the self-subsistence of God. God is the one and only source of all created things; nothing exists which does not ultimately derive from God. This view of God, which many commentators have suggested is due more to Hellenistic philosophy than to Christian theology, clearly raises the question of the relation of the Father to the Son. Arius's critic Athanasius (*c*.296–373) represents him as making the following statements on this point.

> God was not always a father. There was a time when God was all alone, and was not yet a father; only later did he become a father. The Son did not always exist. Everything created is out of nothing . . . so the Logos of God came into existence out of nothing. There was a time when he was not. Before he was brought into being, he did not exist. He also had a beginning to his created existence.

These statements are of considerable importance, and bring us to the heart of Arianism. The following points are of especial significance.

1 The Father is regarded as existing before the Son. "There was when he was not," to quote one of Arius's fighting slogans. This decisive affirmation places Father and Son on different levels, and is consistent with Arius's rigorous insistence that the Son is a creature. Only the Father is "unbegotten"; the Son, like all other creatures, derives from this one source of being. However, Arius is careful to emphasize that the Son is not like every other creature. There is a distinction of rank between the Son and other creatures, including human beings. Arius has some difficulty in identifying the precise nature of this distinction. The Son, he argued, is "a perfect creature, yet not as one among other creatures; a begotten being, yet not as one among other begotten beings." The implication seems to be that the Son outranks other creatures, while sharing their essentially created and begotten nature.

2 An important aspect of Arius's distinction between Father and Son concerns the unknowability of God. Arius emphasizes the utter transcendence and inaccessibility of God. God cannot be known by any other creature. Yet, as we noted above, the Son is to be regarded as a creature, however elevated above all other creatures. Arius presses home his logic, arguing that the Son cannot know the Father. "The one who has a beginning is in no position to comprehend or lay hold of the one who has no beginning." This important affirmation rests upon the radical distinction between Father and Son. Such is the gulf fixed between them, that the latter cannot know the former unaided. In common with all other creatures, the Son is dependent upon the grace of God if the Son is to perform whatever function has been ascribed to him. It is considerations such as these which have led Arius's critics to argue that, at the levels of revelation and salvation, the Son is in precisely the same position as other creatures.

But what about the many biblical passages which seem to suggest that the Son is far more than a mere creature? Arius's opponents were easily able to bring forward a series of biblical passages, pointing to the fundamental unity between Father and Son. On the basis of the controversial literature of the period, it is clear that the Fourth Gospel was of major importance to this controversy, with John 3:35, 10:30, 12:27, 14:10, 17:3 and 17:11 being discussed frequently. Arius's reponse to such texts is significant: the language of "sonship" is variegated in character, and metaphorical in nature. To refer to the "Son" is an honorific, rather than theologically precise, way of speaking. Although Jesus Christ is referred to as "Son" in Scripture, this metaphorical way of speaking is subject to the controlling principle of a God who is totally different in essence from all created beings – including the Son.

The basic elements of Arius's position can be summarized in the following manner. The Son is a creature, who, like all other creatures, derives from the will of God. The term "Son" is thus a metaphor, an honorific term intended to underscore the rank of the Son among other creatures. It does not imply that Father and Son share the same being or status.

Athanasius had little time for Arius's subtle distinctions. If the Son is a creature, then the Son is a creature like any other creature, including human beings. After all, what other kind of creaturehood is there? For Athanasius, the affirmation of the creaturehood of the Son had two decisive consequences, each of which had uniformly negative implications for Arianism.

First, Athanasius makes the point that it is only God who can save. God, and God alone, can break the power of sin, and bring us to eternal life. An essential feature of being a creature is that one requires to be redeemed. No creature can save another creature. Only the creator can redeem the creation. Having emphasized that it is God alone who can save, Athanasius then makes the logical move which the Arians found difficult to counter. The New Testament and the Christian liturgical tradition alike regard Jesus Christ as Saviour. Yet, as Athanasius emphasized, only God can save. So how are we to make sense of this?

The only possible solution, Athanasius argues, is to accept that Jesus is God incarnate. The logic of his argument at times goes something like this:

1   No creature can redeem another creature.
2   According to Arius, Jesus Christ is a creature.
3   Therefore, according to Arius, Jesus Christ cannot redeem humanity.

The second point that Athanasius makes is that Christians worship and pray to Jesus Christ. This represents an excellent case study of the importance of Christian spirituality (especially practices of worship and prayer) for Christian theology. By the fourth century, prayer to and adoration of Christ were standard features of the way in which public worship took place. Athanasius argues that if Jesus Christ is a creature, then Christians are guilty of worshipping a creature instead of God – in other words, they had lapsed into idolatry. Christians, Athanasius stresses, are totally forbidden to worship anyone or anything except God himself. Athanasius thus argued that Arius seemed to be guilty of making nonsense of the way in which Christians prayed and worshipped. Athanasius argued that Christians were right to worship and adore Jesus Christ, because by doing so, they were recognizing him for what he was – God incarnate.

The Arian controversy had to be settled somehow, if peace was to be established within the church. Debate came to center upon two terms as possible descriptions of the relation of the Father to the Son. The term *homoiousios*, "of like substance" or "of like bring," was seen by many as representing a judiciuous compromise, allowing the proximity between Father and Son to be asserted without requiring any further speculation on the precise nature of their relation. However, the rival term *homoousios*, "of the same substance" or "of the same being," eventually gained the upper hand. Though differing by only one letter from the alternative term, it embodied a very different understanding of the relationship between Father and Son.

The Nicene Creed – or, more accurately, the Niceno-Constantinopolitan Creed – of 381 ended the Arian controversy by declaring that Christ was "of the same substance" with the Father. This affirmation has since widely become regarded as a benchmark of Christological orthodoxy within all the mainstream Christian churches, whether Protestant, Catholic, or Orthodox. The Council of Chalcedon (451) subsequently laid down an understanding of the relation of the humanity and divinity of Jesus Christ which became normative for the Christian churches, both east and west. The Council was adamant that Christ must be accepted to be truly divine and truly human, without specifying precisely how this is to be understood. In other words, a number of Christological models are legitimated, providing they uphold this essential Christological affirmation.

> We all with one voice confess our Lord Jesus Christ to be one and the same Son, perfect in divinity and humanity, truly God and truly human, consisting of a rational soul and a body, being of one substance with the Father in relation to his divinity, and being of one substance with us in relation to his humanity, and is like us in all things apart from sin (Hebrews 4:15). He was begotten of the Father before time in relation to his divinity, and in these recent days, was born from the Virgin Mary, the *Theotokos*, for us and for our salvation. In relation to the humanity, he is one and the same Christ, the Son, the Lord, the Only-begotten, who is to be acknowledged in two natures, without confusion, without change, without division, and without separation. This distinction of natures is in no way abolished on account of this union, but rather the characteristic property of each nature is preserved, and concurring into one Person and one subsistence, not as if Christ were parted or divided into two persons, but remains one and the same Son and only-begotten God, Word, Lord, Jesus Christ; even as the Prophets from the beginning spoke concerning him, and our Lord Jesus Christ instructed us, and the Creed of the Fathers was handed down to us.

The classic Christian position is therefore summarized in the "doctrine of the two natures" – that is to say, that Jesus is perfectly divine and perfectly human. This view was definitively stated by the Council of Chalcedon (451). This laid down a controlling principle for classical Christology, which has been accepted as definitive within orthodox Christian theology ever since. The principle in question can be summarized as follows: provided that it is recognized that Jesus Christ is both truly divine and truly human, the precise manner in which this is articulated or explored is not of fundamental importance. The noted patristic scholar Maurice Wiles (1923–) summarized Chalcedon's aims as follows:

> On the one hand was the conviction that a saviour must be fully divine; on the other was the conviction that what is not assumed is not healed. Or, to put the matter in other words, the source of salvation must be God; the locus of salvation must be humanity. It is quite clear that these two principles often pulled in opposite directions. The Council of Chalcedon was the church's attempt to resolve, or perhaps rather to agree to live with, that tension. Indeed, to accept both principles as strongly as did the early church is already to accept the Chalcedonian faith.

Chalcedon simply states definitively what the first five centuries of Christian reflection on the New Testament had already established. It defines the point from which we start the recognition that, in the face of Christ, we see none other than God himself. That is a starting point, not an end. But we must be sure of our starting point, the place at which we begin, if the result is to be reliable. Chalcedon claims to have established that starting point, and whatever difficulties we may find with its turgid language and outdated expressions, the basic ideas which it lays down are clear and crucial, and are obviously a legitimate interpretation of the New Testament witness to Jesus Christ.

Application

The doctrine of the incarnation can be seen to have particular importance for Christian spirituality in three major areas: our knowledge of God; the suffering of God; and the affirmation of the commitment of God to the created order. We shall explore each of these in what follows, beginning with the question of how we know what God is like.

What is God like? If God is invisible and intangible, then we are unable to discern God in any direct manner. Yet if Jesus is God (as the doctrine of the incarnation affirms), then Jesus is to be seen as an excellent visual image of what God is like (see pp. 55–6). The New Testament makes this point in a number of ways. For example, it affirms that Jesus is a reliable representation of what God looks like. Paul refers to Jesus as the "image of the invisible God" (Colossians 1:15). In the letter to the Hebrews, we find Jesus described as the "stamp" or "exact impression" of God's nature (Hebrews 1:3). The Greek word used here could refer to an image stamped upon a coin, conveying the idea of an exact representation of a ruler or monarch. The God who we are dealing with is the "God and Father of our Lord Jesus Christ" (1 Peter 1:3), the God who seeks us, finds us, and meets us, in Jesus Christ.

The Christian theologian thus insists that God is to be most reliably and completely known in the person of Jesus Christ. This is not to say that God may not be known, in various ways and to various degrees, by other means. Christians believe that Jesus Christ is the closest encounter with God to be had in this life. God makes himself available for our acceptance or rejection in the figure of Jesus Christ. To have encountered Jesus is to have encountered God. This line of approach underlies the use of icons in personal and corporate spirituality, to which we shall return presently. However, we may also consider another aspect of the incarnation – what it has to say about God's involvement in the suffering and pain of the creation.

Can God suffer? This is perhaps one of the most poignant questions confronting many Christians, particularly those who are going through a period of suffering themselves. It makes all the difference in the world whether God has experienced suffering at first hand. If God does not know what suffering is, then God will not be able to sympathize with us in our sufferings. On the other hand, if God has experienced the suffering and pain of this world, we can turn to God in prayer knowing that we are in the presence of a fellow-sufferer who knows what we are going through, and can understand our experience, fears, and concerns.

59

The argument for God's first-hand experience of suffering is based upon the doctrine of the incarnation. The structure of the argument may be set out as follows:

1 Jesus is God.
2 Jesus experienced pain and suffering.
3 Therefore God experienced pain and suffering.

Some early Christian writers were reluctant to accept this conclusion, as it appeared to be dishonoring to God. Surely this implied that God's majesty was compromised? How could the immortal God be affected in this manner? However, particularly since the sixteenth century, the insight that God suffered pain in Christ has gained wide acceptance, and has come to feature prominently in Christian devotion and prayer. An early example of this approach can be seen in Origen's commentary on Ezekiel.

> [The savior] descended to earth to grieve for the human race, and took our sufferings on himself before he endured the cross and deigned to assume our flesh. If he had not suffered, he would not have come to share in human life. What is this suffering which he suffered for us beforehand? It is the suffering of love. For the Father himself, the God of the universe, who is "long-suffering and full of mercy" [Psalm 103:8] and merciful, does he not suffer in some way? Or do you now know that, when he deals with humanity, he suffers human suffering? "For the Lord your God has taken your ways upon him as a man bears his son" [cf. Deuteronomy 1:31]. Therefore God has taken our ways upon himself, just as the Son of God bore our sufferings.

Note how Origen sees a close link between incarnation and the suffering of God. If God really became one of us, then God bears all the pain and suffering that human nature knows. That means that God is able to relate to us as human beings. God has trodden the road of pain, suffering and death before us as one of us.

Illustration

To illustrate the importance of the doctrine of the incarnation for spirituality, we shall consider the important issue of the visualization of God in devotion, a matter to which we shall return in much greater detail later (see p. 111). A central aspect of Orthodox spirituality focuses on the use of icons in personal and corporate devotion. An icon is basically a religious picture, which is seen as a visual aid for teaching. In Eastern Orthodox churches, the icons are displayed on an "iconostasis" (a "picture stand"), so that the image can be seen by the congregation. Especially in Russian Orthodox thought, the icon is seen as a window through which divine reality may be apprehended.

Icons depict a range of religious images, including important saints, Mary, and John the Baptist. Our interest here focuses on the particular use of icons in relation to the depiction of Christ. The theological basis of this practice was set out in the eighth-century by John of Damascus (*c.*675–*c.*749), who argued that the theological fact of the incarnation of Christ provides a solid foundation for the use of icons in devotion. An "icon" (*eikon*) is a religious painting or picture, which is understood to act as a window through which the worshipper may catch a closer glimpse of the divine than would otherwise be possible.

> Previously there was absolutely no way in which God, who has neither a body nor a face, could be represented by any image. But now that he has made himself visible in the flesh and has lived with people, I can make an image of what I have seen of God . . . and contemplate the glory of the Lord, his face having been unveiled.

Icons are thus objects of devotion, not in the sense that the picture itself is being adored, but in the sense that God or Christ, to which the icon points, are worshipped. The glory of God – which cannot be taken in by human beings, on account of its brilliance and radiance – is thus presented to us in a manner which is suited for our human abilities and faculties. We shall consider the use of icons in more detail at a later point in this work; our attention now turns to the doctrine of redemption.

Redemption

The redemption of the world through Jesus Christ's death on the cross is of major importance to Christian theology, worship, symbolism, and iconography. In what follows, we shall explore the importance of this theme for spirituality.

Explanation

The Christian faith affirms that the death of Jesus on the cross is of central importance to the salvation of the world. It is therefore of importance to consider the Christian understanding of the grounds and nature of salvation. For Christians, salvation is grounded in the death and resurrection of Jesus Christ. The New Testament affirmation of the necessity and uniqueness of the saving death of Christ has been taken up by Christian writers. Discussions of the meaning of the cross and resurrection of Christ are best grouped around four central controlling themes or images. It must be stressed that these are not mutually exclusive, and that it is normal to find Christian writers adopting approaches which incorporate elements drawn from more than one such category. Indeed, it can be argued that the views of most writers on this subject cannot be reduced to or confined within a single category, without doing serious violence to their ideas.

The cross as a sacrifice
The New Testament, drawing on Old Testament imagery and expectations, presents Christ's death upon the cross as a sacrifice. This approach, which is especially associated with the Letter to the Hebrews, presents Christ's sacrificial offering as an effective and perfect sacrifice, which was able to accomplish that which the sacrifices of the Old Testament were only able to intimate, rather than achieve. In particular, Paul's use of the Greek term *hilasterion* (Rom. 3:25) points to a sacrificial interpretation of Christ's death.

This idea is developed subsequently within the Christian tradition. For example, in taking over the imagery of sacrifice, Augustine states that Christ "was made a sacrifice for sin, offering himself as a whole burnt offering on the cross of his passion." In order for humanity to be restored to God, the mediator must sacrifice himself; without this sacrifice, such restoration is an impossibility.

The sacrificial offering of Christ on the cross came to be linked especially with one aspect of the "threefold office of Christ." (Note that the word "office" here has the older sense of "function" or "responsibility," rather than the modern sense of the building in which these functions or responsibilities are carried out.) According to this typology, which dates from the middle of the sixteenth century, the work of Christ could be summarized under three "offices": prophet (by which Christ declares the will of God), priest (by which he makes sacrifice for sin), and king (by which he rules with authority over his people). The general acceptance of this scheme within Protestantism in the late sixteenth and seventeenth centuries led to a sacrificial understanding of Christ's death becoming of central importance within Protestant soteriologies.

Since the Enlightenment, however, there has been a subtle shift in meaning of the term. A metaphorical extension of meaning of the term has come to be given priority over the original. Whereas the term originally referred to the ritual offering of slaughtered animals as a specifically religious action, the term increasingly came to mean heroic or costly action on the parts of individuals, especially the giving up of one's life, with no transcendent reference or expectation.

The use of sacrificial imagery has become noticeably less widespread since 1945. It is highly likely that this relates directly to the rhetorical debasement of the term in secular contexts, especially in situations of national emergency. The secular use of the imagery of sacrifice, often degenerating to little more than slogan-mongering, is widely regarded as having tainted and compromised both the word and the concept. The frequent use of such phrases as "he sacrificed his life for King and country" in British circles during the First World War (1914–18), and Adolf Hitler's extensive use of sacrificial imagery in justifying economic hardship and the loss of civil liberties as the price of German national revival in the late 1930s, served to render the term virtually unusable for many in Christian teaching and preaching, on account of its negative associations. Nevertheless, the idea remains of importance in modern Roman Catholic sacramental theology, which continues to regard the eucharist as a sacrifice, and find in this image a rich source of theological imagery.

The cross as victory

The New Testament and early church laid considerable emphasis upon the victory gained by Christ over sin, death, and Satan through his cross and resurrection (see pp. 67–71). This theme of victory, often linked liturgically with the Easter celebrations, was of major importance within the western Christian theological tradition until the Enlightenment. The theme of "Christ the victor" brought together a series of themes, centering on the idea of a decisive victory over forces of evil and oppression.

The imagery of Jesus' victory over the devil proved to have enormous popular appeal. The medieval idea of "the harrowing of hell" bears witness to its power. According to this, after dying upon the cross, Christ descended to hell, and broke down its gates in order that the imprisoned souls might go free. The idea rested (rather tenuously, it has to be said) upon 1 Peter 3:18–22, which makes reference to Christ "preaching to the spirits in prison." The hymn "Ye choirs of New Jerusalem," written by Fulbert of Chartres (*c*.970–1028), expresses this theme in two of its verses, picking up the theme of Christ, as the "lion of Judah (Revelation 5:5) defeating Satan, the serpent (Genesis 3:15).

> For Judah's lion bursts his chains
> Crushing the serpent's head;
> And cries aloud through death's domain
> To wake the imprisoned dead.
>
> Devouring depths of hell their prey
> At his command restore;
> His ransomed hosts pursue their way
> Where Jesus goes before.

A similar idea can be found in a fourteenth-century English mystery play, which describes the "harrowing of hell" in the following manner. "And when Christ was dead, his spirit went in haste to hell. And soon he broke down the strong gates that were wrongfully barred against him. . . . He bound Satan fast with eternal bonds, and so shall Satan ever remain bound until the day of doom. He took with him Adam and Eve and others that were dear to him . . . all these he led out of hell and set in paradise."

Perhaps the most well-known portrayal of this powerful image familiar to modern readers is found in that most remarkable of religious allegories – C. S. Lewis' *The Lion, The Witch and the Wardrobe*. In this book, Lewis (1898–1963) tells the story of Narnia, a land which is discovered by accident by four children rummaging around in an old wardrobe. In this work, we encounter the White Witch, who keeps the land of Narnia covered in wintry snow. As we read on, we realize that she rules Narnia not as a matter of right, but by stealth. The true ruler of the land is absent; in his absence, the witch subjects the land to oppression. In the midst of this land of winter stands the witch's castle, within which many of the inhabitants of Narnia have been imprisoned as stone statues.

As the narrative moves on, we discover that the rightful ruler of the land is Aslan, a lion. As Aslan advances into Narnia, winter gives way to spring, and the snow begins to melt. The witch realizes that her power is beginning to fade. In the fourteenth chapter of the book, Lewis describes the killing of Aslan, perhaps the most demonic episode ever to have found its way into a children's story. The forces of darkness and oppression seem to have won a terrible victory – and yet, in that victory lies their defeat. Aslan surrenders himself to the forces of evil, and allows them to do their worst with him – and by so doing, disarms them.

In the sixteenth chapter of this modern version of the "harrowing of hell," Lewis graphically describes how Aslan – Lewis' reworking of the theme of the lion of Judah, who has burst his chains – breaks into the castle, breathes upon the statues, and restores them to life, before leading the liberated army through the shattered gates of the once great fortress to freedom. Hell has been harrowed. It has been despoiled, and its inhabitants liberated from its imprisonment.

The cross and forgiveness

A third approach centers on the idea of the death of Christ providing the basis by which God is enabled to forgive sin. This notion is traditionally associated with the eleventh-century writer Anselm of Canterbury. Anselm's emphasis falls upon the righteousness of God. God redeems humanity in a manner that is totally consistent with the divine quality of righteousness. In the course of his analysis, he argues for both the necessity of the incarnation of the Son of God, and the saving potential of his death and resurrection. The complex argument can be summarized as follows.

1 God created humanity in a state of original righteousness, with the objective of bringing humanity to a state of eternal blessedness.
2 That state of eternal blessedness is contingent upon human obedience to God. However, through sin, humanity is unable to achieve this necessary obedience, which appears to frustrate God's purpose in creating humanity in the first place.
3 In that it is impossible for God's purposes to be frustrated, there must be some means by which the situation can be remedied. However, the situation can only be remedied if a *satisfaction* is made for sin. In other words, something has to be done, by which the offence caused by human sin can be purged.
4 However, there is no way in which humanity can provide this necessary satisfaction. It lacks the resources which are needed. On the other hand, God possesses the resources needed to provide the required satisfaction.
5 Therefore a "God-man" would possess both the *ability* (as God) and the *obligation* (as a human being) to pay the required satisfaction. Therefore the incarnation takes place, in order that the required satisfaction may be made, and humanity redeemed.

Anselm of Canterbury (c.1033–1109). Born in Italy, Anselm migrated to Normandy in 1059, entering the famous monastery of Bec, becoming its prior in 1063, and abbot in 1078. In 1093 he was appointed archbishop of Canterbury. He is chiefly noted for his strong defense of the intellectual foundations of Christianity, and is especially associated with the "ontological argument" for the existence of God.

In taking up Anselm's approach, later writers were able to place it on a more secure foundation by grounding it in the general principles of law. The sixteenth century was particularly appreciative of the importance of human law, and saw it as an appropriate model for God's forgiveness of human sin. Three main models came to be used at this time to understand the manner in which the forgiveness of human sins is related to the death of Christ.

1 *Representation.* Christ is here understood to be the covenant representative of humanity. Through faith, believers come to stand within the covenant between God and humanity. All that Christ has achieved through the cross is available on account of the covenant. Just as God entered into a covenant with his people Israel, so he has entered into a covenant with his church. Christ, by his obedi-

ence upon the cross, represents his covenant people, winning benefits for them as their representative. By coming to faith, individuals come to stand within the covenant, and thus share in all its benefits, won by Christ through his cross and resurrection – including the full and free forgiveness of our sins.

2   *Participation.* Through faith, believers participate in the risen Christ. They are "in Christ," to use Paul's famous phrase. They are caught up in him, and share in his risen life. As a result of this, they share in all the benefits won by Christ, through his obedience upon the cross. One of those benefits is the forgiveness of sins, in which they share through our faith. Participating in Christ thus entails the forgiveness of sins, and sharing in his righteousness.

3   *Substitution.* Christ is here understood to be a substitute, the one who goes to the cross in our place. Sinners ought to have been crucified, on account of their sins. Christ is crucified in their place. God allows Christ to stand in our place, taking our guilt upon himself, so that his righteousness – won by obedience upon the cross – might become ours.

These themes are developed by the modern Swiss Protestant theologian Karl Barth. In his discussion of the theme of "The Judge Judged in Our Place," Barth argues that we can see God exercising his rightful judgment of sinful humanity. The cross exposes human delusions to self-sufficiency and autonomy of judgment, which Barth sees encapsulated in the story of Genesis 3: "the human being wants to be his own judge." Yet alteration of the situation demands that its inherent wrongness be acknowledged. For Barth, the cross of Christ represents the locus, in which the righteous judge makes known his judgment of sinful humanity, and simultaneously takes that judgment upon himself.

> What took place is that the Son of God fulfilled the righteous judgement on us human beings by himself taking our place as a human being, and in our place undergoing the judgement under which we had passed . . . Because God willed to execute his judgement on us in his Son, it all took place in his person, as *his* accusation and condemnation and destruction. He judged, and it was the judge who was judged, who allowed himself to be judged. . . . Why did God become a human being? So that God as a human being might do and accomplish and achieve and complete all this for us wrongdoers, in order that in this way there might be brought about by him our reconciliation with him, and our conversion to him.

> *Karl Barth (1886–1968).* Widely regarded as the most important Protestant theologian of the twentieth century. Originally inclined to support liberal Protestantism, Barth was moved to adopt a more theocentric position through his reflections on the First World War. His early emphasis on the "otherness" of God in his Romans commentary (1919) was continued and modified in his monumental *Church Dogmatics.* Barth's contribution to modern Christian theology has been immense.

The cross and love

A central aspect of the New Testament understanding of the meaning of the cross relates to the demonstration of the love of God for humanity. "For God so loved the world that he gave his one and only Son, that whoever believes in him shall not perish but have eternal life" (John 3:16). "God demonstrates his own love for us in this: While we were still sinners, Christ died for us" (Romans 5:8). "I have been crucified with Christ and I no longer live, but Christ lives in me. The life I live in the body, I live by faith in the Son of God, who loved me and gave himself for me" (Galatians 2:20). This major theme has been developed at some length in the subsequent tradition of biblical interpretation.

Augustine of Hippo was one of many patristic writers to stress that one of the motivations underlying the mission of Christ was the "demonstration of the love of God towards us." Perhaps the most important medieval statement of this emphasis can be found in the writings of Peter Abelard. It must be stressed that Abelard does not, as some of his interpreters suggest, reduce the meaning of the cross to a demonstration of the love of God. This is one among many components of Abelard's soteriology, which includes traditional ideas concerning Christ's death as a sacrifice for human sin. It is Abelard's emphasis upon the subjective impact of the cross that is distinctive.

For Abelard, "the purpose and cause of the incarnation was that Christ might illuminate the world by his wisdom, and excite it to love of himself." In this, Abelard restates the Augustinian idea of Christ's incarnation as a public demonstration of the extent of the love of God, with the intent of evoking a response of love from humanity. "The Son of God took our nature, and in it took upon himself to teach us by both word and example even to the point of death, thus binding us to himself through love."

Peter Abelard (1079–1142). French theologian and spiritual writer, who achieved a considerable reputation as a teacher at the University of Paris. Among his many contributions to the development of medieval theology, his most noted is his emphasis upon the subjective aspects of the atonement.

This theme continues to be of central importance to Christian thinking about the meaning of the cross. The cross demonstrates and affirms the love of God for us. For Christians, the full wonder of the love of God for us can only be appreciated in the light of the cross of Jesus. According to the Christian tradition, God – though angered and grieved by our sin – comes to meet us where we are. Christians believe that Jesus was the embodiment of God, God incarnate, God willingly accepting the suffering, pain, and agony of the world in order to forgive and renew it. Jesus did not come to explain away, or to take away, suffering. He came to take it upon himself, to assume human suffering, and lend it dignity and meaning through his presence and sympathy. It is this which is the full-blooded meaning of the love of God, in the Christian understanding of the idea.

In contemplating the spectacle of Jesus dying on the cross, Christian tradition affirms that we see none other than God taking up the agony of the world which God created and loves. It is this which is the "love of God" in the full-blooded sense of the word. In its deepest sense, the love of God is that of someone who stoops down from heaven to enter into our fallen world, with all its agony and pain, culminating in the grim cross of Calvary.

Having outlined the basic themes of the Christian doctrine of redemption, we shall explore its application, focusing especially on the use of the cross in Christian symbolism.

Application

The doctrine of redemption is central to Christian spirituality, and for this reason the symbol of the cross plays a particularly significant role (see pp. 116–18). It will be helpful to identify some of the more fundamental ways in which the doctrine of redemption relates to spirituality, as follows.

1   The doctrine of redemption stresses *the costliness of human salvation*. Salvation is to be understood as something of enormous intrinsic worth. In one of his parables, Jesus speaks of a "pearl of great price" (Matthew 13:45–46), using this valuable pearl as a symbol of the kingdom of God. The appreciation of the costliness of that pearl is seen as vital to gaining an insight into the nature of the kingdom of God. One of the central tasks of Christian spirituality is thus to allow Christians to gain an enhanced appreciation of the costliness of their redemption, and hence of their own intrinsic value in the sight of God.

2   The doctrine of redemption simultaneously affirms *the reality of human sin and the love of God for sinners*. Several approaches to the cross stress both that Christ died in order that human sin might be forgiven, and that there was no other way in which that sin could be purged. Yet the theme of the love of God for sinners is set alongside this, in such a manner that the affirmation of the reality of human sin does not negate the love of God for sinful human beings. Indeed, the love of God is to be seen in action in the manner in which Christ died in order that human sin might be cancelled and purged, in order that we might achieve true fulfillment in relation to God.

Having considered the central role of the doctrine of redemption (and having hinted at the importance of the symbol of the cross), we may now look at some specific illustrations of its relevance for spirituality.

Illustration

The importance of the cross for Christian spirituality can be illustrated from the rich heritage of devotional literature which centers on its themes. In this section, we shall consider the classic theme of the cross as the basis of Christian meditation upon the costliness and wonder of redemption. This is one of the most common themes in Christian spirituality, and it merits close study. We shall begin by considering a much-loved hymn which is little more than a mediation on the cross, intended to evoke a sense of wonder and commitment on the part of its audience. In his famous hymn "When I survey the wondrous cross," which is still sung widely today, Isaac Watts

(1674–1748) offers a reflection on the cross, designed to allow its audience to see the attractions of the world in their proper perspective. In addition to painting a vivid word-picture of the cross, Watts stresses that all else pales into insignificance in its light.

> When I survey the wondrous Cross
> On which the Prince of Glory died,
> My richest gain I count but loss,
> And pour contempt on all my pride.
>
> Forbid it, Lord, that I should boast
> Save in the Cross of Christ my Lord
> All the vain things that charm me most,
> I sacrifice them to his blood.
>
> See from his head, his hands, his feet
> Sorrow and love flow mingled down;
> Did e'er such love and sorrow meet?
> Or thorns compose so rich a crown?
>
> Were the whole realm of nature mine,
> That were an offering far too small;
> Love so amazing, so divine,
> Demands my soul, my life, my all.

Note how Watts invites the reader (or singer!) of this hymn to meditate on the cross. The hymn builds up a verbal picture of the cross, focusing attention on the pain experienced by the dying Christ, and the fact that this is the means by which the redemption of the world – including the singer! – has been accomplished. The hymn concludes by emphasizing the need to respond to that cross. There is nothing that can equal in magnitude the offering which was made by Christ. But we can at least try – by offering ourselves to Christ in order that his love might be made known to all.

A somewhat different approach is adopted by Ignatius Loyola (1491–1556) in his *Spiritual Exercises* (see pp. 160–1). Loyola, like Watts, wants Christians to focus their thoughts on the cross, and consider its implications for their Christian lives. However, Loyola uses a significantly different technique, inviting his reader to enter into a dialogue with the dying Christ over the costliness of redemption, and the love of the creator in redeeming the creation. In this section from his *Spiritual Exercises*, Ignatius outlines an exercise in which he asks those following his directions to join him in focusing their thoughts on Christ dying on the cross. Using the techniques which he develops in that work (see pp. 85–6), Loyola directs them to project themselves into that situation, and engage in a dialogue with the dying Christ. Initially, that involves reflection on what is happening: the creator suffering for the creation; the one who has eternal life by right choosing to suffer physical pain and death for sinners. Then this meditation is used as a means for self-examination, with a view for setting a future agenda for spiritual growth and discipline.

> Imagine Christ our Lord before you, hanging upon the cross. Talk to him about
> how the creator became a human being, and how he who possesses eternal life

submitted himself to physical death for our sins. Then I shall reflect on myself, and ask:

What I have done for Christ?
What I am now doing for Christ?
What ought I to do for Christ?
As I see him like this, hanging upon the cross, I shall meditate on what comes to mind.

Notice how the dialogue which Loyola wishes those undertaking the exercises to enter into has the effect of moving them from thought to action. The dialogue invites them to meditate on the sufferings of Christ. After reflecting on what Christ has done for us, Loyola requires his followers to ask what life-changing ideas develop, in order to stimulate and catalyze the process of advancement within the Christian life.

The cross is, however, to be set alongside the resurrection of Christ, which is celebrated on Easter Day. In what follows, we shall explore the relevance of the resurrection for our subject.

Resurrection

For many Christians, Easter is the most important event of the year. On that day, the resurrection of Jesus is recalled and celebrated. The gospel accounts of the passion and death of Jesus go on to affirm that he was buried in a borrowed tomb on the evening of the first Good Friday, and that he was raised from the dead on Sunday – the first Easter Day. So important was the celebration of the resurrection to the early Christians that the weekly Jewish day of rest (the Sabbath, which falls on a Saturday) was transferred to Sunday, to allow Christians to celebrate the resurrection of Christ. The importance of the resurrection for Christian spirituality is considerable, as will become clear in the following section.

Explanation

The term "the resurrection" is used to refer to the series of events which took place after the death of Jesus, and which are celebrated on Easter Day. In general terms, "the resurrection" refers to a cluster of related happenings, focusing on what happened to Jesus after his death. We may summarize them as follows.

1   The tomb in which the corpse of Jesus was laid late on the Friday afternoon was discovered to be empty on the Sunday morning. Those who discovered the empty tomb were frightened by what they found; their reports were not taken seriously by many of those in Jesus' close circle of friends.
2   The disciples reported personal appearances of Jesus, and experienced him as someone living.
3   The disciples began to preach Jesus as the living Lord, rather than as a past teacher.

The "empty tomb" tradition is of considerable importance here. It is a major element in each of the four gospels (Matthew 28:1–10; Mark 16:1–8; Luke 24:1–11; John 20:1–10), and must therefore be considered to have a basis in historical fact. The story is told from different aspects in each of the gospels, and includes the divergence on minor points of detail which is so characteristic of eye-witness reports. Interestingly, all four gospels attribute the discovery of the empty tomb to women. The only Easter event to be explicitly related in detail by all four of the gospel writers is the visit of the women to the tomb of Jesus. Yet Judaism dismissed the value of the testimony or witness of women, regarding only men as having significant legal status in this respect. Mark's gospel even names each of them three times: Mary Magdalene, Mary the mother of James, and Salome (Mark 15:40, 47; 16:1), but fails to mention the names of any male disciples who were around at the time. It is perhaps too easy for modern western readers, accustomed to a firm belief in the equality of men and women, to overlook the significance of this point. At the time, in the intensely patriarchal Jewish culture of that period, the testimony of a woman was virtually worthless. In first-century Palestine, this would have been sufficient to discredit the accounts altogether. If the reports of the empty tomb were invented, as some have suggested, it is difficult to understand why their inventors should have embellished their accounts of the "discovery" with something virtually guaranteed to discredit them in the eyes of their audiences.

A further point of interest here concerns the practice of "tomb veneration" – that is, returning to the tomb of a prophet as a place of worship. This is known to have been common in New Testament times, and is probably hinted at in Matthew 23:29–30. The tomb of David in Jerusalem is still venerated by many Jews to this day. But there is no record whatsoever of any such veneration of the tomb of Jesus by his disciples. This would have been unthinkable, unless there was a very good reason for it. That reason appears to be the simple fact that Jesus' body was quite simply absent from its tomb.

It is quite clear that the resurrection of Jesus came as a surprise to the disciples. It must be pointed out that there was no precedent in Jewish thinking for a resurrection of this kind. Most Jews at this time seem to have believed in the resurrection of the dead. Yet the general belief of the time concerned the future resurrection of the dead, at the end of time itself. Nobody believed in a resurrection before the end of history. The Pharisees may be regarded as typical in this respect: they believed in a future resurrection, and held that men and women would be rewarded or punished after death, according to their actions. The Sadducees, however, insisted that there was no resurrection of any kind. No future existence awaited men and women after death. Paul was able to exploit the differences between the Pharisees and Sadducees on this point during an awkward moment in his career (see Acts 26:6–8). The Christian claim thus does not fit any known Jewish pattern at all. The resurrection of Jesus is not declared to be a future event, but something which had already happened in the world of time and space, in front of witnesses.

Luke records one incident which brings out the unexpected nature of the resurrection of Jesus. This is usually referred to as the "road to Emmaus" (Luke 24:13–35). In this narrative, Luke tells of two disciples, one of whom is named Cleopas, who are discussing the day's bewildering events as they walk along the road from Jerusalem to Emmaus (24:13–17). As they talk, they are joined by a stranger. It is only when he breaks bread with them (an important allusion to the Last Supper) that they realize who he is.

Theologically, the resurrection of Christ has particular relevance in relation to two matters.

1 It is an important indication of the identity of Jesus. For Paul, the resurrection was the supreme public demonstration that Jesus was indeed the Son of God (Romans 1:3–4). Any theological account of the significance or identity of Jesus will therefore involve discussion of the resurrection at this point.
2 The resurrection is also an integral aspect of the Christian hope. It is this aspect of the matter that will concern us particularly in this section of the work. If Jesus has been raised, then those who believe in him will be raised from the dead as well. The New Testament speaks of Jesus being the "first-fruits of the dead" (1 Corinthians 15:23) – meaning that others will follow him.

In what follows, we shall explore the relevance of this doctrine to personal and corporate spirituality.

Application

Easter Day marks the resurrection of Jesus, and is widely regarded as the most important festival of the Christian year. The religious importance of the festival is of fundamental importance. In the first place, it affirms the identity of Jesus as the risen Savior and Lord. In the Orthodox tradition, this point is often made through icons or pictures in churches, which show a triumphant and risen Christ (often referred to as *Christos pantocrator*, "Christ the all-powerful") as ruler over the universe as a result of his being raised from the dead. In the second place, it affirms the Christian hope – that is, the fundamental belief that Christians will be raised from the dead, and hence need fear death no more. Both these themes dominate Easter hymns and liturgies.

A good example is provided by a hymn found in the early eighteenth-century collection of hymns known as the *Lyra Davidica*. This collection, first published in 1708, includes a hymn which is widely used at Easter. Note the emphasis on Jesus enduring the pains of the cross for the salvation of the world, and the joy at the knowledge that Jesus is now risen from the grave.

Jesus Christ is risen today, Alleluia!
Our triumphant holy day, Alleluia!
Who did once, upon the cross, Alleluia!
Suffer to redeem our loss. Alleluia!

Hymns of praise then let us sing, Alleluia!
Unto Christ, our heavenly king; Alleluia!
Who endured the cross and grave, Alleluia!
Sinners to redeem and save. Alleluia!

> But the pains that he endured, Alleluia!
> Our salvation have procured; Alleluia!
> Now above the sky he's king, Alleluia!
> Where the angels ever sing! Alleluia!

Similar themes are found in the poems of the Christian tradition. The words of the English poet George Herbert (1593–1633) illustrate this point well. For Herbert, Easter is about the believer's hope of rising with Christ:

> Rise, heart; thy Lord is risen. Sing his praise
>   Without delays,
> Who takes thee by the hand, that thou likewise
>   With him mayst rise.

In the Greek Orthodox church, the following traditional Easter greeting is widely used, and has become familiar within other Christian traditions during the present century:

> *Christos anestos* ("Christ is risen").
> *Alethos anestos* ("he is risen indeed").

Easter is marked in a wide variety of ways throughout the Christian world. In Catholic and Orthodox churches, particular emphasis is often placed on the importance of the symbolism of light and darkness. In the ancient church, baptisms took place on Easter Day, as a way of showing that the believers had passed from darkness to light, from death to life. The custom of giving Easter Eggs, widespread in western culture, seems to go back to the idea of an egg as a symbol of new life, pointing to the new life brought by the Christian gospel.

The liturgy and hymns of the Christian church are a particularly powerful witness to the importance of the message of the resurrection of Jesus Christ from the dead. The "Troparion of Easter" within the Byzantine Liturgy sets out clearly the significance of the Easter event for the world:

> Christ is risen from the dead!
> Dying, he conquered death!
> To the dead, he has given life!

The Christian faith places a particular emphasis on the hope of resurrection and eternal life for believers. This has considerable implications for Christian attitudes towards death. The impact of these beliefs can probably be seen most clearly at Christian funeral services, in which the theme of sorrow at a believer's death is set alongside the theme of rejoicing at the hope of resurrection. This can be seen clearly in the old English order of service for "the burial of the dead" (1662), in which the theme of hope is clearly set out.

The service opens with the priest meeting the funeral party at the churchyard gate, and speaking some words from John's gospel (John 15:25–26), which affirm the reality of the Christian hope in the midst of a world of transience and death:

I am the resurrection and the life, saith the Lord: he that believeth in me, though he were dead, yet shall he live; and whosoever liveth and believeth in me shall never die.

The service then proceeds with the reading of 1 Corinthians 15, a chapter in which Paul stresses the importance of the resurrection, and the difference it makes to Christians. This reading includes the following words:

Death is swallowed up in victory. O death, where is thy sting? O grave, where is thy victory? The sting of death is sin, and the strength of sin is the law. But thanks be to God, which giveth us the victory through our Lord Jesus Christ. Therefore, my beloved brethren, be ye steadfast, unmoveable, always abounding in the work of the Lord, forasmuch as ye know that your labour is not in vain in the Lord.

Finally, as the corpse is lowered into the grave, the priest speaks these words. Again, note the theme of hope.

Forasmuch as it has pleased Almighty God of his great mercy to take unto himself the soul of our dear *brother* here departed, we therefore commit *his* body to the ground; earth to earth, ashes to ashes, dust to dust; in sure and certain hope of the resurrection to eternal life, through our Lord Jesus Christ.

The doctrine of the resurrection has a marked effect on Christian behavior. In the early church, the hope of the resurrection was of considerable importance to martyrs – that is, to Christians who were executed for their faith. The strong belief that they would share in Christ's resurrection is known to have been of major importance in helping them to face death on account of their faith.

Yet the doctrine is also of considerable importance to ordinary Christian believers. It affirms that death is not the final word, and offers a real hope in the face of death. We shall illustrate this in the following section.

Illustration

The theme of the defeat of death through the resurrection has featured prominently in the spiritual writings of the Christian tradition. A theme which predominates is that of "hope" in the strong sense of the word – that is, a sure and confident expectation of eternal life, even in the midst of the death and decay of the world. Our illustration is taken from the writings of the English metaphysical poet John Donne (1571/2–1631), who develops the implications of the doctrine of the resurrection for our attitude toward death. In this famous extract from his "Divine Meditations," Donne sets out the defeat of death through the resurrection. Note the comparison that is drawn between death and sleep.

Death be not proud, though some have called thee
Mighty and valiant, for thou art not so,
For, those, whom thou thinks'st, thou dost overthrow,
Die not, poor death, nor yet canst thou kill me;
From rest and sleep, which but thy pictures be.
Much pleasure, then from thee, much more must flow,

And soonest our best men with thee do go,
Rest of their bones, and soul's delivery.
Thou art slave to fate, chance, kings and desperate men,
And dost with poison, war, and sickness dwell,
And poppy, or charms can make us sleep as well,
And better than thy stroke; why swell'st thou then?
One short sleep past, we wake eternally,
And death shall be no more, Death thou shalt die.

The poem should be read slowly, to appreciate the points which Donne makes. Death is portrayed in personal terms, as someone who claims to have power over humanity. Donne's final point is that death itself has been vanquished. Although the resurrection of Christ is not explicitly mentioned, it is clear that this is the driving force behind the argument.

Consummation

The doctrine of the resurrection is one aspect of the Christian hope; another is the idea of the final consummation of all things, which is often expressed in terms of heaven. In the final section of the present chapter, we shall consider this important theme of Christian spirituality.

Explanation

As we have seen, Christianity is a religion of hope, which focuses on the resurrection of Jesus as the grounds for believing and trusting in a God who is able to triumph over death, and give hope to all those who suffer and die. The word "eschatology" is used to refer to Christian teachings about the "last things" (Greek: *ta eschata*). Just as "Christology" refers to the Christian understanding of the nature and identity of Jesus Christ, so "eschatology" refers to the Christian understanding of such things as heaven and eternal life. In view of the importance of the New Testament material to the shaping of Christian thinking on eschatology, we shall consider some of its leading themes. The two sources of leading importance are generally agreed to be the preaching of Jesus himself, and the writings of Paul. We shall consider each of these in more detail in what follows.

A dominant theme in the preaching of Jesus is the coming of the Kingdom of God. It is clear that this term has both present and future associations. The kingdom is something which is "drawing near" (Mark 1:15), yet which still belongs in its fullness to the future. The Lord's Prayer, which remains of central importance to individual and corporate Christian prayer and worship, includes reference to the future coming of the kingdom (Matthew 6:10). At the Last Supper, Jesus spoke to his disciples of a future occasion when they would drink wine in the kingdom of God (Mark 14:25). The general consensus among New Testament scholars is that there is a tension between the "now" and the "not yet" in relation to the Kingdom of God, similar to that envisaged by the parable of the growing mustard seed (Mark 4:30–32). The term "inaugurated eschatology" has become widely used to refer to the relation of the present inauguration and future fulfillment of the Kingdom.

Paul's eschatology also shows a tension between the "now" and the "not yet." This is articulated in terms of a number of key images, which may be summarized as follows.

1   The presence of a "new age." At several points, Paul emphasizes that the coming of Christ inaugurates a new era or "age" (Greek: *aionos*). Although this new age – which Paul designates a "new creation" (2 Corinthians 5:17) – has yet to be fulfilled, its presence can already be experienced. For this reason, Paul can refer to the "end of the ages" in Christ (1 Corinthians 10:11). The position which Paul opposes in the early chapter of 1 Corinthians clearly corresponds to a realized eschatology, in which each and every aspect of the age to come has been fulfilled in the present. For Paul, there is an element of postponement: the ultimate transformation of the world is yet to come, but may be confidently awaited.

2   The resurrection of Jesus is seen by Paul as an eschatological event, which affirms that the "new age" really has been inaugurated. Although this does not exhaust the meaning of Christ's resurrection, Paul clearly sees Christ's resurrection as an event which enables believers to live in the knowledge that death – a dominant feature of the "present age" – has been overcome.

3   Paul looks forward to the future coming of Jesus Christ in judgment at the end of time, confirming the new life of believers and their triumph over sin and death. A number of images are used to refer to this, including "the day of the Lord." At one point (1 Corinthians 16:22), Paul uses an Aramaic term, *maranatha* (literally, "Come, our Lord!"), as an expression of the Christian hope. The Greek term *parousia* is often used to refer to the future coming of Christ (e.g., 1 Corinthians 15:23; 2 Thessalonians 2:1, 8–9). For Paul, there is an intimate connection between the final coming of Christ and the execution of final judgement.

4   A major theme of Paul's eschatology is the coming of the Holy Spirit. This theme, which builds on a longstanding aspect of Jewish expectations, sees the gift of the Spirit as a confirmation that the new age has dawned in Christ. One of the most significant aspects of Paul's thought at this point is his interpretation of the gift of the Spirit to believers as an *arrabon* (2 Corinthians 1:22; 5:5). This unusual word has the basic sense of a "guarantee" or "pledge," affirming that the believer may rest assured of ultimate salvation on account of the present possession of the Spirit. Although salvation remains something which will be consummated in the future, the believer may have present assurance of this future event through the indwelling of the Spirit.

It will therefore be clear that the eschatology of the New Testament is complex. However, a leading theme is that something which happened in the past has inaugurated something new, which will reach its final consummation in the future. The Christian believer is thus caught up in this tension between the "now" and the "not yet." We have already noted the importance of this point in relation to Christian teaching on the nature of salvation, which includes past, present, and future elements.

The term "heaven" is used frequently in the Pauline writings of the New Testament to refer to the Christian hope. Although it is natural to think of heaven as a future entity, Paul's thinking appears to embrace both a future reality and a spiritual sphere or realm which coexists with the material world of space and time. Thus "heaven" is referred to both as the future home of the believer (2 Corinthians 5:1–2; Philippians 3:20) and as the present dwelling-place of Jesus Christ, from which he will come in final judgement (Romans 10:6; 1 Thessalonians 1:10; 4:16). One of Paul's most significant statements concerning heaven focuses on the notion of believers being "citizens of heaven" (Philippians 3:20), and in some way sharing in the life of heaven in the present. The tension between the "now" and the "not yet" is evident in Paul's statements concerning heaven, making it very difficult to sustain the simple idea of heaven as something which will not come into being until the future, or which cannot be experienced in the present.

Probably the most helpful way of conceiving heaven is to regard it as a consummation of the Christian doctrine of salvation, in which the presence, penalty and power of sin have all been finally eliminated, and the total presence of God in individuals and the community of faith has been achieved (see p. 77). It should be noted that the New Testament parables of heaven are strongly communal in nature; for example, heaven is portrayed as a banquet, a wedding feast, or as a city – the new Jerusalem. Individualist interpretations of heaven or eternal life are also excluded on account of the Christian understanding of God as Trinity. Eternal life is thus not a projection of an individual human existence, but is rather to be seen as sharing, with the redeemed community as a whole, in the community of a loving God.

A major point of difference between Christians should be noted at this point. The Catholic church teaches the existence of "purgatory," while the Protestant and Eastern Orthodox Christians do not. In view of the importance of this difference, we shall consider it in a little detail. Purgatory is perhaps best understood as an intermediate state, in which those who have died in a state of grace are given an opportunity to purge themselves of the guilt of their sins before finally entering heaven. The idea does not have explicit scriptural warrant, although a passage in 2 Maccabees 12:39–45 (regarded as apocryphal, and hence as lacking in authority, by Protestant writers) speaks of Judas Maccabeus making "propitiation for those who had died, in order that they might be released from their sin."

The idea was developed during the patristic period. Clement of Alexandria and Origen both taught that those who had died without time to perform works of penance would be "purified through fire" in the next life. The practice of praying for the dead – which became widespread in the eastern church in the first four centuries – exercised a major impact upon theological development, and provides an excellent case study of the manner in which liturgy influences theology. What was the point of praying for the dead, it was asked, if those prayers could not alter the state in which they existed? Similar views are found in Augustine, who taught the need for purification from the sins of the present life, before entering the joys of the next.

While the practice of praying for the dead appears to have become well established by the fourth century, the explicit formulation of a notion of "purgatory" seems to date from two centuries later, in the writings of Gregory the Great (*c.*540–604). In his exposition of Matthew 12:31, dating from 593 or 594, Gregory picks up the idea of sins which can be forgiven "in the age to come." He interprets this in terms of a future age in which sins which have not been forgiven on earth may be forgiven subsequently. The theme of a fire which purifies – as opposed to a fire which punishes – is developed with particular enthusiasm in Catherine of Genoa's *Treatise on Purgatory*, which probably dates from around the year 1490.

The idea of purgatory was rejected by the Protestant reformers during the sixteenth century. Two major lines of criticism were directed against it. First, it was held to lack any substantial scriptural foundations. Second, it was inconsistent with the doctrine of justification by faith, which declared that an individual could be put "right with God" (or "justified") through faith, thus establishing a relationship which obviated the need for purgatory. Having dispensed with the idea of purgatory, the reformers saw no pressing reason to retain the practice of prayer for the dead, which was henceforth omitted from Protestant liturgies. Contemporary Catholicism maintains both the concept of purgatory and the practice of praying for the dead.

A related idea which must be mentioned at this point is that of "eternal life." The idea of "eternal life" might initially seem to suggest little more than life that goes on and on and on – a perennially extended version of our present existence. This is not what is intended. The Greek language, in which the New Testament was written, has two words for life. One (*bios*) could be understood to mean something like "biological existence"; the other (*zoe*) to mean something like "life in all its fullness." The Christian gospel concerns the gift of fullness of life (John 10:10), a totally fulfilled life which not even death itself can destroy. We are not being offered an endless extension of our biological existence, but rather a transformation of that existence. Eternal life means that our present relationship with God is not destroyed or thwarted by death, but is continued and deepened by it. The fundamental Christian theme of coming to a fulfilled relationship with God through Christ is thus understood to mean that this relationship is begun now, and fulfilled later.

It will therefore be clear that eternal life is not to be seen as something which lies totally in the future. It is something that we can begin to experience now. It is certainly true that eternal life, in all its fullness, is something we can only hope to gain in the age to come (Luke 18:30). Nevertheless, we are able to gain a foretaste of that eternal life now. To come to faith in Jesus Christ is to begin a new relationship with God which is not abolished by death, but which is actually deepened, in that death sweeps away the remaining obstacles to our experiencing the presence of God.

This is not to say that our resurrection has already taken place (a view which is rejected by New Testament writers, as at 2 Timothy 2:18); it is to say that we may catch a glimpse of what eternal life is like here and now. Eternal life is inaugurated, but not fulfilled, in our present life as believers. To enter fully into eternal life is not to experience something totally strange and unknown. Rather, it is to extend and deepen our experience of the presence and love of God.

Application

The theme of the comsummation of all things in the heavenly Jerusalem is of major importance in Christian spirituality. In the medieval period, the Latin term "viator" (literally, a "wayfarer") was used to refer to the believer, who was envisaged as a pilgrim travelling to the heavenly city. The vision of the heavenly city was seen as an encouragement and inspiration to those engaged on this pilgrimage. Many writings of the period direct the believer to focus attention on the glorious hope of final entry into the New Jerusalem, and the rejoicing and delight which this will bring. Such thoughts were widely regarded as an encouragement, enabling believers to deal with the disappointments and hardships which were so often their lot. Much the same theme can, of course, be found in other types of spirituality, such as John Bunyan's famous allegory *The Pilgrim's Progress*, which dates from 1678.

It was, of course, this aspect of the Christian faith which attracted such severe criticism from Karl Marx (1818–83). Marx regarded religion as the "opiate of the people" partly on account of the strongly positive vision set out by Christianity for the future life, which enabled Christians to cope with hardship, suffering, and deprivation in the light of the hope that was set before them. For Marx, this hope deflected them from attending to issues of worldly importance, such as the alleviation of poverty and attending to issues of social justice.

The theme of the Christian hope can also be stated in terms of catching a glimpse of the promised land – seen, as with Moses, from the mountain peak across the Jordan – and finally entering into it. This is demonstrated in many of the sermons of the great African-American civil rights leader Martin Luther King (1929–68), who also illustrates – *contra* Marx – how the theme of the Christian hope can be linked with a call to direct political action. King's final sermon was delivered on April 3, 1968 at the Mason Temple in Memphis, Tennessee (the headquarters of the largest African-American pentecostal denomination in the United States). The sermon is saturated with calls to action, coupled with a strong affirmation of the importance of hope in the future, linked with the imagery of the promised land. The sermon ends as follows:

> We've got some difficult days ahead. But it doesn't matter with me now. Because I've been to the mountaintop. And I don't mind. Like anybody, I would like to live a long life. Longevity has its place. But I'm not concerned about that now. I just want to do God's will. And He's allowed me to go up to the mountain. And I've looked over. And I've seen the promised land. I may not get there with you. But I want you to know tonight that we, as a people, will get to the promised land. And I'm happy, tonight. I'm not worried about the anything. I'm not fearing any man. Mine eyes have seen the glory of the coming of the Lord.

One application of particular interest should be noted: the idea of the "beatific vision." The basic idea which lies behind this is that human beings are simply incapable of fully beholding God in the present on account of the limitations of human nature. The early fathers of the Christian church used to compare understanding God with looking directly into the sun. The human eye is simply not capable to withstanding the intense light of the sun. And just as the human eye cannot cope with the brilliance of the sun, so the human mind cannot cope with the glory and radiance of God. The story of the pagan emperor who visited the Jewish rabbi Joshua ben Hananiah is of interest here. The emperor asked to be shown Joshua's god. The rabbi replied that this was impossible – an answer which failed to satisfy the emperor. So the rabbi took the emperor outside, and asked him to stare at the midday summer sun. "That is impossible!" replied the emperor. "If you cannot look at the sun, which God created," replied the rabbi, "how much less can you behold the glory of God!"

Yet medieval writers stressed that there was no greater privilege nor pleasure than to be able to behold God. This privilege was seen as being reserved for heaven, when the limitations imposed upon human nature by its creatureliness and sinfulness would be thrown aside. In heaven, a final vision of God's radiancy, glory, and beauty would finally be possible – and that was supremely worth waiting for. We find this idea in many medieval writings, perhaps most familiarly in Dante's *Divine Comedy*. This great work, which was probably written over the period 1305–14, describes the gradual ascent of the soul through the various layers of hell, purgatory and paradise – until the final moment, at which the poet catches a glimpse of "the love that moves the sun and the other stars." This is the climax of the book, and of the Christian life: to finally see God face to face for ever, rather than merely catch distant and temporary glimpses in the present life. Bernard of Cluny (*c*.1100–*c*.1150) expresses this hope as follows:

> There God, our King and portion,
> In fulness of his grace
> Shall we behold for ever
> And worship face to face.

Illustration

The theme of heaven is particularly well developed in medieval spirituality. The writings of Bernard of Cluny illustrate the importance of the theme particularly well, and we shall explore one of these in a little detail. In his classic vision of the new Jerusalem, Bernard of Cluny (*c*.1100–*c*.1150) sets out the basic elements of the Christian vision of the comsummation of all things. Note in particular his emphasis upon the inability of human language to do justice to what awaits believers, and also the use of imagery relating to feasting, rejoicing and resting.

> Jerusalem the golden
> With milk and honey blessed,
> Beneath thy contemplation
> Sink heart and voice oppressed.
> I know not, O, I know not
> What joys await us there,
> What radiancy of glory
> What bliss beyond compare.
>
> They stand, those halls of Zion
> All jubilant with song,
> And bright with many an angel,
> And all the martyr throng.

The Prince is ever with them,
The daylight is serene,
The pastures of the blessed
Are decked in glorious sheen

There is the throne of David
And there, from care released,
The shout of them that triumph,
The song of them that feast.
And they, who with their Leader,
Have conquered in the fight
For ever and for ever
Are clad in robes of white.

O sweet and blessed country
The home of God's elect!
O sweet and blessed country
That eager hearts expect!
Jesu, in mercy bring us
To that dear land of rest;
Who art, with God the Father,
And Spirit, ever blessed.

The fundamental theme developed by Bernard in this well-known hym relates to the richness of the New Jerusalem, which is compared to the Promised Land anticipated by Israel. Bernard sets out a vision of what lies ahead as a means of encouraging and sustaining Christian faith at present. Note Bernard's emphasis upon the inability of human language to convey adequately the wonders of heaven, and his insistence that believers can be assured that all these wonderful things are awaiting them. Those who find the life of faith tiring and dispiriting can, according to Bernard, take comfort and encouragement from this vision of heaven, and thus keep going on the road that leads to the celestial city.

Conclusion

With this, we come to the end of our survey of the theological foundations for spirituality. It will be clear that, rightly understood, there are positive and significant interactions between theology and spirituality. The present chapter has not attempted to be exhaustive in its account of this relationship, nor has it explored every area of theology which is of direct relevance to Christian spirituality. A fuller account, for example, would include a detailed exploration of the doctrines of the church and sacraments. Nevertheless, it is hoped that the material set out in this chapter will allow readers to begin to make further connections between theology and spirituality for themselves.

FOR FURTHER READING

All the topics noted in this chapter are surveyed in standard introductions to Christian theology. The most widely used of these introductions is the companion volume to this work:

Alister E. McGrath, *Christian Theology: An Introduction*. 2nd edn. Oxford: Blackwell, 1997.

The following introductions are also recommended for those wishing to explore further some of the issues raised in this chapter.

C. E. Braaten and R. W. Jenson (eds), *Christian Dogmatics*, 2 vols. Philadelphia: Fortress Press, 1984. Very demanding, and written from an explicitly Lutheran perspective; however, it is worth the trouble to read, especially its essays relating to revelation and the doctrine of God.

Millard J. Erickson, *Christian Theology*, 2nd edn. Grand Rapids: Baker, 1998. Written from a broadly baptist and evangelical perspective.

Francis F. Fiorenza and John P. Galvin, *Systematic Theology: Roman Catholic Perspectives*, 2 vols. Minneapolis: Fortress Press, 1991; also published as single-volume edition: Dublin: Gill and Macmillan, 1992. An excellent overview of the leading themes of systematic theology from a Roman Catholic perspective.

P. Hodgson and R. King (eds), *Christian Theology*. Philadelphia: Fortress Press, 1982; also available in an expanded edition, with two extra essays on theological method and the sacraments respectively. Written from a generally liberal perspective; stronger on more recent discussions of classic questions.

Daniel E. Migliore, *Faith Seeking Understanding*. Grand Rapids: Eerdmans, 1991. A useful overview of all the main areas of theology from a generally Reformed perspective by a highly stimulating and engaging writer.

The following are of particular relevance to individual theological topics noted:

Donald M. Baillie, *God was in Christ: An Essay on Incarnation and Atonement*. London: Faber & Faber, 1956.

Leonardo Boff, *Trinity and Society*. London: Burns & Oates, 1988.

David Cairns, *The Image of God in Man*. London: Collins, 1973.

Colin E. Gunton, *The Actuality of Atonement*. Edinburgh: T. & T. Clark, 1988.

Colin E. Gunton, *The Triune Creator: A Historical and Systematic Survey*. Grand Rapids, MI: Eerdmans, 1998.

Robert W. Jenson, *The Triune Identity*. Philadelphia: Fortress Press, 1982.

John Macquarrie, *In Search of Humanity: A Theological and Philosophical Approach*. London: SCM Press, 1983.

John Meyendorff, *Christi in Eastern Christian Thought*. Washington, D.C.: Corpus, 1969.

Jürgen Moltmann, *The Crucified God*. London: SCM Press, 1973.

Jürgen Moltmann, *The Trinity and the Kingdom of God*. London: SCM Press, 1981.

Wolfhart Pannenberg, *Anthropology in Theological Perspective*. London: SCM Press, 1985.

H. E. W. Turner, *The Patristic Doctrine of Redemption*. London: Mowbray, 1952.

Thomas G. Weinandy, *The Father's Spirit of Sonship: Reconceiving the Trinity*. Edinburgh: T. & T. Clark, 1995.

5

BIBLICAL IMAGES AND CHRISTIAN SPIRITUALITY

Christian spirituality involves a number of controlling images, grounded in the Old and New Testaments, each of which offers an understanding of the nature of the Christian life, and the means by which it can be advanced. In the present chapter, we shall explore some of these images, noting how they have been developed and deployed within the rich heritage of Christian spirituality. Our attention first concerns the role of the Bible in Christian spirituality, after which we shall consider some of the images which have had such a major impact on the discipline.

The Bible as a Resource for Spirituality

The Bible is recognized by all Christians as being of foundational importance for Christian thinking and living. The question of how to allow the Bible to shape, nourish, and develop Christian faith has been of major importance since the earliest of times. In what follows, we shall explore the nature of the Bible, and the ways in which its rich potential for spirituality has been tapped and unlocked by generations of Christians.

Before continuing further, it is important to note that the terms "biblical" and "scriptural" are equivalent within Christian theology, as are the terms "Bible" and "Scripture" or "Holy Scripture." The present work will make use of all these terms, and it is important to appreciate from the outset that no theological distinction is presupposed by this usage.

It is important to appreciate that the Bible can be read in a number of different ways. It can be read as an historical document – for example, by someone who is concerned to understand something of the history of Israel and its neighbors around the time of King Solomon. It can also be read as a source-book of Christian ideas – for example, by someone who wants to find out what St Paul thought about the nature of the church. Yet the Bible has been seen by Christians as being about far more than historical or theological information. It is both these things – and yet is more than this. In addition to providing information, Christians have used the Bible – when read in the appropriate manner – as a source of spiritual nourishment and refreshment. This did not mean that this way of reading the Bible was "right," where others were "wrong." Rather, Scripture was seen as a multi-faceted and rich resource, which could – and should! – be read in a number of manners. The mode of inter-pretation of the Bible was related to the concerns, questions, and interests of the reader. For this reason, a number of systems of biblical interpretation were devel-oped, aiming to enable readers to gain the maximum from their engagement with the biblical text.

One of the most important schemes for interpreting the Bible systematically devel-oped during the later Middle Ages. The scheme in question is sometimes known as the "fourfold sense of Scripture," and is sometimes referred to by the Latin term *Quadriga*. The basic idea is that a passage of Scripture can be interpreted in four ways: literally, or according to one of three spiritual senses – *allegorically, tropologi-cally*, or *anagogically*. We shall explain all four senses in what follows, beginning with the *literal* sense of the passage.

The "literal sense" of a passage could be understood as the obvious or natural sense of the passage in question, in which the passage is taken at its face value. Thus the great account of the exodus of the people of Israel from Egypt is taken as a simple historical account of an important moment in the history of God's people. Yet from the earliest of times, Christian writers believed that a deeper and more spiritual meaning could be discerned beneath the surface of Scripture. The identification of this deeper meaning thus became a matter of considerable importance. Thus Augustine of Hippo argued that Old Testament passages possessed a deeper spiritual meaning which was "veiled"; once that veil was removed, the true spiritual meaning of the passage would become clear.

In these precepts and commands of the Law which Christians may not now lawfully obey, such as the Sabbath, circumcision, sacrifices, and the like, there are contained such mys-teries that every religious person may understand there is nothing more dangerous than to take whatever is there literally, and nothing more wholesome than to let the truth be revealed by the Spirit. For this reason: "The letter kills but the Spirit brings life" (2 Corinthians 3:6). And again: "The same veil remains in the reading of the Old Testament and there is no revelation, for in Christ the veil is removed" (2 Corinthians 3:14). It is not the Old Testament that is abolished in Christ but the concealing veil, so that it may be understood through Christ. That which without Christ is obscure and hidden is, as it were, opened up. . . . [Paul] does not say: "The Law or the Old Testament is abolished." It is not the case, therefore, that by the grace of the Lord that which was covered has been abol-ished as useless; rather, the covering which concealed useful truth has been removed. This is what happens to those who earnestly and piously, not proudly and wickedly, seek the sense of the Scriptures. To them is carefully demonstrated the order of events, the reasons for deeds and words, and the agreement of the Old Testament with the New, so that not a single point remains where there is not complete harmony. The secret truths are conveyed in figures that are to be brought to light by interpretation.

Augustine of Hippo (354–430). Widely regarded as the most influential Latin patristic writer, Augustine was converted to Christianity at the northern Italian city of Milan in the summer of 386. He returned to north Africa, and was made bishop of Hippo in 395. He was involved in two major controversies – the Donatist controversy, focusing on the church and sacraments, and the Pelagian controversy, focusing on grace and sin. He also made substantial contributions to the development of the doctrine of the Trinity, and the Christian understanding of history.

So what are these "secret truths," which can be revealed and understood by proper interpretation? Three general spiritual senses were identified during the Middle Ages.

1   The *allegorical* sense of the passage. Here, the passage was taken to have a symbolic meaning related to Christian doctrine. For example, the story of the exodus from Egypt could be understood as an allegory of the redemption of the world through Christ. This interpretation did not, it should be noted, involve denying that the exodus happened in history, or that it was of enormous importance to Israel. Rather, it involved the discernment of a deeper meaning beneath the surface of this historical event, so that the exodus can be seen as a kind of anticipation of redemption in Christ.

2   The *moral* sense of the passage. Here, a spiritual meaning was discerned which concerned the conduct of the believer. Where the allegorical sense of Scripture concerned matters of doctrine, the moral sense (also referred to as the "tropological" sense by some writers) concerned matters of ethics.

3   The *anagogical* sense of the passage. This unusual word means "leading upward" or perhaps "uplifting," and refers to a spiritual meaning which affects the ways in which believers hope. Medieval exegetes would frequently note the way in which some biblical passages encouraged believers to gain a fresh vision of the wonder of God, and look forward with excited anticipation to the final encounter with God in heaven.

One of the most important medieval discussions of the correct way to read Scripture is provided by the Carthusian writer Guigo II (died around 1188). According to Guigo, four stages were to be discerned within the process of reading the biblical text:

1   reading (*lectio*);
2   meditation (*meditatio*);

3   prayer (*oratio*); and
4   contemplation *(contemplatio)*.

Guigo argues that we begin by reading the text of Scripture, in full expectation that we shall encounter something of God in doing so. This leads us on to meditate on what we find – not in the sense of emptying our minds of everything, but rather allowing our minds to focus and concentrate upon the meaning and imagery of the text, with all external thoughts being excluded. This leads us to prayer as the only appropriate response to what we encounter. Finally, this leads to a quiet entrance into the presence of God in contemplation. Guigo sets out the relationship between these four activities in the following series of terse statements:

Reading without meditation is sterile.
Meditation without reading is prone to error.
Prayer without meditation is lukewarm.
Meditation without prayer is barren.
Prayer with devotion achieves contemplation.

Guigo II (died c.1188). Ninth prior of the Grand Chartreuse, the mother house of the Carthusian Order, from about 1173 to 1180. Guigo was one of the most influential spiritual writers of the Middle Ages, and is remembered particularly for his *Scala claustralium* (a work which was once ascribed to Bernard of Clairvaux).

This general scheme was widely accepted in the Middle Ages, and offered a frame-work for unlocking the devotional richness of Scripture. For example, Geert Zerbolt van Zutphen (1367–1400), who is widely regarded as one of the most important early masters of the *devotio moderna*, adopted the basic themes of Guigo's *scala claustralium* in his major work *de spiritualibus ascensionibus* ("on spiritual ascents").

For Zerbolt, the spiritual reading of Scripture prepares the reader for meditation; meditation prepares for prayer; and prayer for contemplation. To meditate without first reading Scripture is to run the risk of being deluded or falling into error, whereas reading Scripture without turning to prayer is arid and barren. In clarifying this point, Zerbolt offers a definition of meditation which can be regarded as a synthesis of the medieval consensus on the issue:

By meditation is meant the process in which you diligently turn over in your heart whatever you have read or heard, earnestly reflecting upon it and thus enkindling your affections in some particular manner, or enlightening your understanding.

A related approach is associated with Ignatius Loyola (*c.*1491–1556), the founder of the Society of Jesus. Loyola developed a technique of empathetic projection or imaginative engagement, in which the reader of a biblical passage imagines herself to be projected into the biblical narrative, viewing and experiencing it from within. The idea is not original; it can be found particularly well developed in Ludolf of Saxony's *Vita Christi* (1374), in which the author sets out his intention to "recount things according to certain imaginative representations" so that his readers may "make themselves present for those things which Jesus did or said." The process involves the use of the imagination to construct a vivid and realistic mental image of the biblical scene, along with a prayerful engagement with the text in order that it might impact upon the reader in the intended manner. Loyola sets out the basic principles of his method in his "First Exercise," considering how the reader of a gospel passage relating to Jesus should approach the text.

> The first preamble is to form a visual conception of the place. It should be noted at this point that when the contemplation is on something that is visible (such as contemplating Christ our Lord during his life on earth), the image will consist of seeing with the mind's eye the physical place where the object we wish to contemplate is present. By the physical place I mean, for instance, a temple or mountain where Jesus or the Blessed Virgin is to be found, depending on the subject of the contemplation. In meditations on something that is invisible, as here in meditation on sins, the mental image will be imagined, by considering my soul imprisoned in its corruptible body, and my entire being in this valley as an exile among wild animals. By "entire being" I mean body and soul.
>
> The second is to ask God our Lord for what I want and desire. The request must be according to the subject matter. Therefore, if the contemplation is on the resurrection, I shall ask for joy with Christ rejoicing; if it is on the passion, I shall ask for pain, tears and suffering with Christ suffering.

The Protestant Reformation of the sixteenth century is often portrayed as a rediscovery of the Bible, and there can be no doubt that one of its leading themes was increasing the accessibility of the Bible, especially to the laity. One of the most central demands of the Reformation was that the Bible should be made available to all in a language which they could understand. The resulting translations of the Bible often had a major impact on the shaping of western European languages. For example, modern German has been recognizably shaped by the phraseology of Martin Luther's translation of the New Testament, just as modern English still contains many set phrases which derive directly from the King James Version of the Bible.

The centrality of scripture for Reformation spirituality can be seen from the literary resources made available by the reformers. Three are of especial importance.

1 The *biblical commentary* aimed to allow its readers to peruse and understand the word of God, explaining difficult phrases, identifying points of importance, and generally allowing its readers to become familiar with the thrust and concerns of the biblical passage. Writers such as John Calvin (1509–64), Martin Luther (1483–1546) and Huldrych Zwingli (1484–1531) produced commentaries aimed at a variety of readerships, both academic and lay.

2 The *expository sermon* aimed to fuse the horizons of the scriptural texts and its hearers, applying the principles underlying the scriptural passage to the situation of the audience. Calvin's sermons at Geneva are a model of their kind. Calvin made extensive use in his preaching of the notion of *lectio continua* – the continuous

preaching through a scriptural book, rather than on passages drawn from a lectionary or chosen by the preacher. For example, during the period between March 20, 1555 and July 15, 1556, Calvin is known to have preached some two hundred sermons on a single scriptural book – Deuteronomy.

3 Works of *biblical theology*, such as Calvin's *Institutes of the Christian Religion*, aimed to allow their readers to gain an appreciation of the theological coherence of scripture, by bringing together and synthesizing its statements on matters of theological importance. By doing this, it enabled its readers to establish a coherent and consistent world-view, which would undergird their everyday lives. For Calvin, as for the reformers in general, Scripture moulded doctrine, which in turned shaped the realities of Christian life.

An excellent illustration of the importance of the Bible for early Protestant spirituality is to be found in Martin Luther's 1535 work "A Simple Way to Pray." Luther wrote this short work for his barber, Peter Beskendorf. The treatise sets out an approach to prayer which is based on the reading of biblical passages, such as the Lord's Prayer (Matthew 6:9–13) and the Ten Commandments (Exodus 20:1–17). Luther sets out a means of praying which is based on a four-fold interaction with the biblical text. In the case of the Ten Commandments, Luther sets out the method of prayer which he personally finds helpful.

> I take one part after another and free myself as much as possible from distractions in order that I may pray. I then divide each commandment into four parts, so that I fashion a garland of four strands. In other words, I think of each commandment as, in the first place, instruction (which is really what it ought to be). Second, I turn it into a thanksgiving. Third, a confession. And fourth, a prayer.

Luther stresses that this framework is only an aid to prayer, and must not be allowed to obstruct the Holy Spirit. However, the framework proved popular, and was widely adopted within Lutheran circles and beyond. The four basic elements which Luther weaves together to yield his "garland of praise" can be set out as follows.

1   *Instruction*. Luther here expects the believer to be reminded of the need to trust God completely in all things, and not to depend on anything else – such as social status or wealth.
2   *Thanksgiving*. At this point, Luther turns his attention to meditation on all that God has done for him, particularly in relation to redemption, but also recalling that God has promised to be his "comfort, guardian, guide and strength" in times of difficulty.
3   *Confession*. Having reflected on all that God has done, Luther moves on to acknowledge and confess his own failings and weaknesses.
4   *Prayer*. In the light of the three previous items, Luther then composes a prayer, weaving together these elements, in which he asks God to renew his faith and trust, and strengthen his resolve to be obedient and faithful.

Martin Luther (1483–1546). Perhaps the greatest figure in the European Reformation, noted particularly for his doctrine of justification by faith alone, and his strongly Christocentric understanding of revelation. His "theology of the cross" has aroused much interest in the late twentieth century. Luther's posting of the Ninety-Five Theses in Ocober 1517 is generally regarded as marking the beginning of the Reformation.

The importance of meditating on biblical passages was thus firmly established within the Protestant spiritual tradition from its earliest phases. The principle can be illustrated from virtually any period of Protestant spirituality. For our purposes, we shall note the way in which it is taken and developed in the writings of the Baptist preacher Charles Haddon Spurgeon (1834–92), widely regarded as one of the finest preachers of the nineteenth century. For Spurgeon, the danger of an excessively technical approach to reading the Bible could be met by an emphasis upon meditation:

> The Spirit has taught us in meditation to ponder its message, to put aside, if we will, the responsibility of preparing the message we've got to give. Just trust God for that. But first, meditate on it, quietly ponder it, let it sink deep into our souls. Have you not often been surprised and overcome with delight as Holy Scripture is opened up as if the gates of the Golden City have been set back for you to enter? A few minutes silent openness of soul before the Lord has brought us more treasure of truth than hours of learned research.

Biblical Images and Spirituality

As we have seen, reading the biblical text and meditation upon it has been of central importance to Christians down the ages. It should therefore be no surprise to learn that many biblical images have exercised a controlling influence over Christian spirituality. It is much easier to reflect upon an image than upon an idea. In what follows, we shall explore a series of biblical images, and note the way in which they have been deployed and developed within the tradition.

The feast

Jesus frequently compared the kingdom of God to a feast – perhaps like a great banquet thrown in celebration of a marriage (Luke 14:15–24). When the prodigal son returned to his father (Luke 15:11–24), the father threw a feast in celebration of the safe return of the son who he had believed to be lost. This theme is of importance to spirituality, partly on account of the light which it casts on the Christian faith itself, and partly on account of what it suggests needs to be done to advance in that faith.

The image of a feast suggests a number of themes, which can be separated out as follows.

1   The image suggests an abundance of food and drink, which are capable of meeting and satisfying human hunger. A leading theme of the Christian understanding of human nature is that we have been created for fellowship with God, and are empty otherwise. Augustine of Hippo (354–430) made this point in his famous prayer to God: "you have made us for yourself, and our hearts are restless until they find their rest in you."

2   It also suggests the idea of invitation. A feast is something to which we have to be invited before we can share in the rejoicing and feasting. Jesus himself ate at table with those who contemporary Jewish society regarded as social outcasts, making the point that these unfortunate people were welcomed and accepted into his presence. Feasting is about being wanted and welcomed into the presence of someone of dignity and importance. It is a profoundly affirming matter.

3   Feasting is about celebration and rejoicing. A feast is arranged to mark an occasion of importance, such as a wedding, so that all those who know and love those who are to be married may share in and express their joy and delight.

Each of these themes is developed within Christian spirituality, especially in relation to the eucharist. The bread and the wine remind us of both a human need (spiritual hunger and thirst) and the manner in which the gospel is able to identify and meet those needs.

Yet the eucharist is also directed toward the Christian hope. The "feasting" image finds its fulfillment in the vision of "the marriage supper of the Lamb" (Revelation 19.9), of which the eucharist is seen as a foretaste in the present. The Second Vatican Council referred to the eucharist as a "foretaste of the heavenly banquet"; John Wesley (1703–91) termed it a "pledge of heaven." The basic theme is that heaven is to be a place of rejoicing and plenty, into which we shall be welcomed. The celebration of the Lord's Supper in the present is thus both an important reminder of what happened in the past (the death and resurrection of Jesus) but also an assurance of what will happen in the future (being welcomed and received into the presence of the living God).

This point is made particularly clearly by Theodore of Mopsuestia (c.350–428), a writer standing within the Antiochene school of biblical interpretation.

> Every time that the liturgy of this awesome sacrifice is performed, which is the clear image of the heavenly realities, we should imagine that we are in heaven . . . Faith enables us to picture in our minds those heavenly realities, as we remind ourselves that the same Christ who is now in heaven is [also present] under these symbols. So when faith enables our eyes to contemplate what now takes place, we are brought again to see his death, resurrection and ascension, which have already taken place for our sakes.

The basic idea that Theodore develops here is that the eucharist allows us to look backwards and forwards. Looking backwards, we are reminded of Christ's death and resurrection for us. Looking forwards, we can begin to imagine ourselves in heaven, where Christ can be seen in all his glory. The Christ who is seen dimly through the sacramental symbols will then be revealed in all his glory and wonder. Then the sign and symbol will be rendered unnecessary, as we enter into the presence of the risen Christ.

So what insights does this image of a feast offer for our understanding of spirituality? One of the answers that can be given is found in the writings of Blaise Pascal, who saw a human awareness of an inner emptiness as ultimately resting upon the absence of God.

> What else does this longing and helplessness proclaim, but that there was once in each person a true happiness, of which all that now remains is the empty print and trace? We try to fill this in vain with everything around us, seeking in things that are not there the help we cannot find in those that are there. Yet none can change things, because this infinite abyss can only be filled with something that is infinite and unchanging – in other words, by God himself. God alone is our true good.

Pascal's argument is that nothing other than God is able to fill the chasm that lies within us. We may try to fill this void with other things – such as financial success or status – but in the end these will not and cannot satisfy. Only God is able to meet this need. The image of feasting, for Pascal, thus points to our need to ensure that we allow nothing and no one other than God to become the object of our desire. If we do so, they will disappoint and betray us. True spirituality consists in the pursuit of God, and not allowing our desire to become attached to anything or anyone else.

Blaise Pascal (1623–62). An influential French Roman Catholic writer, who gained a considerable reputation as a mathematician and theologian. After a religious conversion experience in 1646, he developed an approach to his faith which was strongly Christocentric and experiential. His most famous writing is the collection known as the *Pensées*, first gathered together in 1670, some years after his death.

Similar points are made by Jonathan Edwards (1703–58) and C. S. Lewis (1898–1963). In his sermon "The Christian Pilgrim," Edwards affirmed that: "God is the highest good of the reasonable creature; and the enjoyment of him is the only happiness with which our souls can be satisfied." For Lewis, the human sense of longing or emptiness is a pointer to God, who alone can satisfy human desire. Lewis addressed this matter fully in a remarkable sermon entitled "Weight of Glory," preached before the University of Oxford on June 8, 1941. Lewis spoke of "a desire which no natural happiness will satisfy," "a desire, still wandering and uncertain of its object and still largely unable to see that object in the direction where it really lies." There is something self-defeating about human desire, in that what is desired, when achieved, seems to leave the desire unsatisfied. Lewis illustrates this from the age-old quest for beauty, using imagery which ultimately derives from Augustine:

> The books or the music in which we thought the beauty was located will betray us if we trust to them; it was not in them, it only came *through* them, and what came through them was longing. These things – the beauty, the memory of our own past – are good images of what we really desire; but if they are mistaken for the thing itself they turn into dumb idols, breaking the hearts of their worshippers. For they are not the thing itself; they are only the scent of a flower we have not found, the echo of a tune we have not heard, news from a country we have not visited.

The journey

Both Old and New Testaments depict journeys, such as Abraham's journey to Canaan, or Paul's great missionary journeys. Perhaps the two most important journeys described in the Old Testament are the wandering of the people of Israel through the wilderness for forty years prior to entering into the Promised Land, and the return of the people of Jerusalem to their native city after decades of exile in the great city of Babylon. Each of these journeys has become an image of considerable importance for Christian spirituality.

One of the most powerful images of the Christian life is that of a journey. Indeed, the New Testament records that the early Christians initially referred to themselves as followers of "the way" (see, for example, Acts 9:2; 24:14). Just as God led the people of Israel out of captivity in Egypt into the Promised Land, so the Christian life can be seen as a slow process of deliverance from bondage to sin before being led triumphantly into the heavenly city.

At several points in the writings of St Paul, we find a modification of the image of a journey. For Paul, the Christian life is like a race – a long and arduous journey, undertaken under pressure, in which the winners receive a crown (see Galatians 2:2; 2 Timothy 4:7). The image is also used in the letter to the Hebrews, which urges its readers to persevere in the race of life by keeping their eyes focused firmly on Jesus (Hebrews 12:1–2). This image allows Paul to stress the importance of discipline in the Christian life.

The role of discipline in the Christian life is traditionally explored in asceticism (which derives from the Greek term *askesis*, "discipline"). This term has acquired unhelpful associations – for example, undertaking absurdly rigorous programs of self-denial, and adopting a generally negative attitude toward the world, people, and sexuality. Asceticism is meant to be about the process of self-discipline which enables Christians to lead more authentic and effective lives as believers. The New Testament models of the athlete and the soldier are intended to convey the importance of discipline and training as a means of ensuring the quality of the person's actions. Both soldiers and athletes require training in order to undertake their tasks properly. Asceticism is thus a means to an end, not an end in itself. Training leads to better Christian living; self-discipline is thus not to be seen as a goal in itself, but as a process which enables a greater goal to be achieved.

Self-denial can thus be seen as a systematic program of eliminating influences – such as pride, self-centeredness, and general lack of consideration and love for others – which are a barrier to spiritual growth. Fasting, for example, is an excellent means of self-discipline, which tests our ability to undertake tasks, and also reminds us of the excesses of consumption to which we are prone, which can distract us from our heavenly goal and lead us to neglect the discipline which enables us to achieve it.

The object of the Christian life is thus to arrive safely in the heavenly homeland. Anything that distracts from this task is to be seen as potentially dangerous. For this reason, many spiritual writers stress the importance of cultivating indifference to the world. In his sermon "The Christian Pilgrim," Jonathan Edwards (1703–58) stresses the importance of this point:

> We ought not to rest in the world and its enjoyments, but should desire heaven . . . We ought above all things to desire a heavenly happiness; to be with God; and well with Jesus Christ. Though surrounded with outward enjoyments, and settled in families with desirable friends and relations; though we have companions whose society is delightful, and children in whom we see many promising qualifications; though we live by good neighbors and are generally beloved where known; yet we ought not to take our rest in these things as our portion. . . . We ought to possess, enjoy and use them, with no other view but readily to quit them, whenever we are called to it, and to change them willingly and cheerfully for heaven.

Note that Edwards is not in any way disparaging the world as God's good creation. His concern is that Christians might come to value the creation more highly than the creator, and as a result settle for something that is good, but not as good as God.

Two works of Christian spirituality which focus on the theme of "journeying" may be noted. The central theme of the *Divine Comedy* of Dante Aligheri (1265–1321) is that of a journey from the darkness of a wood to an encounter with God in the beatific vision. In the course of this long and difficult journey, the poet achieves insight into his own identity, and the nature and means of achieving salvation. Perhaps more familiar is the famous *Pilgrim's Progress* of John Bunyan (1628–88). This work was written while he was imprisoned in Bedford as a result of his opposition to the religious policies of Charles II. Its dominant theme is the journey of Christian from the "City of Destruction" to "the Heavenly City." The work is written in very simple and direct English, and has had a major impact on the shaping of the English language. Once more, the leading theme is the difficulties, temptations, and encouragements which are to be had on the journey to the new Jerusalem, intended to encourage and admonish its readers.

So what insights does this image of a journey offer those wishing to develop their spirituality? The image is rich, and a number of different insights can be identified.

1   Before setting out on a journey, it is usually thought to be wise to get hold of a map, which will indicate how to get to the desired destination. In the case of spirituality, the "map" in question is the shared experience of the many Christians who have undertaken this journey before us, and passed down to us their wisdom, knowledge, and encouragement. Engaging with others – whether by reading books, or by spending time with others trying to live out the Christian life, whether alone or in groups – is one of the most helpful ways of leading the Christian life.

2   One of the best ways of gaining encouragement on a long journey is to anticipate one's arrival. This means picturing one's final destination, anticipating the joy of arrival, and picturing those who will be present. Many of the greatest works of Christian spirituality aim to encourage those on this journey by offering them a vision of the new Jerusalem, so that they will long to be there and savor its delights.

3   For most Christian writers, the journey of faith is not to be seen as an individual pilgrimage, but as a corporate achievement, in which those who are weak help the strong. The Christian journey is, and is meant to be, a corporate and

supportive matter. This points to the importance of fellowship and mutual support in the Christian life, a theme of many works of spirituality, including Dietrich Bonhoeffer's *Life Together* (1938).

Dietrich Bonhoeffer (1906–45). A German Lutheran theologian, influenced by Karl Barth, with a particular interest in ecumenical work during the 1930s. He was arrested in 1943, and hanged by the Nazis in 1945. His letters and papers from prison include significant discussions of the suffering of God, and the need for theology to relate to a "religionless society."

Exile

One of the most important events recounted in the Old Testament is the exile of Jerusalem to Babylon, which took place in 586 BC. In 605 BC, the Babylonian emperor Nebuchadnezzar defeated the massed Egyptian armies at Carchemish, establishing Babylon as the leading military and political power in the region. Along with many other territories in this region, the land of Judah became subject to Babylonian rule, possibly in 604. Jehoiakim, king of Judah, decided to rebel against Babylon. It is possible that he may have been encouraged in this move by a successful Egyptian counter-attack against Babylon in 601, which may have seemed to suggest that Babylon's power was on the wane. It was to prove to be a terrible misjudgment. Judah was invaded by Babylonian forces, which was clearly interpreted by writers of the time as the execution of the promised judgment of the Lord against his faithless people and king. Egypt, once the hope of Judah, was also defeated, and neutralized as a military power. (These same events are also vividly described and analyzed by Jeremiah, the later chapters of whose prophecy should be read in the light of this historical narrative.)

Jehoiachim was succeeded by Jehoiachin (the close similarity of these names being a constant source of confusion to readers) toward the end of 598 BC, shortly before the Babylonians finally laid siege to the city. Early the following year, the king, the royal family, and the circle of royal advisors gave themselves up to the besieging forces. They were deported to Babylon, along with several thousand captives. The Babylonians placed Zedekiah, a relative of Jehoiakin, on the throne as their vassal, and seemed happy to leave things like that for the present. Yet Zedekiah attempted to rebel against Babylon. The Babylonian response was massive and decisive. In January 588, they laid siege to the city; in July 586, they broke through its walls, and took the city. The defending army attempted to flee, but was routed. The next month, a Babylonian offical arrived in Jerusalem to supervise the destruction of the defences of the city and its chief buildings, and the deportation of its people. The furnishings of the temple were dismantled, and taken to Babylon as booty.

It is the interpretation of these events which is of particular interest to New Testament writers. The period of exile is interpreted as, in the first place, a judgment against Judah for its lapse into pagan religious beliefs and practices; and in the second, a period of national repentance and renewal, which would lead to the restoration of a resurgent people of God.

This image of "exile" was developed within Christian spirituality, particularly by writers of the medieval period. The basic theme of exile was taken from the history of Jerusalem, as just noted. However, it was interpreted and developed in a particular manner. Drawing on Paul's image of Christians as "citizens of heaven," and the Christian hope of finally entering the new Jerusalem, such writers argued that life on earth was to be thought of as a period of exile from the heavenly Jerusalem. The world is not our homeland; it is the place to which we have been exiled.

An excellent example of this approach can be found in the writings of Peter Abelard (1079–1142), especially his hymn *O quanta qualia sunt illa sabbata*. In this hymn, Abelard contrasts the present situation of Christians as exiles in Babylon with the hope of return to Jerusalem:

> Now, in the meanwhile, with hearts raised on high,
> We for that country must yearn and must sigh;
> Seeking Jerusalem, dear native land,
> Through our long exile on Babylon's strand.

A related approach can be found in the "Prayer to Christ" of Anselm of Canterbury (*c.*1033–1109). In this prayer, Anselm addresses his longing to be with Christ in heaven. The thought of being with Christ simultaneously heightens his sense of sadness at not being with Christ at present, and offers him hope and encouragement that he one day will be in this presence. Again, the image of exile controls his thoughts at this point:

> All this I hold with unwavering faith
> And weep over the hardship of exile.
> Hoping in the sole consolation of your coming
> Ardently longing for the glorious contemplation of your face.

On the basis of this model, medieval spiritual writers began to develop a series of insights which illuminated the status of Christians, and offered them guidance as to how they should behave in the world. For example, they stressed the importance of cultivating the hope of return to the homeland. Many writers of the period offered powerful visual images of the heavenly Jerusalem, in order to encourage their readers to set their hearts firmly on heaven. The Old Testament indicates that some exiled inhabitants of Jerusalem actually came to prefer Babylon, and chose to stay on in that city when others returned home. Bernard of Clairvaux (1090–1153) and others discern a similar danger in the Christian life – that Christians will come to prefer their place of exile to their homeland, and in effect choose to remain in exile.

The struggle

Christianity is often portrayed as a struggle between God and the world, or good and evil. This should not necessarily be taken to imply that Christians regard the world as an evil place; the predominant tendency within the Christian tradition, as noted earlier, is to see the world as God's good creation. The concern is that something which is not God might be substituted for God; that Christians might settle for the lesser good of the world in preference to the greater good of God. The world may point to God; yet it is not itself God, and cannot be accepted as a substitute for God.

This understanding of a tension within the Christian life lends itself especially well to the image of a struggle. St Paul speaks of "putting on the full armor of God" (Ephesians 6:10–18) as protection against spiritual attack. Christians are compared to soldiers, who must be disciplined if they are to persevere in the struggles that lie ahead for them (2 Timothy 2:3).

The image of struggle is deployed in three different contexts within Christian spirituality.

1   *External struggle against those hostile to Christianity, or one of its forms.* It is thought by many that Christianity appears at its most authentic when it is under attack, or forced to suffer. The New Testament frequently assumes that Christians will suffer at the hands of, for example, the Roman authorities on account of their faith. Puritan writers often felt that they were victimized by the Anglican authorities in England, yet their spirituality was deepened by their experiences. In such contexts, the image of faith leading to struggle encourages Christians to persevere in their faith under difficult circumstance. The development of Russian Orthodox spirituality under Stalin brings out this point with particular poignancy, as can be seen from the writings of Anatolii Zhurankovskii (1897–1939) or Tavrion Batotskii (1898–1979).

2   *Internal struggle against temptation.* Many spiritual writers stress the importance of identifying sin, and struggling against it. An excellent example is provided by the *Interior Castle* by Teresa of Ávila (1515–82). This work encourages its readers to look into their souls, understand themselves, and combat the sins which they discern within them. This theme of fighting sins within oneself is found throughout the entire spectrum of Christian spirituality, and is of major importance. A work which develops the theme in some detail, yet which has been somewhat neglected of late, is Lorenzo Scupoli's *Combattimento Spirituale* ("Spiritual Combat"), which appeared in 1589, and went through 250 editions between then and 1750.

3   *Struggle with God.* It must not be thought that the struggle is simply between faith and the world. One of the most remarkable aspects of the Christian tradition is the idea that the believer also struggles with God. In part, that struggle concerns the desire to apprehend God fully. The biblical image which is often deployed in this connection is the mysterious night-time struggle between Jacob and an unidentified man by the ford of the River Jabbok (Genesis 32:22–32). This struggle is widely interpreted as an allegory of the human struggle to comprehend God. Prayer is thus seen (e.g., by writers as different as Thomas Aquinas and John Wesley) as a struggle with God, through which it is hoped to gain insights into God's will and purposes for the individual.

The use of the "struggle" motif is particularly associated with Puritanism. Although the origins of the term "Puritanism" remain unclear, and debate over its precise meaning continues, for our purposes we may define the movement as a version of Reformed theology and spirituality which flourished in England and the North American colonies in the seventeenth century, which gave greater recognition to the importance of experiential and pastoral issues than many of their continental Reformed colleagues. The Puritans saw the Christian life as a sustained struggle against sin and unbelief, in which the believer was sustained and supported by God.

The main lines of this approach can be see in one of the most influential writings of John Owen (1616–83): "On the Mortification of Sin in Believers." The theme of "mortification" was of considerable significance to Puritans writers, in that it denoted the idea of "putting sin to death." Sin was conceived as a personal force, hostile toward God, which threatened to imprison the believer in its shackles, and prevent the believer from attaining fulfillment. In this work, Owen stresses that the struggle against sin is not undertaken by believers in their strength alone; the Holy Spirit is given to believers as an active resource for combatting sin.

> The Holy Ghost works in us and upon us, as we are fit to be wrought in and upon; that is, so as to preserve our own liberty and free obedience. He works upon our understandings, wills, consciences, and affections, agreeably to their own natures; he works *in us* and *with us*, not *against us* or *without us*, so that his assistance is an encouragement as to the facilitating of the work, and no occasion of neglect as to the work itself. And, indeed, I might here bewail the endless, foolish labour of poor souls, who, being convinced of sin and not able to stand against the power of their convictions, do set themselves, by innumerable perplexing ways and duties, to keep down sin, but, being strangers to the Spirit of God, all in vain. They combat without victory, have war without peace, and are in slavery all their days. They spend their strength for that which is not bread, and their labour for that which profiteth not. This is the saddest warfare that any poor creature can be engaged in. A soul under the power of conviction from the law is pressed to fight against sin, but hath no strength for the combat. They cannot but fight, and they can never conquer; they are like men thrust on the sword of enemies on purpose to be slain. The *law* drives them on, and sin beats them back. Sometimes they think, indeed, that they have foiled sin, when they have only raised a dust that they see it not; that is, they distemper their natural affections of fear, sorrow, and anguish, which makes them believe that sin is conquered when it is not touched. By that time they are cold, they must to battle again; and the lust which they thought to be slain appears to have had no wound.

Although Owen's English is archaic, the points which he makes remain significant. One of the most important themes in this passage is that the Christian who trusts in his or her own strength in the struggle against sin is doomed to failure and misery, in that the battle simply cannot be won using purely human resources. Christian assurance rests on the realization that God struggles within the believer against sin, and will eventually win.

Purification

One of the most important biblical images relating to Christian spirituality is that of purification. It is important to appreciate that a distinction must be made between spiritual and physical purification; although the latter may serve as an analogy or illustration for the latter, they are quite distinct. In the Old Testament, considerable emphasis is placed upon the need for preparation before entering into the presence of God. The Day of Atonement ritual, described in detail in Leviticus 16, indicates the importance of purity on the part of those, such as the High Priest, who are allowed to draw close to God. The same theme is also of importance in relation to the sins of individuals. For example, Psalm 51 is traditionally seen as a psalm of contritition on the part of David after his adulterous affair with Bathsheba (2 Samuel 11). The theme of "cleansing from sin" recurs throughout the Psalm, as the following extracts make clear (Psalm 51:2, 7):

> Wash away all my iniquity
>   And cleanse me from my sin . . .
> Cleanse me with hyssop, and I shall be clean;
>   Wash me, and I shall be whiter than snow.

This Psalm has found its way into the Ash Wednesday liturgy. Ash Wednesday is the first day of Lent, the period before Easter which is traditionally seen as a period of repentance and personal preparation for the remembrance of Good Friday and Easter (see pp. 126–7).

This theme of human sinfulness is developed further in the New Testament. One of the central themes of the Letter to the Hebrews is that Christ is the perfect sacrifice, who has taken away the stain of sin so that believers may enter into the presence of God with confidence (Hebrews 4:14–16). The letter uses the imagery of cleansing to refer to the purification from sin which results from the appropriation of Christ's death (see p. 61). Christ's death on the cross "sprinkles the hearts" of believers (a reference to an Old Testament purification rite) and "cleanses guilty consciences" (Hebrews 10:22). This imagery is further developed in relation to the sacrament of baptism, in which the water of baptism is seen partly as a symbol of the cleansing which results from the work of Christ on the cross.

A particularly striking New Testament image for this process of cleansing is that of "being washed in the blood of the Lamb" (Revelation 7:14). This image is initially puzzling, perhaps even paradoxical, in that blood is normally the case of stains on clothing, rather than a means of removing them. Yet the image is intended to convey the fact that Christ's death on the cross (of which the "blood of the lamb" is a symbol) is the means by which sin may be taken away from humanity. This image features prominently in much evangelical hymns. A particularly clear example can be found in the "Hymns of the Passion," a classic Icelandic writing by Hallgrimur Péterson (1614–74). The poem, which dates from 1659, focuses on the effects of the suffering and death of Christ for believers, and makes frequent reference to the idea of being cleansed from sin by Christ's blood. This work, widely regarded as a classic in the Icelandic language, sets out classic Lutheran ideas on the nature of Christ's passion and its benefits in a highly dramatic and visual manner.

The imagery of "contamination" or "stain" has been widely used within Christian spirituality as a way of understanding the nature of sin. For example, Origen (c.185–c.254) argues that, on account of its origins, humanity enters into the world polluted by sin. Only Jesus Christ remains uncontaminated in this manner, on account of the virgin birth.

Everyone who enters the world may be said to be affected by a kind of contamination. . . . By the very fact that humanity is placed in its mother's womb, and that it takes the material of its body from the source of the father's seed, it may be said to be contaminated in respect of both father and mother. . . . Thus everyone is polluted in father and mother. Only Jesus my Lord was born without stain. He was not polluted in respect of his mother, for he entered a body which was not contaminated.

For Origen, the process of salvation includes the gradual elimination of this pollution, as human nature is transformed by the action of God, and is eventually made divine itself.

Origen (c.185–c.254). Leading representative of the Alexandrian school of theology, especially noted for his allegorical exposition of Scripture, and his use of Platonic ideas in theology, particularly Christology. The originals of many of his works, which were written in Greek, have been lost, with the result that some are known only in Latin translations of questionable reliability.

The idea of "contamination by sin" has often been linked with the idea of the "image of God." The Old Testament affirms that humanity has been created in the image and likeness of God (Genesis 1:26–7). Yet this image of God has, in some way, been deformed or covered on account of human sin. The image has thus not been obliterated, but obscured. In order to restore it to its former state, it is necessary to cleanse human nature, both through the grace of God and human discipline. As Bernard of Clairvaux (1090–1153) put it in his *Sermon on the Song of Songs*: "We are repairing the image of God within us, and the way is being prepared, by the grace of God, for the retrieval of that honor which we once possessed, but which we forfeited on account of sin."

This notion was developed in a number of ways within the Middle Ages, of which the most important is probably the notion of the "purgative way" (*via purgativa*). The thirteenth-century writer Hugh of Balma distinguished three "ways" or "paths" in Christian spirituality, of which the first was the purgation of the soul from the sin which, by contaminating it, prevented it from achieving its proper and intended spiritual growth. Once this sin was purged, the believer could progress further by the *via illuminativa* (the "way of illumination," in which the soul is enlightened by rays of divine wisdom through meditation on Scripture and prayer) and the *via unitiva* (the "way of union),"在 which the soul is united with God (see p. 151).

Within the Puritan school of thought, the concept of purification was developed with special reference to the idea of "mortification of sin." John Owen (1616–83) devoted a number of major works of pastoral theology, including *On the Mortification of Sin in Believers*, to the issue of how indwelling sin might be "mortified" (that is, put to death). The characteristic Puritan emphasis on the Christian life as a struggle, noted above, allowed its writers – including Owen and John Bunyan – to describe purification in terms of a struggle to the death with indwelling sin.

One of the most significant related themes to that which we have just considered is that of "internalization." In what follows, we shall explore this in more detail.

The internalization of faith

As we noted earlier, the concept of spirituality is closely linked with the internalization of religious faith. Christianity recognizes a distinction between the formal outward observance of certain religious duties (such as going to church) and the internal appropriation of faith. There need be no tension between an inwardly appropriated faith and its external observance, in that the latter naturally leads to the former. However, one of the main concerns addressed by many writers within the Christian tradition is the fear that some Christians content themselves merely with going through the motions of faith. Religion is seen simply as a code of conduct which is to be observed, which does not have any deep interior origins or basis.

The issue is addressed at some length in the Bible, particularly in the prophetic literature. A common complaint of the Old Testament prophets is that Israel, which once had an intense and passionate love for God, had fallen into a state of religious degeneracy in which mere external compliance with the law had replaced this love. Isaiah complains that Israel simply continues with the external formalities of religion – such as sacrifices, incense, and the observation of the new moon (Isaiah 1:10–17). Similar complaints can be found elsewhere. Their basic common theme is that external compliance with religious requirements has displaced a deeply rooted and internalized faith. The people of Israel may "honor God with their lips," but that God has no place in their hearts (Isaiah 29:13).

In challenging this trend toward a purely external understanding of religion, the Old Testament prophets stressed the need for faith to be a matter of the heart. The phrase "circumcision of the heart" (Deuteronomy 10:16; Jeremiah 4:4) indicates the need for the external sign of faith (circumcision) to relate to the internal emotions. The prophet Jeremiah spoke of the Lord renewing a covenant with Israel; in this case, the covenant would be written on the hearts of the people (Jeremiah 31:33). No longer would the law or the covenant be a matter of external regulations; they would be part of the intellectual and emotional life of the people of God.

Similar themes can be found in the New Testament, particularly in Paul's emphasis on the importance of the role of the Holy Spirit (Galatians 5:16–26). For Paul, the Holy Spirit transforms the inner life of believers, causing them to possess "love, joy, peace, patience, kindness, goodness, faithfullness, gentleness and self-control." These "fruit of the Spirit" (Galatians 5:22) do not come about by external observance of regulations, but by internal transformation through the Holy Spirit.

The importance of this theme within western spirituality is best seen by considering the monastic reforms of the eleventh and twelfth centuries. Prior to this, emphasis had been placed upon the external features of the religious life – for example, conformity to the rule of life of a religious order, the wearing of specified forms of clothing, and the observance of certain fixed patterns of prayer. These could easily be seen in terms of a preoccupation with the external matters of religion, and a relative lack of interest in interior religion.

The religious reforms of the period saw a new emphasis being placed upon the "interior life." The Socratic motto *scito te ipsum* ("know yourself") came to be of major importance, and led to a turn toward personal meditation and prayer with a corresponding reduction in interest in the external matters of religion. While most religious orders of the period retained a "rule of life," this was increasingly interpreted as a means of enhancing the interior life of prayer and contemplation, rather than merely a series of regulations which were to be formally obeyed. This can be seen particularly clearly in the writings of Anselm of Canterbury (*c*.1033–1109) during the eleventh century, where we find the traditional external forms of the religious life maintained and defended – but interpreted in terms of their benefits for the interior life of the soul. Anselm argued that monastic clothing is laden with symbolism, which assists the monk to pray and contemplate:

> The heavy black clothes remind the monk that he is a sinner. They cover him from head to feet in order to direct him to this thought from the beginning to the end of his life. They also present the form of the cross and re-establish the passion of the Lord in him . . . To wear the religious habit serves no purpose unless at the same time an effort is made to be internally what one appears to be externally.

This concern to enhance the internal life of prayer, and ensure that religious faith was never a matter of purely external observance of rules, became of renewed importance at the time of the Reformation. Martin Luther (1483–1546) and John Calvin (1509–64) were both critical of monastic religious observances on the grounds that these encouraged or implied the belief that it was through the observation of external regulations that salvation could be achieved and secured. For Luther, faith was something that was alive within the human soul, nourished by the word of God. Similar concerns were expressed by many writers within the Counter Reformation, including Johann Scheffler (1624–77), who wrote under the name "Angelus Silesius" ("The Silesian Angel"). Perhaps his best-known work is *Der cherubinische Wandersmann* ("The Cherubic Wanderer," 1676), in which the need for a personally-appropriated faith is stressed.

61. God must be born within you
Were Christ to be born a thousand times in Bethelehem,
And yet not be born in you, you will remain lost.

62. External things do not help
The cross of Golgotha cannot save you from sin,
Unless that cross is raised within you.

63. Raise yourself from the dead!
It does not help you that Christ is risen
If you remain bound to sin and death.

Especially within Pietist circles, the emphasis upon the need for an interiorized faith was often linked with the theme of conversion. Conversion is generally understood to be the total internal transformation of the individual. Nicholas Ludwig von Zinzendorff (1700–60), perhaps the best-known German Pietist writer, wrote of conversion in terms of total personal renewal:

Something must happen to us, which Luther calls "the divine work within us," which changes us, gives us new birth, and makes us completely different people in heart, spirit, mind and all our powers.

Similar ideas can be found in the writings of John and Charles Wesley, and subsequently within revivalist traditions in North American Protestantism, including the evangelists Billy Sunday and Billy Graham. This tradition (exemplified by much modern evangelicalism) resists being described as "religious," in that this is seen as placing the emphasis on the outward aspects of the life of faith, where it should, according to this tradition, be placed firmly upon the inner life of faith.

The desert

The desert is to be understood as a lonely place, devoid of distraction, in which the individual is alone with God, and thus has the opportunity to reflect on spiritual issues. A major biblical image which lies behind the use of the "desert" motif in Christian spirituality is the wanderings of Israel in the wilderness prior to their entry into the promised land (an episode, incidentally, which links the themes of "journey" and "desert"). Certain Old Testament prophets (especially Jeremiah and Hosea) spoke of the desert as a place of purification and renewal of Israel. The prophets often looked back to Israel's period of wandering in the wilderness as a period in which the nation was close to God, before becoming corrupted by increasing wealth in the eighth century BC.

The desert is seen as a place of prayer, as well as purification; Elijah and John the Baptist are both associated with the desert in this manner. The gospels often refer to Jesus withdrawing into the wilderness for prayer. In particular, the gospels report that, after his baptism, Jesus withdrew into the wilderness for a period of forty days, during which he was subject to various temptations which he successfully resisted (Luke 4:1–13). This period is recalled during Lent (see p. 126).

Interest in the desert or wilderness was developed in two different manners within third-century eastern Christianity. Some chose to take the image *literally*. Thus Antony of Egypt (*c.*251–356), increasingly alarmed at the growing wealth and corruption of city life, withdrew into the desert with his followers to establish a new community, uncontaminated by the sins of the city. By withdrawing from human society into the desert, Anthony believed that he would be able to address his own spiritual state with a degree of concentration which would be impossible elsewhere. The desert offered an antidote to distraction and temptation, leaving one free to focus on God and the spiritual life.

A similar idea can be found in the writings of Cassian (360–435), who initially entered a monastery in Bethlehem before finally settling down in Egypt. For Cassian, the desert was the place in which individuals could confront and deal with their sins. Nevertheless, those who failed to resolve these difficulties would find that they became worse than before.

> It is the perfect ones, purged of every sin, who ought to go into the desert. And when their faults have been purged in their monastic life, they should enter solitude – not because they are cowards who are running away from their sins, but because they are pursuing the contemplation of God, and long for a more sublime vision [of God] which can only be found in solitude, and then only by those who are perfect. For every sin that we bring into the desert unpurged will still exist within us, hidden and not destroyed. For a life that has been purged of sin, solitude can open the door to the purest contemplation and unfold the knowledge of spiritual mysteries. But, in the same manner, it usually preserves and occasionally worsens faults which have not been cured.

For Cassian, the desert offers unrivalled opportunities for contemplation of God – but only to those who have prepared themselves fully for this privilege.

This theme of "retreat into the desert" was developed in slightly different ways subsequently. For example, the Carmelites were originally a group of hermits associated with St Berthold, based on Mount Carmel. Under Albert of Jerusalem (1206–14), an order of life was established appropriate to this desert location. However, growing political instability in the region obliged the order to move to Europe. The idea of the "desert" was retained in that under the reforms introduced in the sixteenth century, provision was made for regular retreats to isolated centers, in which the solitude of Mount Carmel could be recreated.

A more recent example of one who found spirituality to be enhanced by the desert is provided by Charles de Foucault (1858–1916). During his time as a French cavalry officer serving in North Africa, he came to develop a love for the Sahara. He eventually settled in this region, living in remote desert regions, and exulting in the solitude and insecurity which this brought.

A second approach was to interpret the desert *allegorically*, meaning the spiritual journey of increasing faith and holiness. Origen regarded the desert wanderings of Israel as an allegory of the Christian life, not simply a description of a particularly important moment in the history of Israel. The Christian must expect to wander in the wilderness, and finally enter over the Jordan into the promised land.

> Before the soul comes to perfection, it dwells in the desert, where it can be exercised in the commandments of the Lord, and where its faith may be tried by temptations. Thus when it overcomes one temptation and its faith has been tried in that, it comes to another. And so it passes from one stopping-place to another, and when it has gone through what happens there, it goes on to yet another. And thus by passing through all the trials of life and faith, it is said to have stopping-places, in which the growth in the virtues is the real issue, and there is fulfilled in them the saying of Scripture: "They shall go from strength to strength," until they come to the last, the highest stage of the virtues, and cross the river of God, and receive the promised inheritance.

A variant on this approach drew upon God's gracious provision of manna to Israel during their period of wandering in the wilderness. Many writers argued that this could be interpreted allegorically, in terms of God graciously providing spiritual nourishment (for example, through the preaching of the word or through the sacraments) to Christians as they journeyed through the wilderness to the promised land. An excellent example of this is found in the works of Rupert of Deutz (c.1075–1130), a twelfth-century abbot.

> As often as the Holy Spirit opens the mouths of the apostles and prophets and even teachers to preach the word of salvation and unveil the mystery of the Scriptures, the Lord opens the gates of heaven to rain down manna for us to eat. As long as we are going through the desert of this world, walking by faith and not by sight, we need these provisions desperately. We are fed in our minds by reading and hearing the word of God. We are fed in our mouths by eating the bread of life from the table of the Lord, and drinking the chalice of eternal salvation. Yet when we finally come to the land of the living, to Jesusalem the blessed, where the God of gods will be seen face to face, we shall no longer need the word of doctrine nor shall we eat the bread of angels under the appearances of bread and wine, but in its own proper substance.

Rupert here develops the image of wandering in the wilderness to include both the means by which we are sustained and the consequences of our final arrival. Just as Israel no longer needed manna when it finally settled in the land flowing with milk and honey, so Christians will no longer need the ministries of word and sacrament when they see God face to face. For what they foreshadowed is now to be seen in all its fullness.

Ascent

The theme of ascension – particularly that of ascending mountains – is of considerable importance within both Old and New Testaments. Moses ascended Sinai to receive the Law; Jesus ascended a mountain in order to be transfigured. In each case, the idea of ascent is linked with that of drawing closer to God. This should not be considered as some kind of naïve idea that the higher one climbs, the closer one gets to God. The notion is much more complex than this, and involves the symbolism of transcendence. The image of ascending a mountain was thus a natural choice to illustrate or undergird one central theme of Christian spirituality – drawing closer to God in the Christian life.

The idea of ascent, of course, is not limited to the imagery of mountains. When Jacob dreams of a ladder set up between heaven and earth (Genesis 28:12), the issue at stake is how the eternal and transcendent can break into the human world of transitoriness, with the image of a ladder symbolizing the possibility of transition between the two worlds. This is the issue which is at stake in Christian discussions concerning the nature of revelation. However, our concern focuses rather on the spiritual question of drawing close to God. In what follows, we shall explore the biblical theme of ascent with particular reference to the images of mountains and ladders.

The image of climbing a mountain has become deeply rooted in the Christian spiritual tradition. In his *Itinerarium Mentis in Deum* ("Journey of the Mind into God"), written in 1259, the major Franciscan theologian and spiritual writer Bonaventure (c.1217–74) develops the notion of contemplation as a means of ascent into God. The journey up the mountain begins with a love of Christ, which is sustained and nurtured by mediation on the crucified Christ. "There is no other path," Bonaventure wrote, "except through the burning love of the one who was crucified, a love which so transformed Paul into Christ when he was carried up into the third heaven." Through the passion of Christ, we have access to the Father.

The sixteenth-century Spanish writer St John of the Cross (1542–91) wrote a highly influential work entitled *The Ascent of Mount Carmel*, which includes a hand-drawn map of the mountain for the benefit of those wishing to ascend it. The mountain is, of course, interpreted symbolically, with the process of ascent being interpreted in terms of gaining certain insights and mastering certain difficulties to spiritual growth and development. But the point of the image is clear: spirituality is about progression in the Christian life, in which one draws closer to the presence of God. Thus in his *Divine Comedy*, Dante climbed Mount Purgatory, drawing closer to God and leaving behind sins as he did so. A similar image (although used in another manner) is found in Thomas Merton's *Seven Storey Mountain* (1946), which is basically an autobiographical text in which Merton spoke of his own spiritual development in terms of seven mountains (Canigou; The Calvaire; Brooke Hill; The Pasture; Mount Purgatory; Mount Olivet; Kanchenjunga).

Earlier in this chapter (p. 84), we noted Guigo II's four-fold pattern for reading the Bible, in which the monk passed from reading to meditation, from meditation to prayer, and from prayer to contemplation. The title of the work in which he set forth this framework – *The Ladder of Monks* – is highly significant. Guigo clearly understands his four "steps" as being more than stages in a process; they are a means, like steps on a ladder, by which their user may ascend to higher levels of spiritual awareness. Other uses of the "ladder" motif can be found in the fourteenth-century Walter Hilton's *Scale of Perfection*. In this work, Hilton (*c*.1343–96) develops a four-fold set of steps, based on the Pauline themes of calling; being reformed (Hilton actually uses the word "righting" here – I have used a paraphrase); magnifying; and glorifying. These are seen as means of ascent into God.

Darkness and light

The themes of darkness and light are often deployed in Scripture, and have played a leading role in Christian spirituality. In the Genesis creation account, darkness is linked with the idea of chaos and confusion (Genesis 1:1–3). When God creates light, the universe becomes a radically different place. At times, God's presence and power is described in terms of illumination – for example, the people who walked in darkness see a great light (Isaiah 9:2). Jesus is described as the "light of the world," who will overcome darkness (John 8:12). Yet there are points where God's presence is spoken of in terms of darkness (Exodus 20:21; Deuteronomy 5:23), a reference which is probably best understood in terms of human inability to fully grasp the reality of God. Moses is spoken of approaching God through darkness and cloud; this imagery has been widely taken to symbolize the human inability to grasp God. Similarly, Paul spoke of our present sitation as being that of "seeing through a glass darkly," even though finally we would be able to see God face to face (1 Corinthians 13:12).

The imagery of light and darkness is powerful and highly effective, and it is not surprising that many writers should have chosen to develop this biblical imagery. An emphasis on spiritual illumination can be found in the writings of the influential German spiritual theologian Meister Eckhart (*c*.1260–*c*.1328), especially in his discussion of "breaking through" the limits of human nature, in which the believer is inundated with divine goodness. This aspect of Eckhart's teaching ("der Durchbruch") is difficult to understand, and is noted here primarily to bring out the close link which Eckhart sees between the presence of God and light.

> One property of this birth is that it comes with fresh light. It always brings a great light to the soul, in that it is the nature of the good to diffuse itself wherever it finds itself. In this birth, God flows into the soul in such abundance of light that the nature and ground of the soul are both flooded, and it flows over and floods into the powers of the outward man.

In this section, however, we shall focus particularly on the more negative aspects of our theme, noting the way in which the theme of "darkness" is used by spiritual writers. The main uses to which the image of darkness has been put include the following:

1 *Darkness as an image of doubt.* In this case, darkness is linked with the inability to see properly, and hence to gain a full understanding of what is happening. To "be in the dark" is to fail to understand what is going on. Doubt often arises from concerns about an inability to understand God's mysterious workings and presence within the world; it is easy to see how darkness can be linked with doubt. Light is thus linked with the abolition of doubt.

2 *Darkness as a symbol of sin.* For many spiritual writers, human sin causes a barrier to be placed between God and humanity, so that God is not known or honored on account of human sinfullness. Although some writers suggest that human blindness in regard to the divine is more a consequence of being a creature than being sinful, there are others who choose to stress that spiritual blindness is linked to slavery to sin. As a result, spiritual discipline is seen as a means of obtaining spiritual illumination.

3 *Darkness as a symbol of divine unknowability.* This theme is often found within the apophatic tradition (see p. 118), which stresses the limits placed upon human knowledge of God. For writers such as Gregory of Nyssa (*c*.330–*c*.395) and Gregory of Nazianzus (329–89), the human believer is plunged into a "divine night," in which God remains unknowable, even though the presence of God is beyond doubt. Precisely because of the limitations placed upon creatures, they cannot fully apprehend their creator.

This third approach can be seen particularly in the fourteenth-century writing *The Cloud of Unknowing*. The author of the work is unknown, although some have attributed it to Walter Hilton (*c*.1343–96). Its basic theme is that there is always "a sort of cloud of unknowing" which is always placed between the believer and God, with the result that God can never be seen clearly, understood by the mind, or experienced in the human affections. Although there are excellent reasons for thinking that the writer has been influenced by the apophatic theology of Dionysius the Pseudo-Areopagite (see p. 118), it is clear that the writer develops his own distinctive approach at points of importance. Just as Moses entered into a cloud to experience

105

God, so believers must learn to follow the dark road of unknowing and inner suffering in the present life. Despite occasional moments of rapture corresponding to a partial and temporary grasp of God, the full and permanent possession of God lies beyond the present life.

Many spiritual writers have drawn their imagery of darkness from the Old Testament writing usually referred to as the "Song of Songs," which depicts a meeting of lovers in the darkness. This is interpreted allegorically, as a reference to the encounter of the believing soul and God in the "darkness of faith." For example, John of the Cross (1542–91) uses the image of darkness to refer to the idea of escaping at night to meet the object of the soul's desire – God. In his poem *The Dark Night*, we find him contemplating with excitement a nocturnal meeting with his beloved.

Yet perhaps the best-known exploration of the theme of darkness found in the writings of John of the Cross concerns the famous "dark night of the soul." John used the phrase "the dark night of the soul" to describe the way in which the soul is stripped of its self-assurance and self-reliance in order to open the way to a closer relationship with God. The "dark night of the soul" can be thought of in two different manners, in one of which God is active, in the other of which the believer is active. The active aspect of the "night" is voluntary discipline and self-submission on the part of the believer, in which the Christian learns to avoid sin and achieve detachment from worldly satisfaction and spiritual temptations. This is the normal way of life for most Christian believers.

Yet John also affirms that God may open up another path for those few who are thought to be ready for it. In this case, the believer is passive, and God is active. The passive aspect of the "night" involves the Christian being led or directed by God to achieve new depths of insight through comtemplation. This, however, involves letting go of familiar ways of praying, and can be immensely confusing and bewildering in its early stages. In order to be led by God, it is necessary to let go of the familiar routines and insights which have sustained the spiritual life thus far.

In particular, John argues that, up to this point, the believer has relied upon the mind and imagination to depict God as a means of devotion. The passive "dark night of the soul" involves the recognition that anything concerning God that can be grasped or apprehended must be left behind. John makes extensive use of apophatic themes at this point, stressing the limitations of mediated knowledge of God. To achieve unmediated and direct knowledge of God is like being blinded by the sun, unable to see on account of its brilliance. At points, John speaks of the distress which the "dark night" causes to believers. They may feel alone, abandoned, and confused. It is thought that this aspect of John's spirituality has given him an especial appeal in more recent times, resonating with the anxiety and ambiguity of the modern world.

A further image of darkness which has proved fruitful within the Christian spiritual tradition is that of the dark wood. The theme of a great dark forest, in which individuals can become completely lost, is a major theme in many European folk tales. The Brothers Grimm, for example, collected a number of stories which center on the theme of people who find themselves lost in the great forests of Germany. In Dante's *Divine Comedy*, written in the first decades of the fourteenth century, we find this image used as a symbol of human lostness as a consequence of sin. Dante's *Divine*

Comedy takes the form of an imaginary journey through hell and purgatory into paradise, set in Holy Week 1300. The drama can be read as an account of personal redemption, as well as a carefully phrased commentary on some aspects of Italian politics of the thirteenth century (especially in relation to the city of Florence). The poem opens with Dante being lost in a wood at the foot of a hill, exhausted by the journey of his life. The "dark wood" is a symbol of human lostness in a world of sin. It is from this point that his journey begins, culminating in the vision of God, "the love which moves the sun and the other stars."

Silence

Humanity is reduced to silence when confronted with the majesty of God. It must be noted that other biblical passages affirm the importance of prayer, adoration and praise in the presence of God, so that silence is by no means to be understood as the only appropriate response. Nevertheless, a number of biblical passages suggest that silence is an appropriate human recognition of the inability of human words to do justice to the reality of God. This theme is clearly expressed within the prophetic tradition of the Old Testament – for example, Habakkuk's declaration that the whole earth should be silent in presence of the Lord in the temple (Habakkuk 2:20). The same theme is also present in the wisdom tradition. The book of Job, noted for its radical questioning of the nature and purposes of God, ends with Job being reduced to silence, aware of his foolishness in the sight of God (Job 40:1–3). The book of Revelation refers to a "silence in heaven" (Revelation 8.1), apparently as an expression of human awe in the presence of God.

In this sense, the theme of "silence" can be seen to be related to the apophatic theme of the mystery of God – that is, the recognition that human language is never able to do justice to God. As we noted in our discussion of the theme of "darkness," one of the points being made by the use of this image is the inability of the unaided human mind to penetrate into the mystery of God. The theme of "silence" relates directly to this, in that it affirms that human words are unable to articulate the full wonder of God. Rather than utter platitudes of truisms, the proper response to being confronted with the full wonder of God is silence.

The theme of silence has been of major importance within Christian spirituality, not least because it liberates the mind and imagination to focus and center on God's living presence. "Be still, and know that I am God" (Psalm 46.10). To be silent is often seen as the precondition for effective prayer (which can be thought of as "listening to God"). Many monastic orders encourage silence as a means of facilitating meditation. Thomas Merton's account of his decision to enter a Trappist community, set out in the autobiographical work *Elected Silence* (1949), indicates the high value of silence as an aid to reflection. The Anglican spiritual writer Arthur Michael Ramsey (1904–88), sometime Archbishop of Canterbury, indicates the value of silence in a manner which would be echoed by many, whatever their Christian allegiance:

> Silence enables us to be aware of God, to let mind and imagination dwell upon his truth, to let prayer be listening before it is talking, and to discover our own selves in a way

that is not always possible when we are making or listening to noise. There comes sometimes an inner silence in which the soul discovers itself in a new dimension of energy and peace, a dimension which the restless life can miss. . . . Into the Christian's use of silence there may flow the wonder of God the creator, the recollection of the life and death and resurrection of Jesus, the recalling of scenes in his life, often a passage of the Bible, the glories of nature in which the finger of God is present, gratitude for personal blessings or the words of poets who tell of wonder and beauty.

One of the most important movements in Eastern Christianity takes its name from the Greek term for "silence" or "stillness." The Greek word *hesychia* can have a range of meanings, but basically denotes the idea of tranquillity and quietness. The school of thought widely known as "Hesychasm" stresses the importance of silence in the Christian life, particularly valuing its role in promoting reflection and meditation. Although the term can refer to "outward" silence (that is, to physical isolation from other people, as practised by recluses and hermits), the term is more generally used to refer to "interior" silence, in which the believer is isolated from all distractions in order to focus on God.

This process of quiet meditation is often linked with the "Jesus prayer." This takes the form of a slight adaptation of the words spoken to Jesus by the blind man outside Jericho (Luke 18:38), and is usually stated in the following form: "Lord Jesus Christ, Son of God, have mercy on me." (Occasionally, the words "a sinner" are added at the end.) The prayer was established in its standard form in the eighth century, and is widely used in Orthodox spirituality. Many writers suggest that the prayer should be accompanied by certain physical postures – for example, with a bowed head, and with the breathing coordinated with the rhythm of the words. The development of hesychasm is especially associated with the fourteenth-century writer Gregory Palamas (*c*.1296–1359), who taught that inward prayer allowed a vision of the divine energies, even though the divine essence remained beyond human knowledge.

The practical details of the hesychastic approach are set out in the writings of Gregory of Sinai (*c*.1295–1346), particularly his *Instructions to Hesychasts*. Gregory stresses the importance of physical posture in enabling the believer to concentrate on prayer, and comments as follows on the various ways of using the "Jesus Prayer" in personal devotion.

Sitting in your cell, remain patiently in prayer, as Paul instructs us (Romans 12.12). Gather your mind into your heart, and send out your cry to the Lord Jesus, asking for his help and saying: "Lord Jesus Christ, have mercy on me." . . . Some of the fathers taught us that this prayer should be said in full: "Lord Jesus Christ, Son of God, have mercy upon me." Others have advised us to use half of it, as in: "Jesus, Son of God, have mercy on me," or "Lord Jesus Christ, have mercy on me." Alternatively, sometimes it may be said in full, at other times in a shorter form. Yet it is not wise to give in to laziness by altering the words too often; instead, keep going for a certain length of time as a test of your patience. Some have taught that the prayer should be said using the lips; others that it should be said in the mind. In my view, both should be used.

Conclusion

In the present chapter, we have surveyed a selection of biblical images which have found widespread application within Christian spirituality. Only a representative selection of this rich range of imagery has been explored; it is hoped that the material presented in this chapter will indicate both the spiritual utility and significance of these images. Images have a potential to stimulate the human imagination, and control and guide the thoughts of those who wish to use them to deepen their grasp of the intellectual and existential aspects of their faith. This naturally raises the issue of "visualization" – that is, the need for human beings to be able to "picture" spiritual matters before applying them. In the chapter which follows, we shall develop this important matter in greater detail.

FOR FURTHER READING

George B. Caird, *The Language and Imagery of the Bible*. London: Duckworth, 1980.

David Cairns, *The Image of God in Man*. London: Collins, 1973.

E. W. T. Dicken, *The Crucible of Love: A Study of the Mysticism of St. Teresa of Jesus and St. John of the Cross*. New York: Sheed & Ward, 1963.

Gordon D. Fee and Douglas Stuart, *How to Read the Bible for All Its Worth: A Guide to Understanding the Bible*, 2nd edn. Grand Rapids, MI: Zondervan, 1993.

Thomas M. Gannon and George W. Traub, *The Desert and the City: An Interpretation of the History of Christian Spirituality*. New York: Macmillan, 1969.

Arthur Holmes, *Dante*. Oxford: Oxford University Press, 1980.

William Johnston, *The Mysticism of the Cloud of Unknowing*. Wheathampstead: Anthony Clark, 1978.

Alan W. Jones, *Soul Making: The Desert Way of Spirituality*. San Francisco: Harper & Row, 1985.

David Knowles, *The English Mystical Tradition*. London: Burns & Oates, 1961.

Jean Leclerc, *The Love of Learning and the Desire for God: A Study of Monastic Culture*, 3rd edn. New York: Fordham University Press, 1982.

Tim Lehman, *Seeking the Wilderness: A Spiritual Journey*. Newton, KN: Faith and Life Press, 1993.

Vladimir Lossky, "Darkness and Light in the Knowledge of God," in *In the Image and Likeness of God*. London: Mowbray, 1974, 31–44.

Gregory Mayers, *Listen to the Desert: Secrets of Spiritual Maturity from the Desert Fathers and Mothers*. Liguori, MO: Triumph Books, 1996.

Susan Annette Muto, *John of the Cross for Today: The Ascent*. Notre Dame, IN: Ave Maria Press, 1991.

Hallgrimur Pétursson, *Hymns of the Passion*. Reykjavik: Hallgrims Church, 1978.

David Runcorn, *Space for God: Silence and Solitude in the Christian Life*. London: DLT, 1990.

Philip Sheldrake, *Living Between Worlds: Place and Journey in Celtic Spirituality*. London: DLT, 1995.

6

FACES, PLACES, AND SPACES: VISUALIZATION AND SPATIALIZATION IN CHRISTIAN SPIRITUALITY

One of the most significant issues relating to Christian spirituality concerns *visualization*. How can the often complex themes of the Christian faith be dealt with in such a way that they can be pictured? The issue is of major importance in relation to many areas of life, and can be illustrated particularly well from the natural sciences. We shall explore this by considering an episode in the history of quantum theory, widely regarded as one of the most important developments in theoretical physics since the time of Isaac Newton (1642–1727).

One of the themes which dominated the development of quantum mechanics in the 1920s was the need to be able to "picture" or "visualize" the various entities which the Copenhagen school of quantum theory was proposing, including what came to be known as the "photon." The Danish physicist Niels Bohr (1885–1962) suggested that the photon could be visualized by thinking of it as something which sometimes behaved like a wave, and sometimes like a particle. Both waves and particles were easily visualized. A wave results when a pebble is dropped into a pool of water; the pebble itself can be thought of as a particle. The "photon" is neither – but it can be visualized as if it were one or the other. This approach (generally referred to as the "principle of complementarity") thus allows us to "picture" a complex and abstract entity in terms which are familiar and helpful.

Yet the theme of "visualization" is also important philosophically. Paul Elmer Moore (1864–1937), unquestionably one of America's greatest Platonist philosophers, eventually became a Christian as a result of concerns relating to this point. Moore had always been fascinated and deeply satisfied by the world of beautiful Platonic forms, the world of the purely ideal. But gradually, a process of disillusionment set in. He began to experience a sense of unutterable bleakness and solitariness. He was driven to search for God by "the loneliness of an Ideal world without a Lord." He longed for those impersonal forms to become personal – to turn into a face. "My longing for some audible voice out of the infinite silence rose to a pitch of torture. To be satisfied I must see face to face, I must, as it were, handle and feel – and how should this be?"

Moore's spiritual reflections indicate the importance of being able to see the face of God, to be able to *touch* God. These are vitally important elements of Christian spirituality, given theological foundation in the doctrine of the incarnation. Christ allows us to see God in the flesh – as one who can be seen, felt, and heard. In the present chapter, we shall be exploring some of these issues, beginning with the crucially important theme of visualizing God.

The Visualization of the Divine

God is invisible, and cannot be seen by mortal human beings. This insight is fundamental to most religions with a strongly transcendent understanding of God. Yet throughout the history of Christian thought, human beings have shown a marked longing to be able to depict God in some manner. If God cannot be visualized, the idea of God becomes potentially abstract and impersonal, remote from the world of human experience. One of the most significant themes in Christian spirituality is that of *visualization* – the development of ways in which the divine may be represented visually, as something to be contemplated, without compromising the transcendence of God. Can the face of God be seen?

In an earlier chapter, we explored the importance of the doctrines of the creation (see pp. 36–41) and incarnation (see pp. 54–60) in this matter. It is, however, important to begin our discussion of this issue by considering an issue which inevitably emerges in this matter – the problem of idolatry. To create an image of God runs the risk of constructing something which we ourselves have generated. In other words, every image of God which we generate could become an idol. We shall consider this point in what follows, in that this concern looms large over the entire issue to be considered in this section.

A problem? The challenge of idolatry

The Old Testament absolutely prohibited the production of any images of God. The Second Commandment – regarded as binding by all Christians – is quite explicit on this point (Exodus 20:4–5):

> You shall not make yourself an idol in the form of anything in heaven above or on the earth beneath or in the waters below. You shall not bow down to them or worship them.

This concern has been of major importance within the Reformed tradition within Christianity. This tradition, which is grounded in the works of the Protestant reformer John Calvin (1509–64), holds that there is at least a theoretical risk of worshipping something of our own construction associated with the production of any form of religious imagery. The Reformed tradition therefore discourages any form of religious art, including the depiction of God or Jesus Christ.

In an earlier section, we noted the importance of icons within the Orthodox tradition. It is important to note that the Orthodox use of icons has not met with universal approval. The iconoclastic controversy within the Byzantine world (715–843) raised the question of whether icons were, in fact, idols. Leading defenders of icons (including John of Damascus and Theodore of Studios) insisted that it was perfectly legitimate to represent the humanity of Christ in icons. Through faith, it was possible to pass through the humanity of Christ, and discern his divinity.

It will also be clear from what has just been said that the Reformed tradition within western theology generally holds that the use of icons is potentially idolatrous, in that it encourages the worship of images which have been constructed by human hands. The Orthodox response to such criticisms is that it is not the image, but the reality that it attempts to depict, which is the object of worship. However, it is important to appreciate the importance of this tension within Christian spirituality. The Heidelberg Catechism (1563) sets out the general lines of the Reformed objection to the use of icons. It also indicates why religious art never developed within the Reformed churches to anything like the same extent as within Catholicism or Orthodoxy. This Catechism, written in German in 1563, develops the idea that images of God are neither necessary nor helpful for Christian believers. There is an interesting parallel with Islam here, in that both Islam and Reformed theology are concerned to avoid images of God becoming objects of worship in themselves, instead of being aids to the worship of God.

> Question 96. What does God require in the next commandment?
> Answer: That we should not portray God in any way, nor worship him in any other manner than he has commanded in his Word.
>
> Question 97. So should we not make any use of images?
> Answer: God cannot and should not be depicted in any way. As for creatures, although they may indeed be depicted, God forbids making use of or having any likeness of them, in order to worship them or to use them to serve him.
>
> Question 98. But should we allow pictures instead of books in churches, for the benefit of the unlearned?
> Answer: No. For we should not presume to be wiser than God, who does not want Christendom to be taught by means of dumb idols, but through the living preaching of his Word.

Note how the Heidelberg Catechism indicates that biblical preaching (see p. 86) should take the place of religious art as a means of instruction and devotion. This concern serves to distinguish the Reformed tradition from other Reformation churches (including Lutheranism and Anglicanism), as well as from Catholicism and Orthodoxy. Most other Christian traditions regard religious art as a helpful aid to devotion, and encourage the display of appropriate works of religious art in places of worship. It may also be noted that several recent theologians within the Reformed tradition have used works of religious art as a means of encouraging theological reflection and personal devotion. Thus Karl Barth (1886–1968) had a copy of Matthias Grünewald's Isenheim altarpiece, depicting the crucifixion, on his desk. Jürgen Moltmann (1926–) had a copy of Marc Chagall's "Crucifixion in Yellow" in front of him as he wrote *The Crucified God*, widely regarded as one of the theological masterpieces of the twentieth century.

So how can the charge of idolatry be avoided, if religious imagery is to be used to depict the divine? The simplest answer is perhaps the most persuasive: *because we are meant to*. We shall explore this in the section which follows.

Visualizing God: the incarnation

The New Testament affirms that Jesus is the "image of the invisible God" (Colossians 1.15) and the "exact representation" of God (Hebrews 1.4). St John's gospel includes a number of important sayings of Jesus which indicate that to have seen him is to have seen God (see, for example, John 14.6). The basic theme that emerges from such texts is that Jesus is the authorized visual image for God. In other words, Jesus makes God known in a visible and tangible manner.

This insight has enormous implications for Christian spirituality, some of which we have already explored (pp. 58–61). God is like Jesus. To focus our thoughts upon Jesus is to pass through a window into the living God. The love of Jesus for the outcast, poor and helpless mirrors the love of God for these people. The importance of this insight for Christian spirituality is immense. It allows us to visualize God in a manner of which God approves. It is not as if we have decided to treat Jesus as if he were an image of the invisible God. It is that we have been told that Jesus is indeed an image of that God, and we are meant to act upon that knowledge. The noted Scottish theologian Hugh Ross Mackintosh (1870–1936) expressed this insight as follows: "When I look into the face of Jesus, and see there the very face of God, I know that I have not seen that face elsewhere and cannot see that face elsehow."

The relevance of this point for spirituality can be demonstrated from a number of sources. We shall examine a particularly well-known case. On May 8, 1373, the English religious writer Julian of Norwich experienced a series of visions concerning the love of God. These were triggered off by a very specific stimulus. Julian had become ill, and those around her were convinced that she was about to die. The local parish priest was sent for, and held before her a crucifix (that is, a carving of Christ upon the cross), and spoke these words to her: "I have brought you the image of your Creator and Saviour. Look at it, and be strengthened." The image of Christ upon the cross proved to be a gateway to a series of extended meditations on the goodness of God, and God's overwhelming generosity and courtesy to sinners.

A development of this point can be seen in religious art. If contemplation of the life and person of Jesus led people to a deeper knowledge of God, it seemed to many that vivid depictions of incidents in the life of Christ could assist that process still further. The Middle Ages and Renaissance witnessed a dramatic increase in the use of religious art for both public and private devotion. Panel painting was widely used to depict narratives concerning Jesus, or static portraits of Jesus and his mother. In the early Middle Ages, the two dominant religious images were the madonna and child, and the crucifixion. By the later Renaissance, the same attention once paid to the crucifixion was being devoted to other religious subjects. Renaissance artists regarded many incidents in the life of Jesus as of potential importance. Particular attention was paid to the Annunciation (that is, to the scene in Luke's gospel in which Gabriel informs Mary that she is to bear a son), the baptism of Jesus, and the resurrection. The appearance of the risen Jesus to Mary Magdalene (John 20:17) was also the subject of many classic works, including Fra Angelico's fresco *Noli me tangere* ("do not touch me"), painted over the period 1440–41 in the convent of San Marco in Florence. In addition, emotions – especially pain and sadness – came to be conveyed through the expressions on the faces of those being depicted. Painted panels could be displayed singly in churches, but were often combined in the form of diptychs, triptychs, or even polyptychs, as in the Ghent Altarpiece by Hubert and Jan van Eyck or the Isenheim altarpiece by Matthias Grünewald.

Visualizing God: the creation

As we noted earlier, one corollary of the Christian doctrine of creation is that something of the character of God can be known from nature. The hand of the creator can be discerned within the creation. Hildegard of Bingen (1098–1179) was one of many writers to argue that "all creatures are an indication of God," and went on to insist that "it is God whom we know in every creature." Hugh of St Victor (died 1142) argued that nature was like a book, which was capable of being read by those who wished to know more of the invisible God:

> For the whole sensible world is like a kind of book written by the finger of God – that is, created by divine power – and each particular creature is somewhat like a figure, not invented by human decision, but instituted by the divine will to manifest the invisible things of the wisdom of God.

In other words, the likeness between the creation and God is intrinsic to the creation, and is not the result of some arbitrary human imposition or decision.

This concept of natural theology received a particularly significant development within the Reformed tradition. The Gallic Confession of Faith (1559) argues that God reveals himself to humanity in two manners:

> First, in his works, both in their creation and their preservation and control. Second, and more clearly, in his Word, which was revealed through oracles in the beginning, and which was subsequently committed to writing in the books which we call the Holy Scriptures.

A related idea was set out in the Belgic Confession (1561), which expanded the brief statement on natural theology found in the Gallic Confession. Once more, knowledge of God is affirmed to come about by two means:

> First, by the creation, preservation and government of the universe, which is before our eyes as a most beautiful book, in which all creatures, great and small, are like so many

characters leading us to contemplate the invisible things of God, namely, his eternal power and Godhead, as the Apostle Paul declares (Romans 1:20). All of these things are sufficient to convince humanity, and leave them without excuse. Second, he makes himself known more clearly and fully to us by his holy and divine Word; that is to say, as far as is necessary for us to know in this life, to his glory and our salvation.

The two themes which emerge clearly from these confessional statements can be summarized as follows:

1 There are two modes of knowing God, one through the natural order, and the second through Scripture.

2 The second mode is clearer and fuller than the first.

It will therefore be clear that a significant foundation was laid for the active investigation of the natural world *as a spiritual activity*. To deepen one's knowledge and appreciation of the natural order was to deepen one's knowledge and admiration of its creator. Reformed theologians might not approve of religious art – but they certainly encouraged study of God's handiwork in creation.

The doctrine of creation thus proved to be of especial importance in relation to the development of the spirituality of the natural sciences. The scientist was frequently portrayed as a priest within God's creation. Thus the noted English physicist Robert Boyle frequently spoke of human beings as priests of God's creation, thus stressing the religious and spiritual aspects of the scientific study of creation.

This idea does not necessarily rest upon Christian assumptions. Thus in his *Commentary on the Dream of Scipio,* possibly written as early as 380, the Roman writer Ambrosius Aurelius Theodosius Macrobius defined the world as the visible temple of God, within which the creator could be found and worshipped:

> In order to show, therefore, that the omnipotence of the Supreme God can hardly ever be comprehended and never witnessed, he called whatever is visible to our eyes the temple of that God who is apprehended only in the mind, so that those who worship these visible objects as temples might still owe the greatest reverence to the Creator, and that whoever is inducted into the privileges of this temple might know that he had to live in the manner of a priest.

While there are reasons for thinking that Macrobius may have been influenced by Christianity at this point, the nature and extent of such influence remains disputed. Nevertheless, it will be clear that the Christian understanding of God as creator readily allows the kinds of insights to which Macrobius alludes.

Visualizing God: the sacraments

Most Christians, irrespective of their backgrounds, regard the sacraments as important signs of God's grace and presence. For Luther, sacraments were like promises with signs attached, intended to reassure us of the reality and trustworthiness of those promises. The bread and wine of the eucharist, and the water of baptism, are visible and tangible signs of the spiritual reality which lies behind them. The bread and wine point to the richness of life which the gospel offers, and the water to the cleansing which it brings.

This aspect of the role of sacraments in spirituality is brought out clearly in the famous hymn *Adore te devote*, traditionally ascribed to Thomas Aquinas (*c.*1225–74). We shall cite three verses from this work, and note the general line of its argument.

> Godhead here in hiding, whom I do adore
> Masked by these bare shadows, shape and nothing more;
> See, Lord, at thy service low lies here a heart
> Lost, all lost in wonder at the God thou art.
>
> O thou our reminder of Christ crucified.
> Living bread the life of us for whom he died,
> Lend this life to me then: feed and feast my mind,
> There be thou the sweetness man was meant to find.
>
> Jesus whom I look at shrouded here below,
> I beseech thee send me, what I thirst for so;
> Some day to gaze on thee, face to face in light
> And be blessed forever, with thy glory's sight.

The initial idea is that the sacrament offers a means of discerning the presence of God, even though that presence takes the form of "bare shadows" rather than reality. Yet even though the sacrament is only a sign of the greater reality to which it points, it nevertheless possesses the ability to focus the worshipper's thoughts on God. More specifically, the sacrament reminds us of the saving death of Christ, and the benefits which this brings to humanity. It also serves to uplift the mind to think of its future contemplation of the face of God in heaven. The sacrament thus serves as an impor- tant *visible and tangible* reminder of the Christian hope, as well as a reminder of the pain and suffering of the cross.

The importance of the cross in visualizing aspects of the Christian faith may help us understand why it has become the universally recognized symbol of the Christian faith, a matter which we shall explore in what follows.

Christian symbolism: the cross

We have already seen how the figure of Jesus Christ dominates the Christian faith. In particular, we noted how the death of Jesus on the cross is understood by Christians to be the foundation of the salvation of humanity. The cross is thus a symbol of salvation. It is also a symbol of the Christian hope, in that it affirms that death has been defeated through the resurrection of Jesus. The cross – an instrument of execution – thus became a sign of the hope and transformation which are funda- mental to Christianity.

The cross has been the universally acknowledged symbol of the Christian faith from a very early period, probably as early as the late second century. Indeed, it is fair to suggest that there is no symbol other than the cross which carries such weight, authority, or recognition within the Chrisian faith. Christians are baptized with the sign of the cross. Churches and other Christian places of meeting do not merely include a cross; they are often built in the shape of a cross. The Christian emphasis on the cross has had considerable implications for the design of churches. Indeed, it is probably at this point that Christian theology has had its most profound impact on western culture. To walk around a great medieval cathedral or church is to view theology embodied in stone.

Many Christians find it helpful to make the sign of the cross in times of danger or anxiety. The graves of Christians – whether Catholic, Orthodox, or Protestant – are marked with crosses. Careful studies of the origins and development of Christian symbolism have made it clear that the cross was seen as the symbol of the Christian gospel from the earliest of times. Even in the earliest writings of the New Testament, the phrase "the message of the cross" is used as a shorthand summary of the Christian gospel (see 1 Corinthians 1:18–25). Two second-century writers bring out the importance of the cross with particular clarity: for Tertullian, Christians are "those who believe in the cross"; for Clement of Alexandria, the cross is "the supreme sign of the Lord." There is an anti-Christian graffito which has been preserved from ancient Rome, which depicts a man adoring a crucified man with the head of an ass. The inscription reads: "Alexander worships his god."

The final stage in the global acceptance of the cross as the supreme symbol of the Christian faith is generally regarded as having been the conversion of the Roman emperor Constantine. At some point shortly before or after the decisive battle of the Milvian Bridge (312), Constantine is related to have seen a vision of a cross, which ordered him to place the sign on his soldiers' shields. During the reign of Constantine, crosses of various types were erected in Rome, and began to appear on Roman coinage. Crucifixion had continued as a means of execution under previous Roman emperors. Constantine outlawed the practice, and directed that the scaffolds used for execution would no longer be referred to as "crosses (*cruces*)" but as "patibula."

There is evidence that Christians in the first century were reluctant to portray the crucifixion of Jesus. It was one thing to make the sign of the cross; it was quite another to depict Jesus on the cross of Calvary, especially on account of the issues of taste and decency involved in portraying Jesus naked. However, these inhibitions were gradually overcome. Christian art, both in the east and west, began to focus on the crucifixion for devotional purposes. In response to the view that Jesus was purely divine, lacking any real human nature, Christian leaders encouraged artists to produce depictions of the crucifixion of Jesus as a way of emphasizing his full humanity. What better way of stressing the suffering and death of Jesus than to portray him on the cross? The implications of these considerations are considerable, and help us to understand the importance attached by many Christian writers to the devotional depiction of the crucifixion, which we noted earlier.

The cross remains of fundamental importance today. This point underlines the widespread use of crosses in Christian worship, both public and private. Many churches are built in the shape of crosses, and display crosses prominently within them. Of particular importance to many Christians is the *crucifix* – that is, a wooden carving of Jesus stretched out on the cross, with the inscription "INRI" above his head (these letters spell out the Latin words *Iesus Nazarenus Rex Iudaeorum*, which are to be translated as "Jesus of Nazareth, King of the Jews." See John 19:1–16 for the background). The crucifix is intended to remind Christians of the sufferings of

Jesus, and thus emphasize the costliness and reality of the salvation which resulted from his death on the cross.

A corrective: the apophatic tradition

What has been said thus far might convey the impression that there is a generally positive attitude within the Christian tradition towards the possibility of positively picturing God. The danger of idolatry, once noted, can be reduced to the point where it is no longer signficant. In fact, however, a cautionary note needs to be added at this point. The apophatic tradition within Christian theology and spirituality offers a corrective to the use of imagery just described. One of its central themes can be seen in the treatise *On the Incomprensibility of God* by John Chrysostom (347–407). Chrysostom stresses the limits to human (or angelic!) knowledge and comprehension of God:

> Let us invoke him as the inexpressible God, incomprehensible, invisible and unknowable. Let us affirm that he surpasses all power of human speech; that he eludes the grasp of every mortal intelligence; that the angels cannot penetrate him; that the seraphim cannot see him clearly; that the cherubim cannot fully understand him. For he is invisible to the principalities and powers, the virtues and all creatures, without exception. Only the Son and the Holy Spirit know him.

Chrystostom's point is that only God truly knows God. Any creature – whether human or angelic – must accept the serious limitations which creatureliness imposes upon their grasp and vision of God.

The word "apophatic," used to refer to this perception of radical limitation upon human knowledge of God, needs explanation. The term "apophatic" is probably best translated as "negative." The term is first used by the sixth-century writer Dionysius the Pseudo-Areopagite to refer to an approach to theology which rejects all positive ideas or images of God, and stresses instead the unknowability of God. The soul is understood to enter into a "darkness that is beyond understanding," in which it finds itself quite at a loss to use words or images to describe what it encounters. Apophatic theology identifies and stresses the limitations of human knowledge of God, and especially the ability of human ideas and images to convey the full reality of God.

It must be noted, however, that Dionysius also allows positive statements concerning God; his concern is to stress their limitations, and avoid falling into the fallacy of assuming that we know all that there is to be known about God. However, some of Dionysius' later interpreters chose to stress the more negative aspects of his thought. This particular approach is found in the fourteenth-century work of English mysticism, *The Cloud of Unknowing*, which picks up and develops the negative elements of Dionysius' thought.

The apophatic tradition reminds us that there are limits to what can be known about God, and that a distinction must always be drawn between the images of God and the reality of God. (A related distinction can be found in Gregory Palamas, who distinguishes the energies and essence of God, of which the former may be known, and the latter not.) To perceive the likeness of God in the creation is thus not to have direct access to the reality of God. This point is important, and must be conceded. On the positive side, however, it must also be pointed out that, if many human beings need images to help them think and pray, the existence of authorized images of God have a vital role to play. Their limitations must be recognized – but so must their value in the visualization of the divine.

Telling the Story: Faith in Life

As we have stressed, Christianity is most emphatically not simply a set of ideas; it is about a way of life, focusing on a new relationship with God, brought about through Christ in the Holy Spirit. This insight helps us understand the importance of "stories" in spirituality. The word "story" is potentially ambiguous, and can cause confusion. The word can mean something like "a fictional tale" – in other words, it suggests something that has been made up, rather than something that corresponds to real life. That is not the sense intended in this discussion. In the sense in which the word is used in both Christian theology and spirituality, the word "story" means a narrative of a person's life. It emphasizes the fact that this person's story represents the embodiment of a set of ideas and values. Beliefs and values affect the way in which people live; the story of how they live thus shows us the way in which those ideas and values shape their real historical existence.

Both the Old and the New Testament include narratives which explain how the people of God came into being, and indicate the kind of behavior which is appropriate for their identity as the people of God. The growing recognition of the "narrative" character of the Bible has been one of the more noticeable features of recent theology. For example, many recent works of New Testament scholarship have pointed out the way in which Paul's theology and ethics is grounded in the story of Jesus.

To become a Christian is not merely to learn the Christian story; it is to enter into it, and accept it as part of our own existence. The same pattern can be seen in Judaism down the ages. At the festival of Passover, the story of the exodus from Egypt is retold to the family members, who understand this as shaping their present identity and future hopes. For Christians, the story of Jesus, particularly his death and resurrection, shape the values, beliefs, and hopes of the Christian community. From New Testament times, Christians gathered together on a Sunday to retell the story of the crucifixion of Jesus, and celebrate its implications for their lives.

So what is the importance of narrative for spirituality? Stories are about finding one's identity, and learning the story of one's own people. This point was brought home to me particularly clearly back in 1990, when I heard an American professor of literature describe how he dicovered the importance of learning one's story. This professor, who taught at a leading university in Southern California, was a Kiowa Indian, a native American from the Oklahoma region. He told us how he learned the story of his people when he was still a young boy. One day, just after dawn, his father woke him, and took him to the home of an elderly squaw. He left him there, promising to return to collect him that afternoon.

All that day, the squaw told this young boy the story of the Kiowa people. She told him of their origins by the Yellowstone River, and how they then migrated southward. She told him of the many hardships they faced – the wars with other Indian nations and the great blizzards on the winter plains. She told him of the glories of the life of the Kiowa nation – of the great buffalo hunts, the taming of wild horses, and the great skill of the braves as riders. Finally, she told him of the coming of the white man. She told him about the humiliation of their once-proud nation at the hands of the white soldiers, who forced them to move south to Kansas, where they faced starvation and poverty. Her story ended as she told him of their final humiliating confinement within a reservation at Oklahoma.

Shortly before dark, his father returned to collect him. His words on leaving the home of the squaw remain firmly planted in my mind. "When I left that house, I was a Kiowa." He had learned the story of his people, to which he was heir. He knew what his people had been through. Before he had learned that story, he had been a Kiowa in name only; now he was a Kiowa in reality.

The same principle is clear within Christian spirituality. Throughout the Old Testament, we find Israel being reminded of her identity by being reminded of her story. The Passover celebration involves the recollection of Israel's exodus from Egypt. The Psalms often recall God's great acts of deliverance and providence, both in bringing Israel into being and sustaining her through all her hardships, suffering, and infidelity. The New Testament tells the story of Jesus, the story of the expansion of the church, and looks forward to the culmination of that story in the entry into the new Jerusalem. It affirms that believers are part of that story, and that authentic Christian spirituality depends upon recognizing and accepting that place in the story.

The story is told at two points in particular in the regular Christian cycle of worship and prayer – baptism and the Lord's Supper or Eucharist. Cyril of Jerusalem, writing in the fourth century, argues that the sacrament of baptism calls to mind the story of the exodus of Israel from Egypt, and affirms that those who are about to be baptized share in that great drama of redemption. The exodus from Egypt was an anticipation of the greater redemption to be achieved through Christ's death on the cross. Baptism thus calls to mind the great story of God's saving acts in history.

Let me explain what happened to you on the evening of your baptism. First you entered the antechamber of the baptistery, and turned westwards. When you were told to stretch out your hands, you renounced Satan as though he were there in person. Now you should know that ancient history provides a type of this. When Pharaoh, the harshest and most cruel of all tyrants, oppressed the free and noble people of the Hebrews, God sent Moses to deliver them from this harsh slavery which had been imposed on them by the Egyptians. They anointed their doorposts with the blood of a lamb, so that the destroyer might pass over the houses which bore the sign of this blood, and miraculously set the Hebrew people free from their bondage. After their liberation the enemy pursued them, and on seeing the sea open in front of them, they still continued to pursue them, only to be engulfed in the Red Sea. Let us now pass from the old to the new, from the type to the reality. There Moses is sent by God to Egypt; here Christ is sent by the Father into the world. There, he was to lead an oppressed people from Egypt; here he was to deliver those who are under the tyranny of sin. There the blood of the lamb turned away the destoyer; here the blood of the unblemished lamb, Jesus Christ, puts the demons to flight. In the past, the tyrant pursued the Hebrew people right to the sea; in your case, the devil, the arch-evil one, followed each one of you up to the edge of the streams of salvation. This first [tyrant] was engulfed in the sea; this one disappears in the waters of salvation.

We can see here the clear identification of the Christian church, and individual Christian believers, with the history of Israel. To be a Christian is to stand within this grand narrative of redemption. To tell this story is to affirm that it shapes Christian existence, and defines that Christians *belong* to the community whose origins are to be traced and defined in this way. To tell this story is thus to belong to this story, and to be part of the community whose ideas and values and shaped by it. But perhaps the most important occasion on which the story is told is the celebration of the Lord's Supper, at which the story of the death of Christ is related and applied to the life of the church. Christians disagree over the name to be given to this sacrament; nevertheless, it is of central importance to Christian worship across denominations.

Cyril of Jerusalem (c.315–86). A writer noted especially for his series of 24 catechetical lectures, given around 350 to those preparing for baptism, which are an important witness to the ideas which prevailed in the Jerusalem church around this point. He was appointed bishop of Jerusalem in *c.*349.

Eucharist, Mass, or Supper: What's in a Name?

Christians have proved unable to agree on the best way to refer to the sacrament which focuses on the bread and wine. The main terms used to refer to it are the following. Note the specific associations of each word with particular Christian traditions.

The Mass

This term derives from the Latin word *missa*, which really just means "a service of some sort." As the main service of the western church in the classic period was the breaking of the bread, the term came to refer to this one service in particular. The term "mass" is now especially associated with the Catholic tradition.

Eucharist

This term derives from the Greek verb *eucharistein*, and means "a thanksgiving." The theme of thanksgiving is an important element of the breaking of the bread, making this an entirely appropriate term for the service in question. The term "eucharist" is particularly associated with the Greek Orthodox tradition (although the phrase "the liturgy" is often used), but has found acceptance beyond this, as in Anglicanism.

Holy Communion

The phrase "holy communion" points to the idea of "fellowship" or "sharing." It highlights both the bond of fellowship between Jesus and the church, and also between individual Christians. The term is used in more Protestant circles, particularly in churches tracing their origins back to the English Reformation.

> *Lord's Supper*
> This phrase picks up the theme of the breaking of the bread as a memorial of the last supper. To share in the "Lord's Supper" is to recall with thanks all that Jesus achieved for believers though his death on the cross. The term is used in more Protestant circles, particularly in churches tracing their origins back to the English Reformation. This is sometimes abbreviated to the simple term "supper."

Not only do Christians differ over what they call the sacrament which focuses on the bread and the wine; they also disagree over precisely what its significance might be. One approach, particularly associated with Catholicism, holds that the bread really becomes the body of Christ, and the wine his blood (a position usually known as "transubstantiation," which literally means "a change of substance"). At the opposite end of the theological spectrum, radical Protestants argue that the bread and wine simply function as reminders of Christ's death (a view especially associated with the Swiss reformer Huldrych Zwingli (1484–1531), and often termed "memorialism").

Despite these differences, some common strands can be discerned across theological traditions concerning the role of this sacrament. One of these common strands is that the bread and the wine call to mind the story of the last supper, and the death of Jesus. In other words, they are symbols of the Christian story. It must be stressed that many Christians would wish to add immediately that there is more to the sacrament than this minimalist position! However, the point being made here is that this is a common strand within the rich and complex diversity of Christian understandings of the place of the eucharist in Christian devotion. Other understandings may be added to this without in any way compromising this particular aspect of the role of the sacrament.

Earlier, we identified the sixteenth-century Swiss reformer Huldrych Zwingli as holding a minimalist view of the eucharist. In what follows, we shall look at the way in which Zwingli views the sacrament as a means of recollecting the story of the foundational event of the Christian church. To make sense of his discussion, we need to explain something about Swiss history. During the fourteenth century, the Swiss were constantly under threat from neighboring Austria (a tension famously celebrated in the "William Tell" legend). In April 1388, the Swiss Confederacy gained a notable victory over the Austrians at Nähenfels, which secured their independence. Such was the importance of this victory that an annual pilgrimage was made by leading Swiss citizens to the battleside of Nähenfels. Zwingli argues that there is a parallel between this battle and the death of Christ, in that both are foundational events of institutions. Just as a loyal Swiss citizen would commemorate this great victory as a sign of loyalty to the nation, so the Christian celebrates Christ's death as a sign of loyalty to the church. (The "white cross" referred to identified the soldiers from the various cantons as belonging to the same army; the white cross in question is now incorporated into the Swiss national flag.)

The word "sacrament" means a sign of commitment. If a man sews on a white cross, he proclaims that he is a [Swiss] Confederate. And if he makes the pilgrimage to

Nähenfels and gives God praise and thanksgiving for the victory delivered to our fore-fathers, he testifies from his heart that he is a Confederate. Similarly the man who receives the mark of baptism is the one who is resolved to hear what God says to him, to learn the divine precepts and to live his life in accordance with them. And the man who, in the remembrance or supper, gives thanks to God in the congregation declares that he heartily rejoices in the death of Christ and thanks him for it.

Only part of this long discussion has been cited. Zwingli's general point is that sacraments remind believers of the origins and purposes of the Christian community, and offer them an opportunity to recommit themselves to living according to its norms. Those norms (both beliefs and values) are identified and established through the Christian story.

So what general role do stories play in spirituality? Three general types of stories feature prominently in the spiritual literature of the Christian tradition from the earliest of times.

1   *The story of Jesus.* Many works of spirituality take the form of the retelling of the story of Jesus, allowing Christians to understand what a life of obedience to God implies. Sometimes the emphasis falls on the cross. For example, in his *Imitation of Christ*, Thomas à Kempis (*c.*1380–1471) stresses that all who wish to be true followers of Christ must take up that cross, and follow "the royal road of the cross." Other works of spirituality focus on the way in which Jesus relates to others during his ministry, noting in particular his love for those whom he encounters. In both cases, the story of Jesus is understood to be a model for those who call themselves his followers.

2   *Stories of biblical figures.* The Old Testament in particular is richly adorned with the stories of great individuals, from which believers can learn. The New Testament indicates that much can be learned from these figures (note especially the way in which Hebrews 11 appeals to the Old Testament figures of faith as models for Christians). Sometimes those stories illustrate virtues which believers should imitate – for example, the faith of Abraham in setting out from Ur of the Chaldees, not knowing quite what awaited him (Genesis 15). At other times, the story indicates weaknesses which believers are urged to avoid – for example, David's adulterous affair with Bathsheba (2 Samuel 11). Again, the same principle may be discerned: faith leads to a way of life, and today's believers can learn from the lives of those of the past.

3   *Stories of the saints.* A third category of stories concerns individuals who lived after biblical times, who are recognized as having lived lives which were hallmarked with Christian authenticity. Many Christians find it helpful to read biographies of Christians who they admire, and expect to learn from their example and witness. The many biographies of St Francis of Assisi (1182–1226) illustrate the way in which the stories of those who managed to live closer to God than the rest of us can be an inspiration and encouragement to us.

Yet it is not simply the substance of the Christian story that is of relevance in this respect. The manner in which the story is transmitted and relayed is also of note.

We have already considered the important role played by the sacraments of baptism and the eucharist in this respect. The sacrament embodies and relays aspects of the Christian story. Yet other means of transmitting that story must be noted, of which the following are especially important.

1   The Mystery Plays. During the Middle Ages, the great drama of redemption, from creation to final consummation, was acted out in cathedral precincts across Europe, and especially in England. Chester and York in particular were recognized as centers at which the mysteries of salvation would be acted out in popular form, using plain (and occasionally quite bawdy) English. The plays were often performed on mobile platforms, which could be drawn from one site to another. Although these plays were suppressed at the time of the Reformation in England, they have now been revived, and receive regular performances in several English cathedrals.

2   The "Negro spiritual" came to emerge as a distinctive form of song, recalling aspects of the biblical story using popular folk melodies. Although the origins of this genre of song are thought to lie with eighteenth-century American revivalism, the spiritual achieved classic status within Black American Christianity during the nineteenth century. The songs recalled aspects of the Christian story, and related them to the pain and suffering experienced by the negro community at this time. Particular emphasis was placed on the story of the deliverance of Israel from Egypt, which was seen as reflecting the deliverance for which negro slaves passionately longed.

The Rhythm of Faith: Structuring Time

From the earliest of times, Christians developed ways of structuring time which reflected fundamental Christian beliefs and the historical events on which they were grounded. In this section, we shall explore three such ways of structuring time: the Christian week, the Christian year, and the monastic day.

The Christian week

One of the most obvious such developments was the setting aside of Sunday – the first day of the week – as the day on which the resurrection of Christ would be celebrated. The letters of Paul clearly presuppose that Christians were meeting for worship on Sunday, breaking with the Jewish tradition of observing the sabbath (Saturday) as a day of rest. In 321, the Roman emperor Constantine formally declared that Sunday would be the official imperial day of rest.

Sunday was thus seen by Christian writers as a "space" which was set aside, in God's goodness, to allow for physical rest and spiritual refreshment. One of the writers who stresses this point is Susanna Wesley (1669–1742), the mother of John and Charles Wesley, who was persuaded of the importance of creating space for God in the midst of a busy life. For Susanna, Sunday was a space which had been created by God for exactly this purpose, and was meant to be used joyfully and profitably.

This is the Day that the Lord hath made; I will rejoice and be glad therein
Glory be to Thee, Eternal Father of spirits,
   for so kindly and mercifully indulging one Day in seven
   to the souls Thou hast made.
Wherein it is their duty as well as happiness,
   to retire from the business and hurry of a tumultuous and vexatious world,
   and are permitted to enjoy a more immediate and uninterrupted attendance on the
   Divine Majesty.
Oh Blessed Indulgence! Oh most Happy Day!

Lord I can never sufficiently adore Thy Infinite Love and Goodness
   in appropriating this seventh part of my time to Thy Self.
May these sacred moments ever be employed in Thy service.
May no vain unnecessary or unprofitable thoughts or discourse ever rob You of Your due
   honour and praise on this Day;
   or deprive my soul of the peculiar advantages
   and blessings which are to be gained,
   by the conscientious performance of the duties of the Day.

It is also known that early Christian communities set aside Wednesdays and Fridays as fast-days. The reason for the selection of these particular days is not clear; a later explanation suggested that Wednesday was thus observed because it was the day on which Christ was betrayed, and Friday the day on which he was crucified. The practice of eating fish (rather than meat) on Friday, still widely encountered in Catholic circles, reflects this early development.

Perhaps the most important manner of structuring time concerns the Christian year, to which we now turn.

The Christian year

Christianity is not just a set of ideas; it is a way of life. Part of that life is a richly structured yearly pattern of life, in which various aspects of the Christian faith are singled out for particular attention during the course of a year. The two such festivals which are most familiar outside Christian circles are Christmas and Easter, celebrating the birth and resurrection of Jesus respectively.

It should be noted that there are major variations within the Christian world over the festivals of the Christian faith. In general terms, evangelical and charismatic Christians tend to place a relatively low value on such festivals, whereas Catholic and Orthodox Christians tend to place a considerably greater emphasis upon them. Indeed, the importance attached by Christians to festivals such as Advent and Lent is generally a useful indication of the type of Christianity which they have adopted.

In what follows, we shall note the spiritual importance and utility of some features of the western Christian year. Note that this is simply intended to illustrate the spiritual importance of "structuring" the year, and is intended to be illustrative, not exhaustive.

Advent
The term "Advent" derives from the Latin word *adventus*, meaning "coming" or "arrival." It refers to the period immediately before Christmas, during which

Christians recall the background to the coming of Jesus. Traditionally, four Sundays are set apart in order to prepare for the full appreciation of Christmas, of which the first is referred to as "Advent Sunday," and the final as the "Fourth Sunday in Advent." This period of four Sundays is often observed by the making of "advent crowns," consisting of four candles in a wooden or metal frame. A candle is then lit for each of the four Sundays in Advent. Some churches use purple clerical clothing at this time as a symbol of the need for penitence (a custom which also applies to Lent, which also has a penitential character).

Strictly speaking, Advent is intended to focus on the relationship of two "advents" or "comings" of Jesus: his first coming in humility, during his time on earth (which is especially associated with Christmas); and his second coming in glory as judge, which will take place at the end of time. Advent thus serves to stress the spiritual importance of repentance, and the anticipation of the joy of Christmas.

Christmas

Christmas is a fixed or immovable feast, and is always celebrated in the west on 25 December. It must be stressed that this has never been understood to mean that Christians believe that Jesus was born on this date; rather, this date was chosen for the celebration of the birth of Jesus, irrespective of the precise date of that birth. It is likely that the date was chosen at Rome during the fourth century to provide a Christian alternative to a local pagan festival. The date of the festival is actually something of an irrelevance, despite the association with the imagery of winter and snow found in many Christian writings originating in the northern hemisphere.

The central theme of Christmas is the birth of Jesus, which is often commemorated in special carol services. Of these, the most famous is widely regarded as the "Service of Nine Carols and Lessons" associated with King's College, Cambridge. The nine lessons (that is, readings from the Bible) are designed to trace the steady progress of God's work of redemption in the world, beginning with the call of Israel, and culminating in the coming of Jesus Christ. The feast of Christmas is strongly linked with the doctrine of the incarnation, and is traditionally a time at which the spiritual implications of this doctrine are explored. Many traditional Christmas carols focus on this theme (see pp. 54–61).

Lent

The period of Lent begins with Ash Wednesday, which falls in the seventh week before Easter. The term "Ash Wednesday" needs explanation. The Old Testament occasionally refers to putting ashes on one's face or clothing as a symbol of repentance or remorse (e.g., Esther 4:1; Jeremiah 6:26). Lent is seen as a period of repentance; the wearing of ashes was therefore seen as a proper external sign of an inward attitude of remorse or repentance. In earlier periods in the history of the church, particularly during the Middle Ages, the first day of Lent was therefore marked by imposing ashes on the heads of the clergy and people. In more recent years, the ashes in question are made by burning the palm crosses handed out on Palm Sunday during the previous Lent. The theme of repentance is also symbolized in some churches in the wearing of purple clerical dress during this season.

Lent is widely regarded as a time of preparation for Easter, and in the past was widely associated with a period of fasting. Lent is based on the period of forty days spent by Jesus in the wilderness before the beginning of his public ministry in Galilee. Just as Jesus fasted for forty days, so his followers were encouraged to do the same thing. A period of forty days of fasting before Easter was thus encouraged. The origins of this seem to go back to the fourth century. In earlier periods, a shorter period of fasting was recommended (two or three days). The precise nature of the "fasting" varied from one location and period to another. In general terms, the western church has understood "fasting" primarily in terms of a reduced intake of food, and eating fish rather than meat. The emphasis has generally been placed on devotional reading or attendance at church rather than fasting.

The final week of Lent, leading up to Easter Day itself, should be singled out for special mention. This period, which is generally known as "Holy Week," begins with Palm Sunday (the Sunday before Easter) and ends on the day before Easter Day. It includes four days which are of special importance. These are:

Palm Sunday
Maundy Thursday
Good Friday
Holy Saturday

Palm Sunday is the Sunday immediately before Easter. It commemorates the triumphal entry of Jesus into Jerusalem, during which the crowds threw palm fronds into his path (see Matthew 21:1–11). This day, which marks the beginning of Holy Week, is now widely marked by the distribution of crosses made from palm fronds to congregations.

Maundy Thursday focuses on one of the final acts concerning Jesus to be related in John's Gospel – the washing of the disciples' feet by Jesus (John 13:1–15). The ceremony of the "washing of the feet" of members of the congregation came to be an important part of the liturgy of the medieval church, symbolizing the humility of the clergy, in obedience to the example of Christ. The unusual term "Maundy" is related to this medieval practice. In the Middle Ages, church services were held in Latin. The opening words of a typical service on this day are based on the words of Jesus recorded in John 13:34): "A new command I give you: Love one another. As I have loved you, so you must love one another." In Latin, the opening phrase of this sentence is "mandatum novum do vobis." The word "Maundy" is a corruption of the Latin word "mandatum" ("command").

Good Friday is marked as the day on which Jesus died on the cross. It is the most solemn day in the Christian year, and is widely marked by the removing of all decorations from churches. In Lutheran churches, the day was marked by the reading of the passion narrative in a gospel, a practice which lies behind the "passions" composed by Johann Sebastian Bach (1685–1750). Both the St Matthew Passion and the St John Passion have their origins in this observance of Good Friday. The practice of observing a period of three hours' devotion from 12.00 to 3.00 on Good Friday has its origins in the eighteenth century. The "Three Hours of the Cross" often take the form of an extended meditation on the "Seven Last Words from the Cross," with periods of silence, prayer, or hymn-singing. Good Friday is traditionally associated with reflection on the costliness of human redemption, and the pain and suffering of Christ on the cross (see pp. 61–9).

Holy Saturday is the final day of Lent, immediately before Easter Day. Especially in the Eastern Orthodox churches, the day is marked by the "Paschal Vigil" – a late evening service, which leads directly into the following Easter Day, making extensive use of the imagery of light and darkness (see p. 104). Traditionally, the eucharist is never celebrated on this day.

Easter

Easter Day marks the resurrection of Jesus, and is widely regarded as the most important festival of the Christian year. The religious importance of the festival can be summarized as follows. In the first place, it affirms the identity of Jesus as the risen Savior and Lord. In the Orthodox tradition, this point is often made through icons or pictures in churches, which show a triumphant and risen Christ (often referred to as *Christos pantocrator*, "Christ the all-powerful") as ruler over the universe as a result of his being raised from the dead. In the second place, it affirms the Christian hope – that is, the fundamental belief that Christians will be raised from the dead, and hence need fear death no more. Both these themes dominate Easter hymns and liturgies, and are of immense importance for Christian spirituality. Easter is traditionally a time for reflection on the great theme of Christian hope, and its importance for the life of faith.

It will be clear from this very brief discussion of the Christian year that it encourages and allows Christians to focus on different aspects of their faith at different times of the year. For example, Christmas allows believers to focus on the doctrine of the incarnation, and the humility and love of God in coming to redeem us in history. Easter allows believers to celebrate and exult in the hope of their own resurrection, and to see the problems of pain, suffering and evil in the light of the hope of their final defeat. The Christian year thus allows for the superimposition of a rich and regular annual pattern of personal devotion and theological reflection on the individual's own daily or weekly pattern of prayer and bible reading.

The monastic day

One of the most important ways of structuring time developed within the monasteries. Monasticism can be seen, in part, as a reaction against the secularization of the church as a result of the conversion of Constantine. Monasteries were established in part to allow for constant prayer, which was seen as increasingly problematical for Christians who chose to remain active in the world. Increasingly, monasticism came to be seen as an ideal, in which the goal of continuous prayer was pursued with a dedication which was impossible outside a monastic context.

This emphasis upon constant prayer led to the restructuring of the day. The pattern which gradually emerged was that of seven times of prayer during the day, and one during the night. These times of prayer were given the name "offices," from the Latin term *officium*, meaning "an obligation." The biblical basis for this pattern was found in the Psalter. For example, Psalm 119:164 commends prayer at seven points during the day, and many of the psalms refer to prayer during the night. The evolution of the monastic day can be seen as the gradual institutionalization of this pattern of seven day-time offices and one at night.

The precise evolution of this pattern is not completely understood. The following factors seem to have been involved.

1   There was already a widespread trend within ordinary church life to pray corporately in the early morning and evening. These offices came to be referred to as "Mattins" and "Vespers" (from the Latin terms for "morning" and "evening"). The monasteries appear to have incorporated this regular pattern of prayer into their own more rigorous structures. These two times of prayer were often referred to as "the principal offices."
2   A second major factor was the structure of the classical Roman working day. This led to prayer being specified for the third, sixth and ninth hours (that is, 9.00 a.m. noon, and 3.00 p.m.). These were designated as "terce," "sext," and "none" respectively (from the Latin words for "third," "sixth" and "ninth").
3   Two additional offices were specified. *Compline* was, in effect, the final time of prayer before retiring to bed. *Prime* was an early morning form of prayer, apparently introduced by Cassian, who was concerned that monks might go back to bed after the night office, and sleep until 9.00.
4   There appears to have been considerable variation as to the time of the night office, reflecting local patterns of worship and understandings of personal discipline. If the day is divided into eight periods of three hours, it might be expected that the night office would be set for 3.00 a.m.; however, there appears to have been some variation on this matter.

The basic point to be made here is that the monastic day was systematically structured into segments, which included prayer and the reading of Scripture, particularly the Psalms. Psalms 148, 149 and 150 were used with particular frequency. The pattern of daily offices was seen as an important framework for the development of personal and corporate spirituality, offering monks the opportunity to achieve the ideal of continual prayer, and at the same time saturate them with biblical passages. The internalization of Scripture, so important an aspect of monastic spirituality, is partly grounded in the rich use of the Bible in the monastic offices, as well as the emphasis within some monastic traditions on personal devotion on the part of individual monks in their cells.

It should be noted that some aspects of this structuring of the day remain important outside the monastic tradition. An excellent example is provided by the tradition evangelical "Quiet Time," a daily period set aside for private reading of the Bible, meditation and prayer. For many evangelicals, the early morning provides an ideal opportunity to begin the day with the reading of Scripture. Although the pressures of modern life have undermined this practice somewhat, the basic principle remains unaltered. Many study aids have emerged to encourage and assist the practice of the "Quiet Time," typically through assigning a passage to each day, and offering brief devotional comments and reflections on the passage as an aid to prayer. Similarly, Dietrich Bonhoeffer (1906–45) stresses the positive value of setting aside a daily period for personal Bible study and meditation. In his *Life Together* (1938), Bonhoeffer set out the importance of "being alone with the Word," allowing it to challenge and inspire its readers.

Spiritual Geography: Structuring Space

In the previous section, we looked at the issue of the structuring of time. In a post-Einsteinian world, the close connection between time and space cannot be overlooked. It is therefore of considerable importance to explore the theme of the structuring of space in Christian spirituality. We begin by briefly considering some aspects of architecture of relevance to our theme.

Holy spaces: spirituality and architecture

Christian spirituality involves places, whether these are natural locations such as deserts or mountains (which allow and encourage Christians to be alone with God) or human constructions, such as church buildings. It is therefore important to note the way in which architecture relates to spirituality. In what follows, we shall explore some aspects of church architecture for spirituality, noting in particular some denomiational differences of importance.

One clear function of church architecture is to stress the transcendence of God. The great soaring arches and spires of medieval cathedrals were intended to stress the greatness of God, and raise the thoughts of worshippers heavenwards. The symbolism is that of the eternal impinging upon the temporal, with the church building symbolizing the mediation between heaven and earth offered through the gospel. However, apart from this emphasis on the transcendence of God, architecture reflects a concern to focus on what is deemed to be important. Three such *foci* can be singled out.

1. Especially within Catholicism, the altar was singled out for special attention, reflecting an emphasis upon the importance of the mass. Gregory the Great chose to erect an altar over the tomb of St Peter, thus combining a focus on the "sacrament of the altar" with a veneration of the relics of saints.

2. Within the Eastern Orthodox tradition, particular emphasis came to be placed on the iconostasis – that is, the stand on which icons were placed. In later Orthodox churches, the iconostasis became such a prominent feature that it in effect cut off the entire altar area from the sight of the laity. The icon placed upon the iconostasis thus assumed a much higher profile than the altar.

3. Within the Protestant tradition, the emphasis upon preaching led to the pulpit being elevated above the altar, both physically and in terms of the emphasis placed upon it. The noted Swiss reformed theologian Karl Barth (1886–1968) notes how Reformed churches stress God's "otherness" through the design of churches and other liturgical means:

Preaching takes place from the pulpit (a place which by its awesome but obviously intended height differs from a podium), and on the pulpit, as a warning to those who ascend it, there is a big Bible. Preachers also wear a robe – I am not embarrased to say this – and they should do so, for it is a salutary reminder that from those who wear this special garment, people expect a special word.

More recently, church architecture has come to be influenced by other factors. For example, North American revivalism of the late nineteenth century saw worship partly in terms of entertainment, and thus designed church buildings with stages suitable for the performance of music and worship. The rise of "base ecclesial communities" or "house churches" has led to a new informality of worship, often within private homes or borrowed premises, in which the emphasis has been placed on fellowship, prayer and worship, with architectural considerations being of minimal importance. For some, this can be regarded as a return to the primitive Christian practice.

Christian spirituality is unquestionably affected by the space in which spiritual reflection takes place. There is no doubt that the process of *lectio, meditatio, oratio,* and *contemplatio* proposed by the twelfth-century Carthusian writer Guigo II (see p. 84) is greatly assisted by silence and stillness, and that this is encouraged by certain types of buildings in certain locations.

Holy places: the place of pilgrimage

Many Christian traditions ascribe particular spiritual importance to certain places, or the process of travelling to these. Once more, it is necessary to note that this is not a uniform tendency within Christianity. While immediately conceding the dangers of generalization, it seems that Protestantism has generally been more critical than affirmative of the notion of a "holy place." In the present section, we shall explore some aspects of this notion of "holy places," and their significance for spirituality.

The Old Testament clearly regarded the city of Jerusalem as a holy place. Jerusalem and its temple were seen as the central focus of the religion of Israel. God had chosen Jerusalem as a dwelling-place, and the city and its temple were thus set apart as possessing a religious significance denied to other locations in Israel. Earlier in Israel's history, sites such as Shiloh and Mizpah were seen as being of especial religious importance. It was at these sites that shrines were established during the period of the conquest of Canaan. Nevertheless, the temple erected at Jerusalem came to be seen as possessing supreme significance. Some Old Testament passages spoke of Jerusalem or its temple as the "dwelling place" of God. As a result, Jerusalem came to play a special role in Israel's hopes for the future. It was from Jerusalem that the knowledge of God was to spread to all nations (Isaiah 2:2–4; Micah 4:1–3). It was by worshipping God in Jerusalem that the nations of the world would find their true unity (Isaiah 19:23; Zechariah 8:3). The modern Jewish passover ends with the expression of the hope that, next year, the passover will be celebrated in Jerusalem.

It is therefore clear that Jerusalem came to play a special role in Judaism. In that the central events upon which the Christian faith is founded – supremely, the death and resurrection of Jesus – took place in Jerusalem, it might therefore be expected that the New Testament should take over this Old Testament understanding of the special place of the city. This, however, proves not to be the case. The special sacred status of Jerusalem within the Old Testament is not endorsed by the New Testament, which affirms the historical *but not the theological* importance of Jerusalem. The theme of the "new Jerusalem" is certainly found, as a statement of the Christian hope (see Hebrews 12:22; Revelation 21:2). Yet this is not seen as legitimizing any present spiritual significance for the city of Jerusalem.

The significance of Jerusalem is not discussed in any detail by Christian writers of the first three centuries, in itself an indication that this was not seen as being of major importance. Two very different views emerge in the fourth century. Eusebius of Caesarea (*c.*260–339) argued that the spirituality of the New Testament was not concerned with physical entities (such as the "land of Israel" or the "city of Jerusalem"), but was concerned with spiritual matters, of which these physical entities were at best convenient physical symbols. Cyril of Jerusalem (*c.*320–386), in contrast, was quite clear that Jerusalem remained a "holy city." It is, of course, entirely possible that ecclesiastical politics may have entered into this debate. Cyril was anxious to maintain the prestige of his own city; Eusebius was interested in promoting the claims of Rome as the new city to be granted special divine favor.

An important document dating from this period, which illustrates the spiritual importance of pilgrimage, is known as the "Peregrinatio" or "Pilgrimage of Egeria." This document, discovered in 1884 and probably dating from 381–4, is in effect the personal journal of a woman visiting the Holy Land, and records all that she observes. Although the text is often read for its important first-hand testimony concerning liturgical practices in the Holy Land at this time, it is also an important witness to the benefits that such pilgrimages were understood to bring.

In the course of Christian history, a number of sites have emerged as having potential spiritual importance. These include (but are by no means limited to) the following.

1 Jerusalem, the scene of the last supper, betrayal, crucifixion, and resurrection of Jesus.
2 Rome, widely believed to be the site of the martyrdom and burial of both St Peter and St Paul.
3 Canterbury, the site of the martyrdom of Thomas à Becket in 1170. The bawdy escapades accompanying pilgrimages to Canterbury were set out by Geoffrey Chaucer in his *Canterbury Tales*.
4 Santiago de Compostela, in north-western Spain, the traditional burial place of St James the Apostle.
5 Lourdes, in southern France, the site of a vision of the Virgin Mary in 1858, which has become associated with reports of healings.

What role do pilgrimages to such sites play in Christian spirituality? Clearly, the answer to such questions will be complex and nuanced, given the considerable variation within Christianity concerning issues of theology. For example, Protestants generally do not accept any kind of "theology of sacred places," and would not give any particular place of honor to Mary. Pilgrimages to Lourdes, therefore, do not feature prominently in Protestant spirituality. In general, it is thought that the following factors are of major importance in relation to a spirituality of pilrimage.

1   The act of making a pilgrimage involves at least a degree of commitment and hardship. This makes a pilgrimage an act of self-denial or personal discipline, the virtues of which would be widely accepted. The degree of hardship can be enhanced in various ways: for example, medieval penitents were in the habit of placing small stones inside their shoes to make the journey more painful.
2   The pilgrimage offers an opportunity to reflect on the life and teaching of the person who is associated with the pilgrimage site. For example, a pilgrimage to Santiago de Compostela offers an opportunity to read about St James, just as a pilgrimage to Rome can be the focus for reflection on the life and teaching of both St Peter and St Paul.
3   The notion of "pilgrimage" helps reinforce the Christian idea that believers are "strangers and pilgrims on earth" (Hebrews 11:13), whose true home is a city in heaven (Philippians 3:20). The idea of passing through life en route to the heavenly city, rather than making oneself at home in the world, is clearly embodied in the act of pilgrimage.
4   For some, the sites of pilgrimage are themselves endued with some spiritual quality, which can be experienced by those who travel there.

As was noted earlier, Protestants generally regard the notion of "pilgrimage" with suspicion. However, it is important to appreciate that the idea is present, although in a slightly redirected manner, within many Protestant spiritualities. Many Protestants find it helpful to make journeys to the Holy Land or sites of relevance to the New Testament – for example, the seven churches of Asia (mentioned in the Book of Revelation) or the churches established by or written to by St Paul. These journeys are seen, however, primarily as bringing a new depth to bible study, in that biblical passages take on a new personal significance through having visited the site in question. Visiting sites is thus seen as an aid to more effective Bible study.

FOR FURTHER READING

André Biéler, *Architecture in Worship: The Christian Place of Worship*. Edinburgh: Oliver & Boyd, 1965.
Paul J. Bradshaw, *Daily Prayer in the Early Church: A Study of the Origin and Early Development of the Divine Office*. New York: Oxford University Press, 1982.
Donald J. Bruggink and Carl H. Droppers, *Christ and Architecture: Building Presbyterian/ Reformed Churches*. Grand Rapids: Eerdmans, 1965.
Owen Chadwick, "The Origin of Prime," *Journal of Theological Studies* 49 (1948), 178–82.
Peter Cobb, "The History of the Christian Year," in C. Jones, G. Wainwright and E. Yarnold (eds), *The Study of Liturgy* London: SPCK, 1978, 403–18.
Howard M. Colvin, *Architecture and the After-Life*. New Haven, CT: Yale University Press, 1991.
J. D. Davies, *Holy Week: A Short History*. London: Lutterworth Press, 1963.
Peter Hammond, *Liturgy and Architecture*. London: Barrie & Rockliff, 1960.

K. Hughes, "The Changing Theory and Practice of Irish Pilgrimage," *Journal of Ecclesiastical History* 11 (1960), 143–51.

E. D. Hunt, *Holy Land Pilgrimage in the Later Roman Empire*. Oxford: Oxford University Press, 1982.

Philip Sheldrake, *Living Between Worlds: Place and Journey in Celtic Spirituality*. London: DLT, 1995.

Kenneth J. Stevenson, *Jerusalem Revisited: The Liturgical Meaning of Holy Week*. Washington, D.C.: Pastoral Press, 1988.

Robert F. Taft, *The Liturgy of the Hours in East and West: The Origins of the Divine Office and its Meaning for Today*. Collegeville, MN: Liturgical Press, 1986.

Thomas J. Talley, *The Origins of the Liturgical Year*. New York: Pueblo, 1991.

Victor and Edith Turner, *Image and Pilgrimage in Christian Culture*. Oxford: Blackwell, 1978.

P. W. L. Walker, *Holy City, Holy Places? Christian Attitudes to Jerusalem and the Holy Land in the Fourth Century*. Oxford: Oxford University Press, 1990.

J. Walter, "The Origins of the Iconostasis," *Eastern Churches Quarterly* 3 (1970–1), 251–67.

Franz Xavier Weiser, *Handbook of Christian Feasts and Customs: The Year of the Lord in Liturgy and Folklore*. New York: Harcourt Brace, 1958.

Hugh Wybrew, *Orthodox Lent, Holy Week and Easter*. London: SPCK, 1995.

7

CHRISTIAN SPIRITUALITY: ENGAGING THE TRADITION

Up to this point, we have been engaging with some of the themes and issues of Christian spirituality. At certain points, we have looked briefly at texts which illustrate or apply some of the issues under consideration. However, one of the most important themes of Christian spirituality is *engagement with classical texts*. Yet, as Mark Twain (1835–1910) once quipped in his dry humorous style, a classic is the kind of book that "everyone wants to have read but no one wants to read." For many, the use of the word "classic" throws up a barrier between the potential reader and the text, implying that the latter is difficult to read (and probably out of date anyway).

The present section of this work has been written to encourage engagement with the classic texts of the Christian tradition. It needs to be appreciated that a "classic" is not a work aimed at some kind of pretentious elite, but a work which has proved to have value for generation after generation. To engage with this kind of text is to quarry insights that have served and nourished previous generations, and give every indication of doing the same for generations to come. In many ways, the material presented thus far in this work has been in preparation for dealing directly with the classic texts of the tradition. In what follows, we shall offer an introduction to this process of engagement by a process of guided interaction with short, manageable extracts from major works. We begin by looking at some of the difficulties that arise from dealing with older texts.

Spirituality and History

In his major study *The Classic* (1975), the literary critic Frank Kermode points to the way in which classic texts possess a "superfluity of meaning," allowing them to be a resource and stimulus to ages other than their own. Many of the texts relating to

Christian spirituality must be judged to fall into this category. The writings of Thomas à Kempis (*c*.1380–1471), for example, have been read for centuries, with each generation rediscovering his wisdom and relevance. Nevertheless, there are certain difficulties associated with reading classic texts, which need to be appreciated from the outset. In what follows, we shall consider some of the difficulties likely to be encountered in reading classic texts, and the manner in which they can be (at least to some extent) neutralized.

1   *The intended audience.* The first major difficulty is that the original text may presuppose a specific audience. All authors write with a particular audience in mind, and the envisaged audience determines the style of writing; the vocabulary used; the identification of those assumptions which are to be regarded as shared on the one hand, or controversial on the other; and the extent of the assumed background knowledge. In each case, you may find that it is difficult to relate to the text, precisely because you fall outside the readership envisaged by the author.

It is also important to appreciate that some classic texts were never intended to be published. For example, some of the prayers of Anselm of Canterbury were intended to be read only by those to whom they were dedicated. Some of the writings from the Flemish *Devotio Moderna* school were intended for circulation in very limited circles, and only became available to a wider readership by accident.

Some illustrations of the difficulties which arise, and ways in which they can be met, may be helpful at this point. Many works of medieval western monastic spirituality presuppose that their audience is primarily or exclusively monastic. Many monastic orders (such as the Benedictines) read the Bible so frequently and extensively that its language and imagery became second nature to them. As a result, many works of spirituality originating from such contexts assume that their readers are saturated with the text of the Bible, and will therefore easily recognize biblical images, citations, or allusions. Most modern readers do not share this happy situation, and are therefore likely to miss out on much of the richness and subtlety of the text in question.

The situation is not, however, hopeless. The easiest way of dealing with this situation is for a modern commentator to point out these images, citations and allusions in a series of annotations to the text. In this way, the modern reader is enabled to gain at least something of the original and intended meaning of the author.

A second area of potential difficulty concerns analogies which are used by spiritual writers to help their readers understand certain points. These analogies were chosen to be familiar to the intended audience. Particularly in the case of patristic and medieval texts, this often results in an analogy being used which may well have been very familiar to the original audience, but which makes little, if any, sense to a modern reader. Spiritual writers of the sixteenth century, for example, sometimes use monastic routines, practices of royal courts, or contemporary legal or business practice, to make spiritual points. In every case, major changes in western culture have led to these analogies losing their original power to illuminate. Paradoxically, a literary device which was once an aid to understanding has now become an obstacle to the same process!

Again, the situation is far from hopeless. What is required is for someone familiar with the period to explain the intended meaning of the analogy, allowing the reader to regain something of the freshness of the original image. It may occasionally be possible to offer a modern equivalent, which allows at least something of what is assumed to be the intended meaning to be conveyed in an imaginative and helpful manner.

2   *The goals of the writer.* In some cases, the writer has a set of goals which govern the approach of the work. You may find that you are quite out of sympathy with these goals. For example, Thomas à Kempis' classic *Imitation of Christ* is clearly written to encourage the Brethren of the Common Life to believe that they have chosen well in leaving the world behind, and entering a monastery. At a number of critical points, Thomas argues that to remain in the world is to forfeit a whole series of spiritual benefits and insights. Only those who have the integrity to renounce the world and enter a monastic order will gain the full benefits of the Christian gospel. Many modern readers regard this as a questionable assumption.

So how does this affect the manner in which we approach such texts? An extreme reaction is to argue that, unless you can agree with each and every identifiable assumption made by the text's author, there is nothing to be gained by studying the text. This is indefensible. To begin with, it would restrict your reading to a remarkably limited range of works. Perhaps more importantly, it is important to read works which set out viewpoints other than your own, to allow you to continue to think through the issues involved. Some readers will wish to place "Do Not Disturb" notices on their mental faculties, in that they have made up their minds about everything, and do not wish to have to rethink anything. It is important, as a matter of principle, to study and engage with viewpoints which are outside your personal comfort zone.

The most commonly encountered approach to this difficulty is probably also the most effective. We shall term this the *principle of selective attention*. The basic idea is that you pick out the ideas that you like, and disregard others. Thus, to go back to Thomas à Kempis' *Imitation of Christ*, we find that most modern readers of the text (who are generally not monks!) pay selective attention to the work's remarkably fine exposition of life under the cross, but adopt one of two approaches:

1   They choose to disregard or refute some of the work's other themes (such as the need to renounce the world for a monastic life). This approach is somewhat eclectic, but corresponds well to the way in which many people approach texts of this nature.
2   They treat these as aspects of the work which reflect its original circumstances of composition, and which are therefore not necessarily to be seen as binding on readers whose personal circumstances are somewhat different. This could be argued to constitute a "contextualized" approach, where differences in the context of writer and reader lead to certain adjustments being made in consequence.

Interrogating the Text

One of the most important points to appreciate about reading classic texts of spirituality is that the process in question is meant to be interactive. The reader is not a passive participant in the process, but is intended to engage with the text. One of the most rewarding means of doing this is by interrogating the text. At first sight, this might seem to invoke all kinds of unhelpful and unpleasant associations, such as treating the text as if it were the subject of a police investigation. But in reality, something quite different is intended. The idea is that the reader of the text should not be a passive spectator, but an active participant. The reader engages with the text – and one of the most effective ways of doing this is to ask questions of and about the text. The following questions are especially important.

1   *Who is the author?* It is important to appreciate that texts were written by real people, with experience of life and a concern to pass on to others the wisdom which they had accumulated. Identifying the writer and understanding something of the writer's background reminds us that works of spirituality are written by real, living and concerned individuals for other real, living and concerned individuals. The writers have passions, concerns and agendas, often informed by a wealth of experience and insight. The manner in which a reader interacts with a text often reflects that reader's admiration or reservations concerning its author. In that spirituality concerns living Christian experience, it is thus important to appreciate something of the lived Christian life which shaped and informed the text under consideration. For this reason, each text to be considered in the present chapter will be prefaced by a brief biographical study of its author.

2   *For whom was the text written?* Many texts were written with a very specific audience in mind. For example, *The Cloud of Unknowing* was clearly written with the needs of a young man who is pursuing the contemplative life under monastic obedience in mind. The audience which the writer has in mind determines a number of major issues, including the language and imagery to be used; the expectations that the writer has of the reader; the options which the reader has to put the ideas or methods of the text into practice; gender and class related issues – to mention some of the more obvious points. Identifying the intended readership group is especially important if you, the reader, do not belong to that group. If this is the case, you will have to make all kinds of adaptations if you are to benefit from the text. In the present chapter, we will be exploring some of the ways in which this process of adaptation or accommodation can take place.

3   *What is the historical and cultural context of the work?* The rich heritage of the Christian tradition involves many periods in history, cultures and languages. Inevitably, the historical and cultural location of the work affects the manner in which it is read. For example, Anselm of Canterbury's writings on human redemption (which date from the eleventh century) often make allusions to the feudal system which prevailed in western Europe at the time. In order to grasp and appropriate his

ideas, it is necessary to understand the context against which he wrote, which often determines the analogies and terms that he uses to express himself. A process of "translation" or "transferral" is often needed, in which the reader asks this question: "if Anselm were writing today, with the culture with which I am familiar in mind, how would he express himself?" Once more, we shall illustrate ways in which this can be done in the course of this chapter.

4 *What biblical imagery does the work employ?* Many works of Christian spirituality are saturated with biblical images and allusions. Sometimes these are explicitly identified; at other times, they are not specifically identified, and it is left to the reader to work out what they are. Identifying the biblical imagery deployed in a passage is one of the most effective ways of engaging with a work of spirituality. Often, the writer's intention is to force readers to engage with the text of the Bible, in order to deepen their knowledge and familiarity with it, and to set off a cascade of biblical ideas and themes which stimulate and satisfy the reader. We shall explore how this technique is used at several points in the present chapter.

5 *What does the writer want me to think?* One of the goals of spiritual writers is generally to win their readers round to their way of thinking – for example, concerning the excellence of a contemplative life, the importance of prayer, the need to deepen our love of God, and so on. As you read a passage, try to work out what the writer wants you to think, and the ways in which the writer tries to win you over. Identify the arguments, authorities, and approaches which are used in this attempt. For example, some writers make a direct and emotive appeal: "If God loves you this much, why is it that you do not love God in return?" Others use a more rational approach, based on arguments which appeal to your reason.

6 *What does the writer want me to do?* Spirituality, as we have stressed, is not simply about ideas, but about living the Christian life to its full. Many spiritual writers have well-developed ideas about how the full riches of the Christian life are to be achieved, which generally involves doing certain things – for example, praying more often, cultivating a certain attitude toward the world, and so on. Aim to identify what the writer expects readers to do as a result of reading the work.

7 *What can I take away from my engagement with the text?* Note the way in which this question is phrased. You are not being asked what you think that the writer wants you to take away; the issue concerns what you have encountered that you would like to remain with you as helpful, stimulating, encouraging, or challenging. The noted French spiritual writer Francis de Sales (1567–1622) uses the image of gathering flowers from a garden to illustrate this point in his *Introduction to the Devout Life* (1609):

> Those who have been walking in a beautiful garden do not leave it willingly without taking away with them in their hands four or five flowers, in order to inhale their fragrance and carry them about during the day. Even so, when we have considered some mystery in meditation, we should choose one or two or three points which we have

found particularly to our taste, and which are particularly appropriate to our advancement, so that we may remember them during the day, and inhale their fragrance spiritually.

Other questions could be asked of the text; those provided above, however, offer a framework by which the full richness of a classic text of spirituality may be unlocked. In what follows, we shall be using this technique to help explore some of the classic texts of the Christian spiritual tradition.

But we have spent long enough preparing for this engagement with the texts. In what follows, we shall plunge into some of the greatest writings of the Christian spiritual tradition, and allow them to impact upon us.

Classic Texts: An Engagement

Anyone wanting to offer a selection of readings representing the long and rich tradition of Christian spirituality is confronted with a massive problem. There is so much material to choose from that any selection will seem inadequate, arbitrary, and unsatisfactory. The process of selection for inclusion inevitably means a corresponding process of choosing to overlook. Readers are asked to understand that the process of making decisions as to what to include was difficult. Many other texts that demand and deserve to be included have had to be passed over.

However, the present chapter is intended to help you engage with the classic texts of Christian spirituality, as a means of enabling you to move on from here to engage with the texts which you really want to examine. If those texts are not included in this volume, you will at least be able to move on to your preferred text with a good background knowledge which will enable you to gain far more from reading that text than you might otherwise do. It must be appreciated that the selection of texts provided is not meant to be representative, exhaustive, or even illustrative of the enormous riches of the Christian tradition. The object is simply to encourage you in the process of engagement, in order that you can move on to benefit more fully from the texts that you would really like to study!

You are thus invited to see this chapter as a means of acquiring the active reading skills which are essential to the engagement with classic texts of the Christian spiritual tradition. For this reason, you are asked to work your way through *all* the texts provided, even if you are not personally sympathetic to the approaches or presuppositions of the writers. Engagement with the texts which are provided in this chapter will equip you to engage more effectively with those which you particularly want to read at a later stage.

An important part of the process of engagement with any text is the movement from reading to reflection to prayer. In several cases, one of the questions which you will be asked to answer is the following: can you compose a prayer which incorporates and responds to the particular issues raised by the passage under study? While some readers may find this difficult, it is an excellent way of avoiding the "passive reading" of texts which leads to an impoverished appreciation of their importance. If you are asked to respond in this way, try writing a brief prayer, which need not be more than five lines long, incorporating the concerns of the passage. In some cases, the passages in question take the form of a prayer, making the process correspondingly easier.

In what follows, a section is devoted to each of the writers to be studied. To make the process of engagement simpler, each section follows a more or less identical format. Note that line numbers have been printed against the text for study, to facilitate reference to sections within it.

Gregory of Nyssa

Gregory of Nyssa (*c*.330–*c*.395) is widely regarded as one of the most important writers of the Christian east. He became bishop of Nyssa (now in modern-day Turkey) in 371. Gregory was a strong defender of the full divinity and humanity of Christ, and found himself being marginalized during the period in which Arianism (see p. 55) temporarily gained the ascendancy in the region. Gregory made extensive use of Platonic ideas (such as the notion of "the Good") in his exposition and defence of the Christian faith. His more spiritual writings stress the inability of the human mind to fully comprehend or penetrate into the mystery of God. He can thus be thought of as "apophatic" (see p. 118), in that he points out the severe limitations placed upon human knowledge of God as a result of human creatureliness.

The text for study is taken from a collection of eight sermons preached on Matthew 5:1–10, which are generally referred to collectively as the "Commentary on the Beatitudes." The origins of the work are thought to lie in addresses given to congregations at Nyssa. In the third of this series of eight sermons, Gregory deals with the human longing for God, and traces its origins back to the fact that humanity has been created in the image of God. At several points, Gregory makes use of the Platonic notion of "the Good," which, together with the notions of "the True" and "the Beautiful," constitutes what is often referred to as the Platonic triad. Gregory, in common with most Christian writers who make use of Platonist categories, identifies these with God, arguing that these classical notions can be seen as prefiguring the full disclosure of the divine wisdom in Christ.

Gregory of Nyssa on Longing for God

The more that we believe that "the Good," on account of its nature, lies far beyond the limits of our knowledge, the more we experience a sense of sorrow that we have to be separated from this "Good," which is both great and desirable, and yet cannot be embraced fully by our minds. Yet we mortals once had a share in this "Good" which
5   so eludes our attempts to comprehend it. This "Good" – which surpasses all human thought, and which we once possessed – is such that human nature also seemed to be "good" in some related form, in that it was fashioned as the most exact likeness and in the image of its prototype. For humanity then possessed all those qualities about which we now speculate – immortality, happiness, independence and self-
10   determination, a life without drudgery or sorrow, being caught up in divine matters, a vision of "the Good" through an unclouded and undistracted mind. This is what the creation story hints at briefly (Genesis 1:27), when it tells us that humanity was formed

> in the image of God, and lived in Paradise, enjoying what grew there (and the fruit of
> those trees was life, knowledge, and so on). So if we once possessed those gifts, we
> 15 can only grieve over our sadness when we compare our previous happiness to our
> present misery. What was high has been made low; what was created in the image of
> heaven has been reduced to earth; the one who was ordained to govern the earth has
> been reduced to a slave; what was created for immortality has been destroyed by death;
> the one who lived in the joys of Paradise has ended up in this place of drudgery and
> 20 illness ... Our tears would flow even more if we were to list all those physical suffer-
> ings that are an inevitable part of our human conditions (by this, I mean all the dif-
> ferent sorts of illnesses), and when we reflect on the fact that humanity was originally
> free from all of these, and when we compare the joys that we once knew with our
> present misery by setting our sadness alongside that better life. So when our Lord says:
> 25 "Blessed are those who mourn" (Matthew 5:5), I believe his hidden teaching to be
> this: the soul should fix its gaze on "the true Good," and not be immersed in the illu-
> sion of this present life.

Begin by reading the above passage twice. You will find it helpful to read the
Beatitude on which it is based (Matthew 5:5), in that Gregory is dealing with the
sense of sorrow or mourning which he discerns within human existence.

1   According to this passage, for what is humanity mourning? The answer given
is that we mourn the loss of the good that we once possessed.

2   You will need to read Genesis 2:4–20 to make sense of some of what Gregory
argues next. Do this before moving on to the next question.

3   Gregory's basic argument is that humanity enjoyed the life of Paradise, before
losing this through disobedience. Take a piece of paper, and list the contrasts which
he identifies between our present state and that enjoyed in paradise.

4   Gregory thus argues that it is inevitable that we will feel sad and miserable,
when we compare our present situation with that which existed in paradise. Yet the
Beatitude affirms that those who mourn *shall be comforted* (Matthew 5:5). In what
way does Gregory draw hope from our present sorrow?

5   It is important to appreciate that Gregory's general theological outlook brings
together the past, present, and future. The past is about Paradise; the present is about
a loss of God's immediate presence and all the joys of Paradise; the future, however,
is about the potential recovery of those joys of Paradise in heaven. Gregory's argument is that we can set our minds and hearts firmly on the recovery of that lost state
of innocence and joy in the world to come. His analysis thus encourages his readers
to contemplate the future restoration of what was lost in Eden through sin. (For
Gregory, incidentally, one of the leading themes of the doctrine of redemption is that
Christ restores what Adam lost.)

6   Read Genesis 1:26–27. Note that the passage refers to humanity being created
in the image and likeness of God. How does Gregory make use of this point in his

argument? What difference does this insight make to our understanding of human nature and destiny?

7   Finally, what does Gregory want us to *do* as a result of his reflections? Could you compose a prayer which responds to those concerns and reflections?

The passage is clearly telling us that we must learn not to be distracted or overwhelmed by the present world or our present situation. We must fix our gaze on "the true Good," which is none other than God. Gregory's argument is that this prepares us for our future consolation, when what is at present only a hope becomes a reality.

FOR FURTHER READING

Hilda C. Graef, *Gregory of Nyssa: The Lord's Prayer; The Beatitudes.* Westminster, MD: Newman Press, 1957.
Anthony Meredith, *Gregory of Nyssa.* London: Routledge, 1999.

Augustine of Hippo

Augustine of Hippo (354–430) is widely regarded as one of the most important writers of the Christian church. Augustine was born in the Roman province of Numidia (now in modern-day Algeria). His mother, Monica, was a devout Christian, and wished her son to share in her faith. Augustine showed no inclination to do so, and at the age of 17 took a local girl as his mistress, and subsequently came under the influence of the Manichees, a religious group based on the gnostic philosophy of Mani. Augustine settled in Italy, and pursued a career within the Roman civil service. While staying at Milan, however, Augustine underwent a conversion experience in July 386. He returned to his native North Africa in the late summer of 388. While visiting the coastal town of Hippo Regius in 391, he was ordained against his own wishes, and subsequently (probably in 395) became a bishop. Although the local affairs of the North African church figured prominently in his concerns, Augustine devoted himself particularly to the clarification, exposition, and defense of the Christian faith against its external opponents and internal dissidents. His writings deal with the major issues of Christian thought, including the doctrines of the Trinity, the church, and grace (but significantly, not Christology).

One of those writings, from which our extract is taken, is known as the *Confessions*. This work, written in Latin, is widely recognized as one of the most significant works to be written in the west, whether sacred or secular. The *Confessions* were written over the period 398–400, and take the form of an extended meditation on God, interspersed with prayer. Of its thirteen component sections (referred to as "books"), the first nine are essentially autobiographical, describing his youth and early loss of faith; his growing interest in and commitment to the Manichees; his subsequent alienation from the movement, and interest in Platonism; and his conversion in the summer of 386. A particularly moving section toward the end of this autobiographical portion of the work deals with the death of his mother, Monica. The four concluding sections deal with aspects of the relation of the universe to God, focusing on issues such as memory, time and creation.

The major theme found in the passage is that of God as the source of true joy. Augustine's argument is essentially that we have been created for fellowship with God, and that where this potentiality remains unfulfilled, dissatisfaction and restlessness results. For Augustine, true human fulfillment and satisfaction thus come about only when God is known and worshipped. Interestingly, Augustine allows that other things in the world may offer at least the appearance of happiness; for Augustine, the fact that the world has been created by God means that hints of God's goodness and beauty may be found throughout the creation. The creation thus contains some "image of the true joy," which can serve as a signpost to the source and fulfillment of that joy – God.

An integral element of Augustine's spirituality is thus that the creation is to be thought of as good, and divine in its origins. Nevertheless, it possesses the ability to mislead individuals into thinking that the creation itself has the ability to satisfy human longing and desire. For Augustine, this is not correct, and can only lead to sadness and despair. The creation is a sign which points to God, and which has achieved its purpose only when the one to whom it points has been recognized and encountered.

There is no doubt that Augustine's personal experience lies behind this passage. The *Confessions* sets out Augustine's own attempts to find satisfaction in the relationship with his mistress, in the ideas of the Manichees, and in his quest for recognition and promotion within the Roman civil service. Each of these is exposed as inadequate and second-rate in the light of knowing God. Augustine has experienced the longing for happiness himself, and the frustration and sadness which arise when the quest for joy seems to lead to a dead end. He expects his readers to be able to understand this longing for happiness, and identify with the quest for joy. He wants his readers to go away from reading this passage with the realization that the quest for joy is actually a disguised or unrecognized quest for God.

One of the dominant themes of the work is set out in its opening paragraph, in which Augustine – addressing God – declares that: "you have made us for yourself, and our hearts are restless until they find their rest in you." This theme of the human search for joy, which is reflected strongly in Augustine's personal history, permeates the *Confessions*, and is the subject of the extract which we shall consider in some detail. The extract is taken from the tenth book of the work, which deals with the theme of memory.

Augustine on God as the Sole Source of True Joy

Where and when, then, have I experienced the happy life for myself, so that I can remember and love and long for it? The desire for happiness is not in myself alone or in a few friends, but is found in everybody. If we did not know this with certain knowledge, we would not want it with determination in our will. But what does this mean?
5 If two people are asked if they want to serve in the army, it may turn out that one of them replies that he would like to do so, while the other would not. But if they are asked whether they would like to be happy, each would at once say without the least

hesitation that he would choose to be so. And the reason why one would wish to be a soldier and the other would not is only that they want to be happy. Is it then the case that one person finds joy in one way, another in a different way? What all agree upon is that they want to be happy, just as they would concur, if asked, that they want to experience joy and would call that joy the happy life. Even if one person pursues it in one way and another in a different way, yet there is one goal which all are striving to attain, namely to experience joy. Since no one can say that this is a matter outside experience, the happy life is found in the memory and is recognized when the words are uttered.

Far be it from me, Lord, far from the heart of your servant who is making confession to you, far be it from me to think myself happy, whatever be the joy in which I take my delight. There is a delight which is given not to the wicked, but to those who worship you, for no reward save the joy that you yourself are to them. That is the authentic happy life, to set one's joy on you, grounded in you and caused by you. That is the real thing, and there is no other. Those who think that the happy life is found elsewhere pursue another joy and not the true one. Nevertheless, their will remains drawn towards some image of the true joy.

Please read this passage through twice, before moving on to the six points set out below.

1 We begin by noting the unusual style of the work, which takes the form of an extended meditation and prayer. Notice how the work involves both personal reflection and confession, as well as explicit prayer to God. Identify sections of the work where this seems to be seen at its clearest.

2 Notice how often words such as "joy," "delight," and "happy" are used throughout this text. One of the key themes that Augustine wishes to deal with in this text is the question of where true joy is to be found. What is his answer to this question?

3 What is the purpose of the analogy of the two people considering military service?

4 Augustine speaks of setting our "joy on you, grounded in you and caused by you." What does he mean by each of these three affirmations?

5 Notice the final statement. Augustine asserts that, even where people are attracted to something other than God, "their will remains drawn towards some image of the true joy." What does he mean by this?

6 What does Augustine want his readers to do as a result of the kind of arguments he explores in this passage? Could you write a prayer which reflects this?

FOR FURTHER READING

Peter Brown, *Augustine of Hippo*. London: Faber, 1967.
John Burnaby, *Amor Dei: A Study of the Religion of St Augustine*. London: Hodder & Stoughton, 1938.
Henry Chadwick, *Augustine*. Oxford: Oxford University Press, 1986.

Anselm of Canterbury

Anselm of Canterbury (*c.*1033–1109) is widely regarded as one of the most important early medieval theological and spiritual writers. Anselm was born in Aosta in Lombardy, but eventually settled in France. In 1059 he entered the monastery of Bec in Normandy, where he became prior in 1063 and abbot in 1078, In 1093, Anselm became Archbishop of Canterbury. This apparently curious appointment reflects the fact that William I had invaded England from Normandy in 1066, and a general process of appointing Normans to senior English positions had been set in place as a result. Anselm disliked the responsibilities which accompanied this position, and is remembered chiefly for his writings, of which two may be singled out for particular mention. The *Monologion* (1078) is an extended meditation upon God, which includes what has come to be known as the "ontological argument" for the existence of God. The treatise *Cur Deus homo* ("why God became man," 1098) set out a highly influential account of the death of Christ and the necessity of the incarnation. Yet Anselm was also much in demand as a spiritual advisor, and many of his prayers and letters of spiritual guidance have survived.

The passage selected for study is an extract from the work known as the "Prayer to Christ." The basic approach adopted by Anselm is that of stirring the conscience to a deeper love of God, involving the intellect, emotion, and will. As the title of the prayer suggests, there is a strong element of focusing on the passion and death of Christ as a means of deepening the love of the one who prays for the one who is prayed to. Anselm himself wrote that the prayer was intended to "stir up the mind of the reader to the love of God," and urged that it was "not to be read in a turmoil, but quietly; not skimmed or hurried through, but taken a little at a time, with deep and thoughtful meditation." Try to read the text in this way, before we turn to interacting with it.

Anselm's Prayer to Christ

Hope of my heart, strength of my soul,
    help of my weakness,
    by your powerful kindness complete
    what in my powerless weakness I attempt.
5   My life, the end to which I strive,
      although I have not yet attained to love you as I ought,
      still let my desire for you
      be as great as my love ought to be.
My light, you see my conscience,
10   because, "Lord, before you is all my desire,"
      and if my soul wills any good, you gave it me.
Lord, if what you inspire is good,
      or rather because it is good, that I should want to love you,
      give me what you have made me want:

15   grant that I may attain to love you as much as you command.
I praise and thank you for the desire that you have inspired;
    and I offer you praise and thanks
    lest your gift to me be unfruitful,
    which you have given me of your own accord.
20   Perfect what you have begun,
    and grant me what you have made me long for,
    not according to my deserts but out of your kindness
    that came first to me.
Most merciful Lord,
25   turn my lukewarmness into a fervent love of you.
Most gentle Lord,
    my prayer tends towards this –
    that by remembering and meditating
    on the good things you have done
30   I may be enkindled with your love.
    Your goodness, Lord, created me;
Your mercy cleansed what you had created from original sin;
    your patience has hitherto borne with me,
    fed me, waited for me,
35   when after I had lost the grace of my baptism
    I wallowed in many sordid sins.
You wait, good Lord, for my amendment;
My soul waits for the inbreathing of your grace
    in order to be sufficiently penitent
40   to lead a better life.
My Lord and my Creator,
    you bear with me and nourish me – be my helper.
I thirst for you, I hunger for you, I desire you,
I sigh for you, I covet you:
45   I am like an orphan deprived of the presence
    of a very kind father,
who, weeping and wailing, does not cease to cling to
    the dear face with his whole heart.
So, as much as I can, though not as much as I ought,
50   I am mindful of your passion,
your buffeting, your scourging, your cross, your wounds,
    how you were slain for me,
    how prepared for burial and buried;
    and also I remember your glorious Resurrection,
55   and wonderful Ascension.
All this I hold with unwavering faith,
    and weep over the hardship of exile,
    hoping in the sole consolation of your coming,
    ardently longing for the glorious contemplation of your face.

Read this passage through twice, noting Anselm's request to read slowly, before moving on to interact with the text.

1   Anselm begins by confessing the lukewarmness of his love for God. This is an allusion to the situation of the church in the Asian city of Laodicea, as described in

Revelation 3:14–22 – the only point in the New Testament at which the word "luke-warm" is used. Read through this passage, and note the characteristics of this church: you might list these as including being "lukewarm," "self-satisfied," and "unwilling to acknowledge dependence on God." How does this passage cast light on Anselm's understanding of his own spiritual state, and the manner in which it might be changed?

2   Anselm asks (lines 26–30) that the lukewarmness of his love for God might be "enkindled" – that is, set alight. How does he expect this to happen?

3   Anselm's reference to "remembering and meditating on the good things [God] has done" (lines 28–9) picks up on a major theme from the Psalms: recalling the great acts of God in the past. To see what Anselm has in mind, read Psalm 136. Each verse of this Psalm includes the refrain: "[God's] love endures for ever." Note how the Psalm sets out the great acts of God in history – for example, the creation of the world (verses 5–9), the exodus from Egypt (verses 10–15), and the entry into the promised land (verses 16–22). Anselm's approach mirrors that of the Psalms at this point.

4   At several points, Anselm expressed a sense of longing for God, often using imagery which suggests human emptiness. Work through the text, and identify as many images or phrases of this type as you can. What is the cumulative effect of these images and phrases?

5   Identify two images of separation used in this passage by Anselm to indicate his sense of distance from God. We shall explore them presently; at this stage, read the text again, and see if you can identify the images in question.

6   The first of these images is encountered at lines 45–6, and is that of an orphan who longs for a lost father. What emotions does Anselm arouse by his use of this image?

7   The second image is found at line 57, and is that of exile. What associations are linked with this image? And how does Anselm develop them? You may find it helpful to read pp. 93–4 first.

8   Anselm expresses his longing for God, and his sense that he at present does not possess God fully. What does he expect to happen? At what point does he introduce the theme of the "beatific vision" (see p. 78)? And what use does he make of it?

FOR FURTHER READING

G. R. Evans, *Anselm and Talking about God*. Oxford: Oxford University Press, 1978.
R. W. Southern, *St. Anselm and his Biographer*. Cambridge: Cambridge University Press, 1953.

Francis of Assisi

Francis of Assisi (1182–1226) was the son of Pietro di Bernadone, a wealthy merchant in the Italian city of Assisi. As a young man, he opted for a military career. This was not entirely successful, and came to an abrupt halt as he travelled from Assisi to take part in a battle in 1204. About 40 kilometers from Assisi, he experienced a vision and felt he should return home. Soon afterwards, he received a vision of the crucified Christ, and felt that he was being called to some special mission. He renounced the wealth of his father, and took upon himself a life of poverty. In 1224, the imprints of the wounds of the crucified Christ (usually referred to as "the stigmata") appeared on his body. Francis's life and ministry were marked by poverty and simplicity, and a particular closeness to the natural world.

This close affinity with the natural order is particularly important in relation to Franciscan spirituality. This can be seen stated with especial clarity in the famous *Canticle of the Sun*, which we shall consider below. This canticle represents an important affirmation of a positive attitude toward the creation, which is typical of Franciscan spirituality. The Canticle is noted for its theology of providence, in which the benefit of each aspect of creation for humanity is identified. The most famous feature of the canticle is its use of the terms "brother" and "sister" to refer to various aspects of the created order. Traditional English translations of this familiar poem have been heavily influenced by the need to ensure rhyming. My prose translation of the original Italian ignores such considerations in order to convey the sense of the poem, and has retained the lines of the original. Note that the first 23 lines, dealing with nature, date from an earlier point than the final 11, which extend the analysis to the world of human experience.

Francis of Assisi on the Creation

Most high, all-powerful and good Lord!
To you are due the praises, the glory,
the honor and every blessing,
To you only, O highest one, are they due
5   and no human being is worthy to speak of you.

Be praised, my Lord, with all your creatures
especially by brother sun
by whom we are lightened every day
for he is fair and radiant with great splendor
10   and bears your likeness, O highest one.

Be praised, my Lord, for sister moon and the stars
you have set them in heaven, precious, fair and bright.

Be praised, my Lord, by brother wind
and by air and cloud and sky and every weather
15   through whom you give life to all your creatures.

Be praised, my Lord, by sister water
for she is useful and humble and precious and chaste.

> Be praised, my Lord, by brother fire
> by him we are lightened at night
> 20   and he is fair and cheerful and sturdy and strong.
>
> Be praised, my Lord, by our sister, mother earth
> she sustains and governs us
> and brings forth many fruits and coloured flowers and plants.
>
> Be praised, my Lord, by those who have been pardoned by your love
> 25   and who bear infirmity and tribulation;
> blessed are those who suffer them in peace
> for by you, O highest one, they shall be crowned.
>
> Be praised, my Lord, by our sister, physical death
> From whom no one who lives can escape
> 30   woe to those who die in mortal sin
> but blessed are those who are found in your most holy will
> for the second death can do them no harm.
>
> May I bless and praise you, my Lord, and give you thanks
> and serve you with great humility.

Read the canticle twice, and then engage with it along the following lines.

1   One of the most distinctive features of the Canticle is its use of the language of brotherhood and sisterhood to refer to aspects of the created order, such as the sun and moon. Begin by identifying as many of these personifications as you can.

2   What is the effect of referring to the moon as "sister," and so forth? In what ways does it change our attitude to the created order?

3   The text begins by praising God, before moving on to celebrate the created order. How are these connected? In what way does Francis relate the praise of God with a survey of the creation?

4   Work through the first 23 lines of the canticle, noting the way in which each element of the creation is assigned a useful function. Why do you think Francis identified the utility of the wind, fire, water, and so forth?

5   Some scholars suggest that there is a discontinuity between the first section (lines 1–23) and the second (lines 24–34). What do you think?

6   Francis' own ministry acknowledged that every creature was to be thought of as special to God, created for a purpose – and to be respected, valued, and honored for that reason. In what ways does this canticle reflect this attitude?

7   In an age in which much of western society regards nature as something which is to be exploited as we please, what correctives to this attitude can be found in Francis' spirituality?

FOR FURTHER READING

John R. H. Moorman, *St Francis of Assisi: Writings and Early Biographies.* London: SPCK, 1979.

Brother Ramon, SSF, *Franciscan Spirituality: Following Francis Today.* London: SPCK, 1994.

Hugh of Balma

Tantalizingly little is known of this thirteenth-century Carthusian writer. While we know he was active during the thirteenth century, nothing is known for certain concerning the dates of his birth or death. Like many other Carthusian spiritual writers, the writer who is now known as "Hugh of Balma" chose to remain anonymous. It is thought that the author of the work *Viae Sion lugent* ("The Roads to Zion mourn") was prior of the Charterhouse (that is, the Carthusian house) at Meyriat, located roughly halfway between Lyons and Geneva. The work has been spuriously attributed to a number of leading medieval spiritual writers, including Jean Gerson and Bonaventure. The work is known to have been written before 1297 (in that Guigo de Ponte, who died in 1296, refers to it). It is also clearly of Carthusian origins, in that there are important references to the Carthusians at several points. This, incidentally, made the attribution to Bonaventure – who was a Franciscan – highly problematic, and even led some early editors to "modify" these passages to make it appear as if they did indeed refer to the Franciscan rather than the Carthusian order.

The Roads to Zion was widely translated in the centuries following its appearance, and translations are known in a number of western European languages, including English, French, German, and Portugese. Its many attractions include a clear statement of the classic "threefold path" of spiritual advancement through the *via purgativa* (the "way of cleansing," in which the soul is cleansed of sin); the *via illuminativa* (the "way of illumination," in which the soul is enlightened by rays of divine wisdom through meditation on Scripture and prayer); and the *via unitiva* (the "way of union," in which the soul is united with God). Hugh argues that it is essential to begin by confessing one's sins and meditating on Scripture. However, these can be thought of as supports which eventually can be dispensed with, once a certain critical stage has been reached. He uses the analogy of the construction of a stone bridge to make this point, as can be seen from the passage which follows.

Hugh of Balma on the Threefold Path

This way to God is threefold; that is, it consists of a way of cleansing (*via purgativa*), in which the human mind is disposed so that it may discern true wisdom; a way of illumination (*via illuminativa*), in which the mind is set on fire as it reflects with the fire of love; and the way of unity (*via unitiva*) in which the mind is carried upwards by
5 God alone, and is led beyond all reason, understanding and intelligence. Now when a bridge is being build, it should be noted that the builders first erect a wooden framework, over which the solid stonework is assembled. Then, when this has been completed, the wooden framework which had been supporting the stonework is completely removed. In the same way, the human mind (though initially imperfect in love) begins

10 to rise to the perfection of love through meditation until, strengthened by practice in
the love which leads to unity, it is raised far beyond itself ... Thus any new disciple
may rise by stages to the perfection of this knowledge by zealous application of the
way of cleansing. This is the way of novices or children. It begins with these words:
"Righteousness and judgement are the preparation for your throne" (Psalm 89:15).
15 After a short time (perhaps a month or so, as appropriate), the disciple may rise to love
by reflection, surrounded by the radiance of divine illumination. If anyone should think
that it is presumptuous that such a sinful soul should dare to ask Christ for the union
of love, they should recall that there is no difficulty provided that they first kiss his feet
by recalling their sins; then kiss his hand by recognizing his goodness to them; and
20 finally, go on to kiss him on the mouth, desiring Christ and clinging to him through
love alone ... [This leads to a knowledge in which] all reason, knowledge and understanding fall away, and the affection soars upwards, guided by love and passing all
human understanding, directing the mind only by the guidance of the union of love
towards the one who is the source of all goodness.

Read this passage through twice. Notice that the essential idea is that repentance
and understanding (gained, for example, through meditation on biblical passages) are essential to get the believer to the point at which direct knowledge of God
may be had – but, once this point has been reached, they are no longer necessary.
This teaching became the subject of debate in the fifteenth century, when the
"Tegernsee debate" broke out over whether it was possible to achieve mystical union
with God without any preceding or accompanying understanding or knowledge.
Hugh appears to have held that such knowledge and understanding are initially necessary, just as a wooden framework is necessary before a stone bridge can be constructed. But once this initial stage has been achieved and passed, they are no longer
necessary.

We shall explore Hugh's ideas by interacting with the text as follows.

1 What, according to Hugh, are the three stages in the spiritual life? How does
he characterize them?

2 Pay careful attention to the bridge analogy. Try to visualize the process of constructing a stone bridge. The basic analogy presupposes that the bridge is an arch,
held in place by a key-stone. Until that stone is in place, the stonework cannot support
itself – hence the need for the wooden framework to support it until this crucial stage
is reached. Once you can visualize the analogy, identify what its component parts are
meant to signify. According to Hugh, what does the wooden framework represent?
And the stonework?

3 Taking this analogy a stage further: imagine that the stonework of the bridge
is now in place. Is the wooden framework now necessary? And if not, does this mean
that it served no useful purpose? What conclusions does Hugh want you to draw
concerning the role of knowledge and understanding in relation to a mystical union
with God?

4 Notice the language that Hugh uses. There is a clear tension between "knowledge" and "love." How would you distinguish these two ideas?

5 Hugh uses the analogy of three types of kiss to illustrate the "threefold path." Why does he use the analogy of a kiss in the first place? How do they help illustrate the points in question?

6 While the full details of the "Tegernsee debate" need not concern us, that debate partly focused on the role of knowledge and understanding in Christian spirituality. What role does Hugh assign to them? What are the strengths and weaknesses of this approach?

FOR FURTHER READING

There is relatively little available in English on Hugh of Balma.

Robin Bruce Lockhart, *Halfway to Heaven: The Hidden Life of the Sublime Carthusians.* New York: Vanguard Press, 1985.

Dennis D. Martin, *Carthusian Spirituality: The Writings of Hugh of Balma and Guigo de Ponte.* New York: Paulist Press, 1997, 1–47.

Ludolf of Saxony

Ludolf of Saxony (*c*.1300–78) is a somewhat enigmatic figure, of whom relatively little is known. He is known to have entered the Order of Preachers and gained a qualification in theology before joining the Carthusians at Strasbourg in 1340. In 1343, he moved to the Carthusian house at Coblenz, becoming its Prior. However, he does not appear to have been particularly enthusiastic for the responsibilities of this office, and in 1348 he resumed his life as an ordinary monk. The remainder of his life was spent in the cities of Mainz and Strasbourg. It should be noted that this writer is also known as Ludolf the Carthusian, and that the German name "Ludolf" is often spelled in its Latinized forms as "Ludolphus" or "Ludolph."

Ludolf is remembered supremely for his *Vita Christi* ("The life of Christ"), which was first published at Cologne in 1474. The work is based largely on an earlier work by Michael de Massa (died 1337), which took the form of a life of Christ based on a number of highly-focused meditations. Ludolf's *Vita Christi* takes the form of an extended meditation on the life of Christ, interspersed with prayers and citations from earlier writers. Such compilations of earlier sayings or anecdotes were popular in the late Middle Ages, and were widely used both for personal devotion and as sourcebooks for preaching. In this work, Ludolf sets out his intention to "recount things according to certain imaginative representations" so that his readers may "make themselves present for those things which Jesus did or said." The process involves the use of the imagination to construct a vivid and realistic mental image of the biblical scene. The important thing here is the *immediacy* with which the reader may represent the things that Jesus said or did.

Ludolf of Saxony on Entering into Scripture

Draw close with a devout heart to the one who comes down from the bosom of the Father to the Virgin's womb. In pure faith be there with the angel, like another witness, at the moment of the holy conception, and rejoice with the Virgin Mother now with child for you. Be present at his birth and circumcision, like a faithful guardian, with St.
5 Joseph. Go with the Wise Men to Bethlehem and adore the little king. Help his parents carry the child and present him in the Temple. Alongside the apostles, accompany the Good Shepherd as he performs his miracles. With his blessed mother and St. John, be there at his death, to have compassion on him and to grieve with him. Touch his body with a kind of devout curiosity, handling one by one the wounds of your Saviour who
10 has died for you. With Mary Magdalene seek the risen Christ until you are found worthy to find him. Look with wonder at his ascent into heaven as though you were standing among his disciples on the Mount of Olives. Take your place with the apostles as they gather together; hide yourself away from other things so that you may be found worthy to be clothed from on high with the power of the Holy Spirit. If you want to draw
15 fruit from these mysteries, you must offer yourself as present to what was said and done through our Lord Jesus Christ with the whole affective power of your mind, with loving care, with lingering delight, thus laying aside all other worries and care. Hear and see these things being narrated, as though you were hearing with your own ears and seeing with your own eyes, for these things are most sweet to him who thinks on them with
20 desire, and even more so to him who tastes them. And although many of these are narrated as past events, you must meditate them all as though they were happening in the present moment, because in this way you will certainly taste a greater sweetness. Read then of what has been done as though they were happening now. Bring before your eyes past actions as though they were present. Then you will feel how full of wisdom
25 and delight they are.

Please read this passage through twice, before moving on to the seven points set out below.

1 Note the way in which Ludolf is concerned to draw his readers into the life of Christ. In what ways does he do this?

2 Ludolf identifies a number of episodes in the life of Christ which he regards as being of particular importance, and links these specifically with certain individuals who were present on that occasion. Make out a list of the occasions and the witnesses: for example, the circumcision is witnessed by Joseph, and so forth. You will also find it helpful to identify the biblical passages to which he alludes.

3 Now note the way in which Ludolf draws us into the narrative. He does not simply recount what happened; he asks us to do things which draw us into the narrative. In each of the episodes which Ludolf describes, identify what it is he asks you to do. For example, he asks you to help Mary and Joseph carry the baby Jesus to the Temple. Notice how Ludolf portrays you, the reader, as an active participant in the events which are being described. You are to *project yourself* into the action.

4   Read the following sentence again, and try to summarize in your owns words what Ludolf wants you to do. "If you want to draw fruit from these mysteries, you must offer yourself as present to what was said and done through our Lord Jesus Christ with the whole affective power of your mind, with loving care, with lingering delight, thus laying aside all other worries and care."

5   Having rephrased Ludolf, focus on three key phrases from this sentence: "with the whole affective power of your mind, with loving care, with lingering delight." Each of these phrases is of considerable importance. What does he mean by them?

6   One of Ludolf's concerns is to allow his readers to set distractions to one side, and focus on the reading of biblical passages relating to the life of Christ. He wants them to slow down and linger over the events described. His emphasis on "entering into" the scene, and using the "affective power" of the mind to allow us to experience the passages as immediate, direct, and present (rather than distant and past) allows us to get more from the text than we otherwise might. But notice how it has another effect: *it slows us down*. It takes more time to enter into the passage in this way than it does simply to read it. The result – as Ludolf intends – is that we "linger" over the passage, taking longer over it than we otherwise might, and thus gain more from it.

7   Could you compose a prayer which reflects the issues that Ludolf addresses in this passage?

FOR FURTHER READING

There is relatively little available on this neglected fourteenth-century writer. However, the
following works are recommended for those wishing to take things further.
M. I. Bodenstedt, *The Vita Christi of Ludolphus the Carthusian*. Washington, DC: Catholic
University of America, 1955.
M. I. Bodenstedt, *Praying the life of Christ*. Salzburg: James Hogg, 1973.

Julian of Norwich

Julian of Norwich (*c*.1342–after 1416) is perhaps the best known of all the English female spiritual writers, whether of the fourteenth century or beyond. Remarkably little is known about her. "Julian" was not her real name; its origins are due to the fact that she established her "anchorage" (literally, a place of retreat or isolation) next to St Julian's Church in Norwich. In some writings, she is referred to as "Juliana." According to her own account of her "shewings" (the Middle English term which is now usually translated as "revelations"), these were given to Julian at the age of thirty, in May 1373. All other dates in her life are the subject of conjecture, including both her birth and death. The date of her birth is usually established from her own assertion that she was thirty in 1373; the date of her death remains unknown, except that she is known to have received a bequest in 1412 (the last known date relating to her life).

The "Shewings" takes the form of a description of sixteen personal revelations, and subsequent reflection on their meanings, triggered off by Julian's serious illness in May 1373. While there are many themes that can be discerned within the text, two may be singled out for especial comment. The first is Julian's constant emphasis on the goodness and love of God for the world. Despite its weakness and frailty, it is the creation of God, and God loves and cares for it passionately. Despite all its trials and sorrows, in the end "all will be well." This note of reassurance is one of the most distinctive and admired features of the work. The second theme is the importance of prayer. For Julian, prayer is a thing of great delight to God, who rejoices when we pray. We should persevere in prayer, even when that prayer seems dry and useless. It is this theme which we shall explore further in the extract from the "Shewings."

The "Shewings" exists in two versions, which are generally referred to as the "short text" and "long text." The shorter version exists in one manuscript only, and may well represent an abbreviated version of the full text, suitable for the purposes of personal devotion. The extract for study is taken from the longer version.

Julian of Norwich on Prayer

These revelations were shown to a simple and uneducated creature on the eighth of May 1373. Some time earlier she had asked three gifts from God: (i) to understand his passion; (ii) to suffer physically while still a young woman of thirty; and (iii) to have as God's gift three wounds.

5   With regard to the first I had thought I had already had some experience of the passion of Christ, but by his grace I wanted still more. I wanted to actually be there with Mary Magdalen and the others who loved him, and with my own eyes to see and know more of the physical suffering of our Saviour, and the compassion of our Lady and of those who there and then were loving him truly and watching his pains. I would
10 be one of them and suffer with him. I had no desire for any other vision of God until after such time as I had died. The reason for this prayer was that I might more truly understand the passion of Christ.

The second came to me with much greater urgency. I quite sincerely wanted to be ill to the point of dying, so that I might receive the last rites of Holy Church, in the
15 belief – shared by my friends – that I was in fact dying. In this illness I wanted to undergo all those spiritual and physical sufferings I should have were I really dying, and to know, moreover, the terror and assault of the demons – everything, except death itself! My intention was that I should be wholly cleansed thereby through the mercy of God, and that thereafter, because of that illness, I might live more worthily of him.
20 Perhaps too I might even die a better death, for I was longing to be with my God.

There was a condition with these two desires: "Lord, you know what I am wanting. If it is your will that I have it ... But if not, do not be cross, good Lord, for I want nothing but your will."

As for the third, through the grace of God and the teaching of Holy Church, I devel-
25 oped a strong desire to receive three wounds, namely the wound of true contrition, the wound of genuine compassion, and the wound of sincere longing for God. There was no proviso attached to any part of this third prayer. I forgot all about the first two desires, but the third was with me continually.

Read the passage twice, and then interact with it along the following lines.

1   Julian opens by stressing her own lowly condition. She is "simple and uneducated.". What do you think lies behind these statements?

2   The passage deals with three "graces" which Julian hoped to obtain. Read the passage through, and ensure that you can identify all three. Which of them does Julian seem to regard as being the most significant?

3   Why does Julian want to see or experience the suffering of Christ on the cross? This is a recurrent theme in Christian spirituality, and Julian's interest in this theme is an excellent illustration of the way in which the passion of Christ relates to spirituality.

4   Julian's second desire is for physical illness. At first sight, this seems a rather morbid and curious request. What does she hope to gain from it? Note how her hope for a near-death experience is closely linked with her desire to be purified and to live a better life subsequently.

5   Read 2 Corinthians 12:7–10. Here Paul writes of how God humbled him through a "thorn in the flesh" (generally thought to have been an illness, possibly malaria, contracted during his missionary journeys). What lessons does Paul indicate that he learned from this illness? Can you see any parallels between Paul and Julian in this matter?

6   In a brief aside after this second request (lines 21–3), Julian writes of the tension she experiences in prayer. How would you describe this tension? For Julian, the important thing is that God's will should be done. This leads her on (in later sections of the "Shewings") to write of the Christian being united to God and thus joined to God's will. As a result, part of the process of spiritual growth is to learn to desire the things that God wills for us, and then to pray for them.

7   Julian's third request is that she should receive three wounds. What are they? Note that "contrition" can be thought of as "sorrow for sin." Are these three wounds related to each other in any way? And what benefits would they bring to Julian?

8   Julian seems to regard this third desire to be the most important. Why might this be so?

FOR FURTHER READING

Grace M. Jantzen, *Julian of Norwich: Mystic and Theologian*. London: SPCK, 1987.
Paul Molinari, *Julian of Norwich: The Teaching of a Fourteenth-Century Mystic*. New York: Arden Library, 1979.
Joan Nuth, *Wisdom's Daughter: The Theology of Julian of Norwich*. New York: Crossroad, 1991.

Martin Luther

Martin Luther (1483–1546) is one of the more significant figures of the Protestant Reformation. Born to a relatively prosperous German miner, Luther was initially intended by his father for a career in law. He attended the University of Erfurt from 1501 to 1505, and then proceeded briefly to study law. However, following a vow he made during a violent thunderstorm in 1505, Luther became a monk instead, and entered the Augustinian house at Erfurt. He was recognized by his superiors as having theological ability, and in 1512 was appointed professor of biblical studies at the University of Wittenberg. He came to have increasing misgivings over the theology of grace he encountered in some of his theological mentors, and came to place considerable emphasis upon the total gratuity of salvation, focusing particularly on the Pauline theme of "justification by faith." In 1517, he published the Ninety-Five Theses on indulgences; in 1520, he published three reforming pamphlets, from which our extract is taken. He was condemned by the Pope for his theological teachings, and in consequence began a program of reform which resulted in his breaking away from the medieval church. Modern Lutheranism bears many traces of his distinctive approaches to theology, liturgy, and particularly hymnody.

Although Luther is remembered primarily as a theologian and ecclesiastical activist, he had a deep pastoral concern for the spirituality of Christian believers. In addition to offering much practical advice to his readers (for example, when and how to pray), Luther also laid the foundations for an understanding of the mystic union between Christ and the believer. In his 1520 writing *The Freedom of a Christian*, Luther explored the nature and implications of this union for Christian spirituality. The work is written for a lay readership, and is intended to explain, in simple language, some of the theological themes which are of importance to Luther, and their practical relevance. In the passage in question, Luther emphasizes the critical role of faith in establishing this intimate relationship between Christ and the believer (attributing to "faith" many of the qualities which medieval writers tended to attribute to "love"). The passage reflects its sixteenth-century origins, not least in the way it assumes that the dignity of the husband is automatically conferred upon his wife.

Martin Luther on Union with Christ

Faith does not merely mean that the soul realizes that the divine word is full of all grace, free and holy; it also unites the soul with Christ, as a bride is united with her bridegroom. From such a marriage, as St Paul says (Ephesians 5:32–32), it follows that Christ and the soul become one body, so that they hold all things in common, whether
5 for better or worse. This means that what Christ possesses belongs to the believing soul; and what the soul possesses, belongs to Christ. Thus Christ possesses all good things and holiness; these now belong to the soul. The soul possesses lots of vices and sin; these now belong to Christ. Here we have a happy exchange and struggle. Christ is God and a human being, who has never sinned and whose holiness is unconquer-
10 able, eternal and almighty. So he makes the sin of the believing soul his own through its wedding ring, which is faith, and acts as if he had done it [i.e., sin] himself, so that

> sin could be swallowed up in him. For his unconquerable righteousness is too strong
> for all sin, so that is made single and free from all its sins on account of its pledge, that
> is its faith, and can turn to the eternal righteousness of its bridegroom, Christ. Now
> 15 is not this a happy business? Christ, the rich, noble, and holy bridegroom, takes in mar-
> riage this poor, contemptible and sinful little prostitute, takes away all her evil, and
> bestows all his goodness upon her! It is no longer possible for sin to overwhelm her,
> for she is now found in Christ and is swallowed up by him, so that she possesses a rich
> righteousness in her bridegroom.

Read this passage twice, noting the imagery which Luther uses, and particularly the important role of faith. Then interact with the passage as follows.

1   The image of a marriage is used extensively in this passage. What are the main points which Luther bases upon the analogy, or illuminates on its basis?

2   As we noted, Luther makes extensive use of the imagery of marriage in this analogy. Does the passage make any use of the theme of divorce?

3   For Luther, faith unites the soul with Christ. Notice how Luther draws a distinction between "believing that certain things are true" and a personal trust in God which brings about an intimate and personal union with Christ. In one of Luther's later writings, he refers to a "grasping faith" (*fides apprehensiva*) which "takes hold of this treasure, Jesus Christ." How does this later statement relate to the present passage?

4   Examine the marriage analogy closely, and identify the way in which Luther uses it to illustrate the distinction between a personal relationship with Christ, and the benefits which Christ confers upon the believer. What are those benefits?

5   Some scholars suggest that Luther sees the Christian life in terms of a "legal fiction," in that God treats us as if we are righteous when in reality we are sinners. Does the marriage analogy confirm or question this interpretation?

6   What is the point being made by the rather distasteful prostitute analogy?

7   It is clear that Luther intends the prostitute analogy to indicate that believers, even though sinful and lowly in status, are raised up on account of their relationship with Christ, just as a prostitute would find her social status raised considerably if she were to marry a prince. What spiritual conclusions does Luther want his readers to draw from this analogy?

8   Finally, it is clear that one of the themes which hovers around this passage is the question of the believer's struggle with sin. Pastorally, this issue is always of importance in relation to Christian spirituality. What insights does Luther want his readers to gain concerning the nature and power of sin from this passage?

FOR FURTHER READING

Roland Bainton, *Here I Stand: A Life of Martin Luther*. New York: New American Library, 1950.
Alister E. McGrath, *Luther's Theology of the Cross*. Oxford: Blackwell, 1985.
Randall C. Zachman, *The Assurance of Faith: Conscience in the Theology of Martin Luther and John Calvin*. Minneapolis: Fortress Press, 1993.

Ignatius Loyola

It is widely agreed that Ignatius Loyola (*c.*1491–1556) is one of the most important Spanish spiritual writers of the sixteenth century. Initially, Loyola's career was fairly typical of his age. After a period of service in the household of the Royal Treasurer of Castille, he joined the army of the Duke of Nájera. Any hopes he may have held for future advancement were called into question when he was wounded during the siege of Pamplona (May 1521). The leg wound which he received required a prolonged period of convalescence at the family home, the castle of Loyola. He had hoped to alleviate the boredom of this period of enforced rest by reading some novels; the family library, however, was not particularly well stocked. In the end, Loyola found himself reading Ludolf of Saxony's *Life of Christ*. As we noted earlier (p. 153), this work develops the idea of an imaginative projection of the reader into the biblical narrative. Although Loyola read other spiritual works (such as lives of the saints) at this time, there is little doubt that this work stimulated his thinking on the relation of the believer, God and the world.

The result of Loyola's immersion in this work was a decision to reform his life. His initial decision was to sell his possessions, and undertake a pilgrimage to Jerusalem. The latter task proved abortive. He was obliged to spend a period of ten months (March 1522–February 1523) at the town of Manressa waiting to be allowed to travel to Rome, prior to a further journey onward to Jerusalem. During that period, he developed the general approach to spirituality which is now embodied in the *Spiritual Exercises*. This book is primarily intended for those who conduct retreats, and is not really intended to be read by others. However, it has found a wide readership beyond its intended audience.

The most characteristic features of the *Spiritual Exercises* can be summarized as follows:

1   An imaginative approach to the reading of Scripture and prayer, in which those undertaking the exercises (often referred to as "exercitants") form mental images as aids to prayer and contemplation (see p. 85).

2   A structured and progressive program of reflection and meditation, which proceeds sequentially through the major themes of the Christian life. The four weeks specified for the *Exercises* focus on sin and its consequences; the life of Christ; the death of Christ; and the resurrection.

3   The use of a retreat director, who guides the exercitant through the exercises, allowing reflection on both God and self, leading to the taking of decisions for personal reform and renewal.

The "Ignatian retreat" has become a well established feature of modern Christian life, especially within Catholicism, just as Ignatian approaches to prayer have been welcomed by many who have found more cognitive or intellectual approaches to be spiritually dry and unhelpful.

The text chosen for study takes the form of extracts taken from the "Second Exercise" set for the first week of a retreat, focusing on the idea of sin and its consequences for the believer.

Ignatius Loyola on Imagining the Gravity of Sin

This is a meditation on our sins. After the preparatory prayer and two preambles, there are five points and a colloquy. . . .

Second preamble: this is to ask for what I desire. Here it will be to ask for a growing and intense sorrow and tears for my sins.

5 First point. This is the record of my sins. I will call to mind all the sins of my life, considering them year by year, and period by period. Three things will help me in this: first, I shall recall the place where I lived; secondly, my dealings with other people; and thirdly, the positions I have held. . . .
  Third point: I will consider who I am, and humble myself by means of examples:

10 1 What I am compared with all human beings?
   2 What are all human beings compared with the angels and saints of heaven?
   3 What is all creation in comparison with God? So what am I, alone on my own?
   4 I will consider all the corruption and putridity of my body.
   5 I will consider myself as a source of corruption and infection, the source of count-
15 less sins, evil and poison.

Fourth point: I will consider who the God against whom I have sinned really is, comparing myself against God's attributes and their opposites within me; God's wisdom with my ignorance; God's power with my weakness; God's justice with my iniquity; God's goodness with my wickedness

---

Read this passage through twice, and then begin to interact with it, using the following questions as a guide.

1 Notice how Loyola begins by making his intentions clear. The passage is a meditation on sin, and is intended to deepen our sense of shame and sorrow on our sin and its consequences. Note particularly how he engages with the emotional aspects of sin. Sin is not something which is meant to be understood, but something which generates an emotional reaction of sorrow.

2 Notice how Loyola offers a highly structured approach to meditation and reflection. The exercitant is taken through a series of points, each designed to allow maximum engagement with the issue of sin. This is particularly clear with the "first point," in which Loyola offers three frameworks for the recollection of sin: the places in which we have lived; the people with whom we have interacted; and the responsibilities or positions which we have held.

3 Notice also that Loyola is not prepared for exercitants to talk about "sin" in general or abstract terms. He wants them to identify and name their sins. Why do you think that he is so concerned to identify their individual sins, rather than just recognize that they are sinners in general?

4 One of the key points here is that Loyola wants to set an agenda for action on the part of the exercitant. To identify one's sins is one way of identifying the areas of one's life which need to be reformed.

5 Look at the "third point," and consider the first three examples. These can be seen as "examples of scale," which are intended to bring home the insignificance of the exercitant by comparing her with all of creation. Try to identify the logical progression within these three comparisons. What conclusion does Loyola want to be drawn? Notice how the comparisons involve (at any rate, for most people) the generation of mental pictures, a central element of Loyola's general approach.

6 What conclusions does he want to be drawn from the fourth and fifth "examples" of this point?

7 The "fourth point" involves a comparison between the exercitant and God. What purpose does this serve?

8 What prayer might Loyola wish to offer at the end of this section? You might like to reflect on this, and try writing down some ideas, before reading the text which follows. This is the colloquy with which Loyola concludes this exercise, and it indicates the importance of the theme of purposefully intending to reform and renew one's life:

> I will conclude with a colloquy, in which I praise the mercy of God our Lord, pouring out my thoughts and giving thanks that I have been granted life up to this point. I will then resolve, with God's grace, to amend things in the future.

FOR FURTHER READING

David Lonsdale, *Eyes to See, Ears to Hear: An Introduction to Ignatian Spirituality*. London: Darton, Longman and Todd, 1990.
Terence O'Reilly, *From Ignatius Loyola to John of the Cross: Spirituality and Literature in Sixteenth-century Spain*. Aldershot: Variorum, 1995.
Hugo Rahner, *Ignatius the Theologian*. London: Chapman, 1990.

Teresa of Ávila

Teresa of Ávila (1515–82) was born Teresa de Cepeda y Ahumada. She developed an interest in spirituality while still a relatively young girl, and at an early stage reached a decision to enter an order of Carmelite nuns at Ávila in 1535. At this stage, the convent in question did not make particularly severe demands of its members. Teresa found the life of prayer dry, difficult and unrewarding, and came close to abandoning it altogether. However in 1554 she had a powerful religious conversion experience, which led her to the conclusion that she had, up to this point, been trusting in her own efforts, rather than allowing God to refresh and renew her in "sweetness and glory." Her enthusiasm over her new experience of God received something of a setback when the spiritual directors she initially consulted informed her that they were probably satanic. However, Diego de Cetina suggested that her experiences were valid, and recommended that she focus her thoughts on the passion of Christ.

For Teresa, spiritual and institutional renewal were closely linked. She began a program of reform within the Carmelite order in 1562, founding the first "discalced" (that is, shoeless) Carmelite convent with a considerably stricter rule than that found elsewhere. The reform gained momentum, and was extended to male Carmelites in 1568. One of the first male discalced Carmelites was John of the Cross (born Juan de Yepes). Throughout her later career, she encountered serious (and occasionally violent) opposition from the "calced" Carmelites, who took exception to her more rigorous understanding of the religious life. Although her writings were initially placed on the Index of banned books, it was only a matter of time before their spiritual and literary merit were appreciated. She was canonized in 1622.

The three most important of Teresa's writings are her *Life*, *The Way of Perfection* and *The Interior Castle of the Soul*. The passage we shall be interacting with is taken from her *Life*, perhaps the most difficult of her best-known works. The book was written to serve two purposes: to provide an account of her spiritual development on the one hand, and on the other to describe her spiritual experiences and methods of prayer, which were regarded as controversial. (A later work, *The Way of Perfection*, focused on these experiences and methods, and aimed to make them more widely known.) The first draft of the *Life* was completed by June 1562; the work was revised over the period 1563–5 in response to the comments of her advisors. A particularly important addition is the section now contained as chapters 11–22, in which Teresa, at the insistence of García de Toledo, set out a systematic account of her understanding of prayer. Initially, reaction was generally favorable; however, Teresa had made enemies, and the manuscript was confiscated by the Inquisition in 1574. It was only after her death that the work was recovered, and began to be read more widely.

The section chosen for detailed study is taken from the opening part of the major section inserted by Teresa in the revision of the first draft of the text. As noted above, chapters 11–22 aim to set out Teresa's views on prayer in a systematic manner. We shall be focusing on the opening part of that section, in which Teresa uses the analogy of a garden to set out the various modes of prayer.

Teresa of Ávila on a Spiritual Garden

The beginner must think of herself as someone who is setting out to establish a garden on unfruitful ground, full of weeds, in which the Lord is to take delight. His Majesty uproots the weeds and will replace them with good plants. Now let us suppose that

this has already been done. A soul has resolved to practise prayer, and has actually
5 begun to do so. What we have to do now is (like good gardeners!) to make these plants
grow. We must water them carefully, so that they do not die, but may produce flowers
which will send forth a great fragrance to give refreshment to our Lord, so that he will
come to the garden often for pleasure and delight.

So let us consider how this garden may be watered. This will allow us to know what
10 we need to do, what labor will be necessary, and for how long this labor is required.
It seems to me that the garden can be watered in four ways:

- By drawing the water from a well, which is very laborious.
- By a water-wheel and buckets, using a windlass to draw the water. This is less laborious, and produces more water.
15 - By a river or stream, which waters the ground much better. It saturates it more thoroughly and, as there is less need to water it so often, it is correspondingly less laborious.
- By heavy rain, in which the Lord waters it without any labor on our part. This way is vastly superior to the others which have been described.

20   I now come to my point. These four means of watering the garden need to be applied
if it is to be fertile. If the garden has no water, it will be ruined. It seems to me that
this way can be used to explain something about the four stages of prayer to which
the Lord, in his goodness, has occasionally brought me.

Read the text twice, and then begin to engage with it, using the following points
to guide you.

1   Teresa uses the analogy of a garden as she sets out her views on prayers. Why
should she have chosen such an image? You will find it helpful to read Genesis 2:8–10,
and note the language used about the Lord planting a garden. Note particularly the
emphasis placed upon the garden being watered from four sources (Genesis 2:10).
You might also like to note the theme of the Lord "walking in the garden," which
is introduced at Genesis 3:8.

2   Alongside the image of a delightful garden, in which the Lord takes great pleasure, we find the more practical image of the need for this garden to be watered.
Bear in mind that the inland regions of Spain are often hot and dry, especially in
summer, so that the practical necessity of this issue would have been immediately
obvious to her readers. It is also important to note how the importance of water to
plants figures prominently in parts of the Old Testament. Read Psalm 1:3. What
point does it make about the righteous person? And how does the analogy of the
tree illuminate this?

3   Teresa identifies four major ways of watering a garden. Work your way through
them slowly, asking two questions as you do so. First, how much water does each
method deliver? Second, how much effort does it involve on the part of the
gardener?

4 Teresa then compares the watering of the garden to the refreshment of the soul through prayer. How effective is this comparison?

5 Teresa then sets out four models of prayer. We do not have the time to engage with these in detail, although you are strongly encouraged to read further about them, both in the *Life* itself, and also the substantial body of secondary literature concerning Teresa. At this stage, however, use the analogy offered by Teresa to identify the differences between the types of prayer she will later describe.

6 Teresa's early period in her spiritual development turned out to be rather arid. She later attributed this to placing too much reliance on her own efforts, and not relying enough on God. Which of the four models of prayer corresponds to this early stage in her development?

7 Read the first paragraph of the passage again closely. On the basis of the passage, what does Teresa consider one of the main purposes of prayer do be?

FOR FURTHER READING

Stephen Clissold, *St Teresa of Avila*. London: Sheldon Press, 1979.
E. Trueman Dicken, *The Crucible of Love: A Study of the Mysticism of St Teresa of Jesus and St John of the Cross*. London: Darton, Longman and Todd, 1963.
E. Allison Peers, *Mother of Carmel: A Portrait of St Terea of Jesus*. London: SCM Press, 1979.

Charles Wesley

Charles Wesley (1707–88), along with his elder brother John Wesley (1703–91), was one of the leading figures in the evangelical revival within the English church of the eighteenth century, and a founder of the form of Protestant Christianity known as "Methodism." Wesley went up to Christ Church, Oxford, in 1726, and subsequently travelled to the colony of Georgia in North America to undertake pastoral and evangelistic work. This was not an encouraging experience. Wesley underwent a conversion experience in May 1738, in which he recalls for the first time "being at peace with God and rejoicing in hope." Although Wesley gave much time to open-air preaching, the form of spiritual writing which he made his own was the congregational hymn. For both Wesleys, the hymn was a means of theological education and spiritual uplifting, through which the congregations which sang them might both enjoy the process of singing while absorbing the ideas and themes conveyed in and through the words.

Our text for study takes the form of one of his best-known hymns. The particular theme which dominates this hymn is that of assurance. Christians may rest assured that they have been saved through Christ, and delivered from the powers of darkness and sin. The background to the hymn lies in the profound conversion experience which Wesley experienced on May 21, 1738 through the ministry of the Moravian Peter Böhler. In this hymn, written a year after this experience, Wesley put into verse his understanding of the significance of the death of Christ for Christian believers. The hymn brings together a remarkably rich range of images relating to salvation, including liberation and enlightenment. The hymn was originally entitled "Free Grace." Note that the curious form " 'Tis" is an archaic version of "It is"; similarly, "quickening" is an archaic form of "life-giving."

Charles Wesley on Christian Assurance

1   And can it be that I should gain
      An interest in the Saviour's blood?
Died he for me? – who caused his pain?
      For me? – who Him to death pursued?
Amazing love! How can it be
That Thou, my God, shouldst die for me?

2   'Tis mystery all! The Immortal dies!
      Who can explore his strange design?
In vain the first-born Seraph tries
      To sound the depths of love divine.
'Tis mercy all! Let earth adore;
Let angel minds inquire no more.

3   He left his Father's throne above
      (So free, so infinite his grace!)
Emptied himself of all but love,
      And bled for Adam's helpless Race.
'Tis Mercy all, immense and free,
For, O my God! it found out me!

4   Long my imprisoned spirit lay,
      Fast bound in Sin and Nature's Night
Thine eye diffused a quickening ray;
      I woke; the dungeon flamed with light.
My chains fell off, my heart was free,
I rose, went forth, and followed Thee.

5   No condemnation now I dread,
      Jesus, and all in Him, is mine.
Alive in Him, my living head,
      And clothed in righteousness divine,
Bold I approach the eternal throne,
And claim the crown, through Christ my own.

Read the hymn through twice; if you know the tune (Sagina), you might like to try singing it to yourself. Now interact with the text, as follows.

1   Taking the hymn one verse at a time, provide a summary of the key point being made in each. Can you identify a logical progression of thought as the hymn proceeds?

2 What is the central question which dominates the first verse? In what way do the second and third verses offer an answer to this question?

3 Compare the first and final verses. Note how the first verse has a questioning, skeptical and uncertain tone to it, whereas the final verse is marked by confidence and boldness. What reasons can be given for this change of tone?

4 One of the central themes of the hymn is the immensity and availability of the love of God for sinners. In what ways does Wesley convey this theme in the second and third verses?

5 The fourth verse contains a richness of imagery relating to the meaning of the death of Christ. How many different images can you discern? Why do you think Wesley uses so many images in this way?

6 What does Wesley want us to believe as a result of singing this hymn? Note in particular the emphasis upon the love of God for us, the believer's relationship with Christ, and the affirmation of the hope of heaven.

7 What do you think Wesley would like those who have sung this hymn to do? Part of the answer, of course, is to internalize the doctrinal themes which he explores and affirms. However, it is widely thought that one of the most important themes is the assurance of faith – that the believer can get on with the business of living a full and authentic Christian life without constantly having to worry about whether that life has really been begun, or whether God really loves the believer.

FOR FURTHER READING

Frank Baker, *Charles Wesley's Verse: An Introduction*. 2nd edn. London: Epworth Press, 1988.
John Lawson, *A Thousand Tongues: The Wesley Hymns as a Guide to Scriptural Teaching*. Exeter: Paternoster Press, 1987.

John Henry Newman

John Henry Newman (1801–90) is widely regarded as one of the more significant nineteenth-century religious writers. Newman underwent an evangelical conversion while at school at Ealing, and began his religious life with a generally Reformed outlook on the Christian faith. He went up to Trinity College, Oxford, in 1816, and was elected to a Fellowship at Oriel College in 1822. At Oriel, he came into contact with a group of liberal Anglicans (the "Noetics") who had considerable influence upon him. Although initially evangelical in his outlook, Newman found himself increasing moving in a more liberal direction.

This was not, however, to be a permanent feature of Newman's spirituality. Under the influence of John Keble, Hurrell Froude and Robert Isaac Wilberforce (all fellows of Oriel in the mid-1820s), Newman found himself gaining an increasing interest in and respect for more catholic approaches to the Christian life, especially in relation to the doctrine of the church. He was appointed as Vicar of the University Church of St Mary the Virgin, Oxford, in 1828, and remained in this position until his growing disillusionment with the Church of England led him to resign it in 1843. He was received into the Catholic church in 1845, ordained priest in 1847, and created a cardinal in 1879.

Newman is of immense importance in relation to the development of English Christianity. Along with John Keble (1792–1866) and Edward Bouverie Pusey (1800–82), Newman was a leading light of the "Oxford Movement," which sought the recovery of catholic belief and practice within the Church of England. Although Newman declared that he was "not a theologian," he nevertheless produced a number of works of theological importance, including *The Arians of the Fourth Century* (1833) and *An Essay on the Development of Christian Doctrine* (1845). He was instrumental in establishing a Catholic university in Ireland (University College, Dublin), and set out his reflections on the nature of a university in *The Idea of a University* (1873).

Yet Newman was never comfortable with the idea of a purely academic theology, and showed himself to be acutely aware of the importance of forging links between theology and Christian life and experience. Newman's concern for spirituality is probably best studied from the sermons which he preached at the University Church, which were published as *Parochial and Plain Sermons*, the first volume of which was published in March 1834. Although Newman initially modelled his preaching style on that of the noted Cambridge evangelical preacher Charles Simeon, from October 1831 he developed his own distinctive approach. Newman came to dislike evangelical forms of preaching, believing that they deadened the minds of their recipients. He was particularly critical of evangelical preachers who failed to appreciate a point made in the eighteenth century by Bishop Butler (the author of the *Analogy of Religion*), who argued that "if we say things over without feeling them, we become worse, not better." Newman's concern was for the impact of such preaching on children: "Children who are taught, since they were weaned, to rely on the Christian atonement, and in whose ears have been dinned the motives of gratitude to it before their hearts are trained to understand them, are deadened to them by the time they are twenty-one."

Newman's own preaching style shows a real concern for issues of spirituality, particularly in relation to the correlation of faith, reason, and experience. In particular, the issue of "self-knowledge" is identified as of considerable importance. Newman stresses the danger of self-deception in relation to the Christian life, noting especially the dangers of intellectual pride as a barrier to faith. It is perhaps no accident that Newman often feels obliged to mention specifically academic weaknesses, characteristic of communities such as Oxford University. The text which we shall be examining, taken from the *Parochial and Plain Sermons*, addresses the issue of academic arrogance as a barrier to true faith and spiritual development. The text on which Newman comments is 1 Corinthians 3:18–19.

John Henry Newman on the Sin of Academic Arrogance

Among the various deceptions against which St Paul warns us, a principal one is that of a *false wisdom*; as in the text. The Corinthians prided themselves on their intellectual acuteness and knowledge; as if anything could equal the excellence of Christian love. Accordingly, St Paul writing to them says, "Let no man deceive himself. If any
5   man among you seemeth to be wise in this world" (i.e., has the reputation of wisdom in the world). "let him become a fool" (what the world calls a fool), "that he may [really] be wise". . . . This warning of the Apostle against *our trusting our own wisdom* may lead us, through God's blessing, to some profitable reflections today.

The world's wisdom is said to be *foolishness* in God's sight; and the end of it error,
10 perplexity and then ruin. "He taketh the wise in their own craftiness." Here is one especial reason why professed inquirers after truth do not find it. They seek it in a wrong way, by a vain wisdom, which leads them away from the truth, however it may seem to promise success. Let us then inquire what is this *vain wisdom*, and then we shall the better see how it leads men astray . . .
15 The false wisdom of which St Paul speaks in the text is a trusting in our own powers for arriving at religious truth, instead of taking what is divinely provided for us, whether in nature or revelation. . . . The first sin of men of superior understanding is to *value* themselves upon it, and look down upon others. They make intellect the measure of praise and blame; and instead of considering a common *faith* to be the bond of union
20 between Christian and Christian, they dream of some other fellowship of civilization, refinement, literature, science, or general mental illumination, to unite gifted minds one with another. Having thus cast down moral excellence from its true station, and set up the usurping empire of mere reason, they next place a value upon all truths exactly in proportion to the possibility of proving them by means of that mere reason.
25 Hence moral and religious truths are thought little of by them, because they fall under the province of *conscience* far more than of the intellect. Religion sinks in their estimation, or becomes of no account; they begin to think all religions alike; and no wonder, for they are like men who have lost the faculty of discerning colours, and who never, by any exercise of reason, can make out the difference between white and black.
30 . . . And all these inducements to live by sight and not by faith are greatly increased, when men are engaged in any pursuit which properly *belongs* to the intellect. Hence sciences conversant with experiments on the material creation tend to make men forget the existence of spirit and the Lord of spirits.

Read this passage twice, and then interact with it as follows.

1   The passage relates to 1 Corinthians 3:18–19. Read this through, preferably in a modern translation. (Newman uses the King James Version.) Note how Newman glosses the text, placing a particular interpretation on "wise" and "fool." This allows him to relate the text to his predominantly academic audience.

2   Newman clearly regards academic pride as a serious obstacle to faith and spiritual growth. Why?

3 Newman establishes a link between academic pride and rationalism. Make sure that you can follow his argument on this point. How convincing do you find the argument?

4 The sermon was preached at a time when the natural sciences were beginning to emerge as significant at Oxford University. What reference does Newman make to this discipline? And what spiritual danger does he identify as arising from it?

5 What do you think Newman wanted his audience to do as a result of hearing this sermon?

6 Could you write a prayer which echoes the main concerns of this sermon?

FOR FURTHER READING

Owen Chadwick, *Newman*. Oxford: Oxford University Press, 1983.
Sheridan Gilley, *Newman and His Age*. London: DLT, 1990.
Ian Ker, *Healing the Wound of Humanity: The Spirituality of John Henry Newman*. London: DLT, 1993.

James I. Packer

At first sight, it might seem strange to include a twentieth-century writer in this section. To speak of a "classic" text immediately suggests an *old* text. Yet it is clear that a number of twentieth-century writers have achieved classic status in the eyes of their readers, such as Thomas Merton and Simone Weil. The final author to be included in this section has been recognized by many as having achieved this status. However, he has been included because, in many ways, he represents an *older* tradition of spirituality – that associated with the Puritans. Part of the significance of James I. Packer (1926–   ) is that his approach to spirituality, particularly in its relation to theology, represents a significant restatement and development of the spirituality of the Puritans. To study his writings is thus to engage with this classic tradition; Packer is one of its most creative contemporary exponents.

Packer was converted to Christianity in the 1940s while a classics student at Oxford University. After periods in parish ministry and theological education in England, he emigrated to Canada in 1979 to become professor of theology at Regent College, Vancouver. Regent College has subsequently established a reputation for its creative attempts to bring theology and spirituality together.

Although Packer has published many works, he is best known for the work entitled *Knowing God*, which has become a landmark in modern evangelical spirituality. The work had its origins in a series of articles published over a period of five years in *The Evangelical Magazine*, an obscure publication with a limited readership. The objective which Packer set himself in writing the work was to allow his readers to encounter and experience the *reality* of God, rather than just refine the way in which they *thought* about God. God is one who is *known*, not merely *known about*. Underlying *Knowing God* can be discerned a set of theological guidelines which –

like the title of the book itself – can be argued to derive from the reformer John Calvin (1509–64), for whom Packer had considerable admiration. Packer identifies four main themes which occur in Calvin's writings.

1 "Knowledge of God" does not refer to some natural human awareness of God, but to a knowledge which arises within a relationship.
2 Knowledge of God is more than any particular experience of God. Faith is about trust in God, from which particular experiences of God have their origins.
3 Knowledge of God is "more than knowing *about* God," although knowing about God is its foundation. Packer here draws a distinction between "knowledge by description" and "knowledge by acquaintance." While it is necessary to have a correct understanding of God as the righteous, wise and merciful creator and judge, true knowledge of God must also be "relational knowledge, knowledge that comes to us in the relation of commitment and trust, faith and reliance."
4 To know God is also to know God's relationship to us. Calvin affirmed that all human wisdom could be summed up as "knowledge of God and of ourselves," and stressed that these two were inseparable. To know God is to know ourselves; to know ourselves truly, we must know God. "Knowing God" is therefore "not knowing God in isolation; it is knowing God in his relationship to us, that relationship in which he gives himself and his gifts to us for our enrichment." To know God, we need to know his gracious gifts to us, and our need for such gifts in the first place.

On the basis of this analysis, Packer concludes by declaring that "knowing God" consists of three components, which must be taken together:

1 apprehension of what God is;

2 application to ourselves of what God is and what God gives;

3 adoration of God, as the one who gives these gifts.

Packer's major work *Knowing God* can be seen as a careful exposition of these three components, which are presented in a closely interrelated manner. Packer's general strategy is to begin by allowing his readers to apprehend the reality of God; then to move on to allow them to apply these insights to their lives; and finally, to respond to God in adoration.

Packer's spiritual insights are rigorously grounded in theology. The application of theology to life – a key theme in Puritan writings – can be seen at point after point in Packer's writings, especially *Knowing God*. The passage following below is a remarkably fine application of the doctrine of providence to the personal life of the Christian believer. Notice how Packer uses a series of phrases and statements to develop and explore what is substantially the same rich theme – the providential care of God for his people. In this case, Packer focuses this theological theme on the individual; elsewhere, he applies this and other themes to different contexts, such as the life of the church. Packer does not merely state a theological premise; he aims to apply it to the life of the believer – in short, he seeks *to make it real*. In the section of the work which we shall be studying, Packer explores the theme of "knowing God" with particular reference to the converse of this – namely, that God knows us.

James I. Packer on Being Known by God

What matters supremely, therefore, is not, in the last analysis, the fact that I know God, but the larger fact which underlies it – the fact that *he knows me*. I am graven on the palms of his hands. I am never out of his mind. All my knowledge of him depends on his sustained initiative in knowing me. I know him, because he first knew me, and con-
5 tinues to know me. He knows me as a friend, one who loves me; and there is no moment when his eye is off me, or his attention distracted from me, and no moment, therefore, when his care falters.

This is momentous knowledge. There is unspeakable comfort – the sort of comfort that energises, be it said, not enervates – in knowing that God is constantly taking care
10 of me in love, and watching over me for my good. There is tremendous relief in knowing that his love to me is utterly realistic, based at every point on prior knowledge of the worst about me, so that no discovery now can disillusion him about me.

Read this passage twice, and then begin to interact with it as follows.

1   Note the powerful imagery used: we are "graven on the palms of his hands." This image derives from Isaiah 49:16 "See, I have engraved you on the palms of my hands." The King James Version uses the older term "graven"; Packer here alludes to this classic translation. The image acts as a stimulus to the human imagination, in that it immediately evokes the image of the hands of God the creator (an image used extensively in the Christian tradition – see Irenaeus of Lyons for its use) being wounded in order to save his creation. The creator and redeemer are one and the same.

2   More specifically, the image evokes the deeply moving scene of the crucifixion, in which Christ's hands were pierced by nails. It also calls to mind the remarkable scene of recognition in which Thomas – the one who doubted the reality of the resurrection – was reassured of the reality of the presence of the risen Lord, by being allowed to see the wounds in the hands of Jesus (John 20:24–28). Packer's imagery is thus grounded in Scripture, and evokes the recollection of appropriate biblical passages on the part of his readers.

3   Note how Packer's prose is rich in allusions to passages of Scripture, none of which are explicitly identified. Once more, the effect is to generate a cascade of biblically-focused reflection on the part of the reader. For example, the use of the phrase "I am never out of his mind" will immediately evoke the memory of a whole series of biblical passages, particularly those in the prophetic literature referring to God's constant love for and attention to his wayward people. "Can a mother forget the baby at her breast and have no compassion on the child she

has borne? Though she may forget, I will not forget you!" (Isaiah 49:15). The reference to God knowing us before we knew him immediately calls to mind the affirmation of the priority of God's love for us in the First Letter of John (1 John 4:19). The affirmation of the constant watch of God over his people ("there is no moment when his eye is off me") will call to mind the great statements, particularly in the Psalter, concerning the Lord's continual watch over and care for his people: "He who watches over Israel will neither slumber nor sleep" (Psalm 121:4).

4   What are the differences between "knowing" and "knowing about"? How could you illustrate the point at issue? How important do you think it is? Is it fair to suggest that theology concerns *knowing about God*, whereas spirituality is about *knowing God*?

5   What is the point being made in the second paragraph? Read Psalm 139:1–6. In what way does Packer develop the themes of that Psalm? And what does he mean by the "comfort that energises, not enervates?"

FOR FURTHER READING

Alister McGrath, *To Know and Serve God: A Biography of James I. Packer.* London: Hodder & Stoughton, 1997. North American edition: *J. I. Packer: A Biography.* Grand Rapids, MI: Baker, 1998.

Conclusion: Where Next?

This chapter has stressed the importance of actively engaging with works of Christian spirituality, and offered a number of single case studies designed to encourage and guide you in this process of engagement. Once more, it must be stressed that the works selected for engagement in this way are not being treated as if they are totally representative of the extensive tradition of writing in this field. They have been selected on the basis of the ease with which it is possible to interact with them, which it is hoped will encourage you to move on and engage with more demanding texts in the future.

The present chapter has aimed to develop your ability to engage and interact with texts by studying short sections from much larger works. While this exercise is thoroughly worthwhile, it should be noted that you should consider your final goal to be the engagement with entire works. Extracts from longer works can only be fully appreciated by understanding the argument up to that point, the writer's personal style and distinctive use of imagery, and the point at which the writer wishes to leave you. Now that you have begun to gain confidence in interacting with classic texts, you should consider wrestling with a text in its entirety. For example, on p. 146 we looked at a section of Anselm of Canterbury's "Prayer to Christ." You might like to look at the full version of that prayer, which is relatively compact.

The following suggestions are intended to help you take your interest in the subject further.

1   As has been stressed throughout this book, spirituality is about *doing*, not just thinking or reflecting. To learn more about evangelical Bible studies, you should join an evangelical Bible study group. To learn more about Ignatian spirituality, you should go on an Ignatian retreat. Try to find out ways in which you can get involved with groups or organizations which will help you take your interest further.

2   Many colleges, seminaries, and churches organize conferences and summer schools which focus on spirituality. These often take the form of historical surveys or focus on one specific writer or school. This book will have taught you enough to allow you to gain the maximum benefit from such further study, and you are strongly encouraged to take this study further in this way. The increase in interest in spirituality has reached such levels that many seminaries and colleges now offer part-time courses in the subject; if you have the time available, this can be a fascinating and helpful way of developing your personal faith.

3   You can develop your interest in a particular spiritual writer, or group of writers, either by reading on your own, or attending courses dealing with them. In the case of leading spiritual writers, you can easily obtain full details of their main writings, as well as access the secondary literature about them. Writers that you may find helpful to study in this way include Bonaventure, Thomas à Kempis, Julian of Norwich, Martin Luther, Ignatius Loyola, John of the Cross, Jonathan Edwards, or Thomas Merton. You may also find it interesting to explore groups of writers – for example, female spiritual writers of the Middle Ages. Alternatively, you can develop your interest by focusing on a school of thought. Such schools of thought might include Benedictine, Carthusian, or Dominican spirituality of the thirteenth and fourteenth centuries; the *Devotio Moderna*; English mysticism in the fourteenth century; English or North American Puritanism; or the French religious writers of the seventeenth century. A further possibility is to focus on a particular theme in spirituality – for example, the theme of solitude.

4   You will also find it invaluable to explore the immense range of resources relating to Christian spirituality now available on the Internet, some of which are noted in this work (pp. 175–7).

At this point, our introduction to the field of Christian spirituality must end. Its purpose has been to acquaint you with the basic themes, personalities, and schools of thought in this field, to enable you to get the maximum enjoyment and satisfaction from the further exploration of the field that lies ahead for you. It is hoped that this book will have stimulated your interest in the subject of Christian spirituality, and encouraged you to want to learn more.

CHRISTIAN SPIRITUALITY: INTERNET RESOURCES

The Internet is such a rich source of materials that it would be unthinkable to omit any reference to the resources which it makes available. The following site locations are correct at the time of publication; please note that Internet addresses often change rapidly, making it difficult to keep this section up to date. One of the most effective ways of locating resources of potential value is to search for the words "Christian spirituality" using your favorite search engine. What follows constitutes a representative and useful sample of key resources.

MAJOR INDIVIDUALS OR SCHOOLS OF THOUGHT

Augustine
http://ccat.sas.upenn.edu/jod/augustine.html

Dietrich Bonhoeffer
http://www.cyberword.com/bonhoef/

Carmelite Spirituality
http://www.frontiernet.net/~ocarmvoc/spiritua.html

Carthusian Spirituality
http://www.users.dircon.co.uk/~marcpip/cart/c-spirit.htm

John Cassian
http://www.osb.org/osb/gen/topics/lectio/cassian/inst/index.html

Celtic Spirituality
http://www2.gol.com:80/users/stuart/celtihs.html

English Mystics
http://www.mindspring.com/~mccolman/unknowing.ht

Gregory of Nyssa
http://www.ucc.uconn.edu/~das93006/nyssa.html

Bede Griffiths
http://www.ecsd.com/~grace/jmabry/bede.html

Hildegard of Bingen
http://www.uni-mainz.de/~horst/hildegard/ewelcome.html

John of the Cross
http://www.ocd.or.at/ics/others/cs6.html

C. S. Lewis
http://ernie.bgsu.edu/~edwards/lewis.html
http://cslewis.drzeus.net/

Thomas Merton
http://acad.smumn.edu/merton/merton.html
http://edge.net/~dphillip/Merton.html

Therese of Lisieux
http://www2.dcci.com/ocdokla/

Teresa of Ávila
http://www.ocd.or.at/lit/teresa/life/main.html

READINGS IN CHRISTIAN SPIRITUALITY

Excellent collections of texts are maintained at the following locations:

http://ccel.wheaton.edu/
http://www.ewtn.com/New_library/library1.htm
http://www.chass.utoronto.ca:8080/~degregor/spirituality.html
http://www.mcgill.pvt.k12.al.us/jerryd/cm/spirit.htm

In addition, the following specific sites may be consulted:

John Cassian
http://www.osb.org/osb/gen/topics/lectio/cassian/inst/index.html

Cyril of Alexandria
http://www.nwmissouri.edu/~0500074/cyrlhome.html

John Donne
http://www.users.csbsju.edu/~eknuth/jd/index.html

Gregory of Nyssa
http://www.ucc.uconn.edu/~das93006/nyssa.html

Madame Guyon
http://ccel.wheaton.edu/guyon/auto/autobi.htm

John of the Cross
http://www.ocd.or.at/ics/john/works.htm
http://ccel.wheaton.edu/john_of_the_cross/

Julian of Norwich
http://140.190.128.190/merton/julian.html

Lasallian Spirituality
http://www.catholic.org/delasalle/1.3.2.html

Brother Lawrence
http://ccel.wheaton.edu/bro_lawrence/practice/practice.html

Ignatius Loyola
http://ccel.wheaton.edu/ignatius/exercises/exercises.html

Monastic Spirituality
http://www.christdesert.org/noframes/scholar/monastic_spirituality.html
http://www.csbsju.edu/osb/cist/melleray/html/primer.html
http://www.csbsju.edu/library/internet/theomons.html

Mysticism
http://www.clas.ufl.edu/users/gthursby/mys/index.htm

Blaise Pascal
http://www.users.csbsju.edu/~eknuth/pascal.html

Jan Ruysbroeck
http://ccel.wheaton.edu/ruysbroeck/US_ONLY/adornment/

Servite Spirituality
http://www.weblifepro.com/vocations/osm_spir.html

Evelyn Underhill
http://ccel.wheaton.edu/underhill/mysticism/

GENERAL THEMES IN CHRISTIAN SPIRITUALITY

What follows is a loose collection of material relating to prayer, spiritual direction, journal-keeping and other related issues.

http://landru.i-link-2.net/shnyves/prayer.html
http://www.mcgill.pvt.k12.al.us/jerryd/cm/devotion.htm
gopher://gopher.luc.edu:7000/11/spirituality/prayers
http://www.nwu.edu/lutheran/luther.html
http://maple.lemoyne.edu/~bucko/retreat.html#1
http://www.io.com/~lefty/Centering_Prayer.html
http://maple.lemoyne.edu/~bucko/krivak.html
http://www.mother.com/~flindahl/devnexus.htm

GLOSSARY OF TERMS

What follows is a brief discussion of a series of technical terms that the reader is likely to encounter in the course of reading works relating to Christianity in general, or Christian spirituality in particular. Many of the terms are considered in greater detail within the text of this work.

Abandonment
This term, which is often used to translate the French word "abandon," refers to a trusting acceptance in divine providence, and a willingness to live out the Christian life on the basis of that trust. It is particularly associated with writers such as Jean-Pierre de Caussade (p. 46), but can be found in other writers of the period, such as St Francis de Sales and Jacques Benigne Bossuet.

Adoptionism
The heretical view that Jesus was "adopted" as the Son of God at some point during his ministry (usually his baptism), as opposed to the orthodox teaching that Jesus was Son of God by nature from the moment of his conception.

Alexandrian School
A patristic school of thought, especially associated with the city of Alexandria in Egypt, noted for its Christology (which placed emphasis upon the divinity of Christ) and its method of biblical interpretation (which employed allegorical methods of exegesis). A rival approach in both areas was associated with Antioch.

Anabaptism
A term derived from the Greek word for "re-baptizer," and used to refer to the radical wing of the sixteenth-century Reformation, based on thinkers such as Menno Simons or Balthasar Hubmaier.

Analogy of being (*analogia entis*)

The theory, especially associated with Thomas Aquinas, that there exists a correspondence or analogy between the created order and God, as a result of the divine creatorship. The idea gives theoretical justification to the practice of drawing conclusions from the known objects and relationships of the natural order concerning God.

Analogy of faith (*analogia fidei*)

The theory, especially associated with Karl Barth, which holds that any correspondence between the created order and God is only established on the basis of the self-revelation of God.

Anthropomorphism

The tendency to ascribe human features (such as hands or arms) or other human characteristics to God.

Antiochene School

A patristic school of thought, especially associated with the city of Antioch in modern-day Turkey, noted for its Christology (which placed emphasis upon the humanity of Christ) and its method of biblical interpretation (which employed literal methods of exegesis). A rival approach in both areas was associated with Alexandria.

antiPelagian writings

The writings of Augustine relating to the Pelagian controversy, in which he defended his views on grace and justification. *See* "Pelagianism."

Apocalyptic

A type of writing or religious outlook in general which focuses on the last things and the end of the world, often taking the form of visions with complex symbolism. The book of Daniel (Old Testament) and Revelation (New Testament) are examples of this type of writing.

Apologetics

The area of Christian theology which focuses on the defense of the Christian faith, particularly through the rational justification of Christian belief and doctrines.

Apophatic

A term used to refer to a particular style of theology, which stressed that God cannot be known in terms of human categories. "Apophatic" (which derives from the Greek *apophasis*, "negation" or "denial") approaches to theology are especially associated with the monastic tradition of the Eastern Orthodox church.

Apophthegmata

The term used to refer to the collections of monastic writings often known as the "Sayings of the Desert Fathers." The writings often take the form of brief and pointed sayings, reflecting the concise and practical guidance typical of these writers.

Apostolic era

The period of the Christian church, regarded as definitive by many, bounded by the resurrection of Jesus Christ (*c*.AD 35) and the death of the last apostle (*c*.AD 90?). The ideas and practices of this period were widely regarded as normative, at least in some sense or to some degree, in many church circles.

Appropriation

A term relating to the doctrine of the Trinity, which affirms that while all three persons of the Trinity are active in all the outward actions of the Trinity, it is appropriate to think of those actions as being the particular work of one of the persons. Thus it is appropriate to think of creation as the work of the Father, or redemption as the work of the Son, despite the fact that all three persons are present and active in both these works.

Arianism

A major early Christological heresy, which treated Jesus Christ as the supreme of God's creatures, and denied his divine status. The Arian controversy was of major importance in the development of Christology during the fourth century.

Asceticism

A term used to refer to the wide variety of forms of self-discipline used by Christians to deepen their knowledge of and commitment to God. The terms derives from the Greek term *askesis* ("discipline").

Atonement

An English term originally coined by William Tyndale to translate the Latin term *reconciliatio*, which has since come to have the developed meaning of "the work of Christ" or "the benefits of Christ gained for believers by his death and resurrection."

Barthian

An adjective used to describe the theological outlook of the Swiss theologian Karl Barth (1886–1968), and noted chiefly for its emphasis upon the priority of revelation and its focus upon Jesus Christ. The terms "neo-Orthodoxy" and "dialectical theology" are also used in this connection.

Beatific Vision

A term used, especially in Roman Catholic theology, to refer to the full vision of God, which is allowed only to the elect after death. However, some writers, including Thomas Aquinas, taught that certain favored individuals – such as Moses and Paul – were allowed this vision in the present life.

Calvinism

An ambiguous term, used with two quite distinct meanings. First, it refers to the religious ideas of religious bodies (such as the Reformed church) and individuals (such as Theodore Beza) who were profoundly influenced by John Calvin, or by documents written by him. Second, it refers to the religious ideas of John Calvin himself. Although the first sense is by far the more common, there is a growing recognition that the term is misleading.

Cappadocian Fathers

A term used to refer collectively to three major Greek-speaking writers of the patristic period: Basil of Caesarea, Gregory of Nazianzen and Gregory of Nyssa, all of whom date from the late fourth century. "Cappadocia" designates an area in Asia Minor (modern-day Turkey), in which these writers were based.

Cartesianism

The philosophical outlook especially associated with René Descartes (1596–1650), particularly in relation to its emphasis on the separation of the knower from the known, and its insis-

tence that the existence of the individual thinking self is the proper starting point for philosophical reflection.

Catechism
A popular manual of Christian doctrine, usually in the form of question and answer, intended
for religious instruction.

Catharsis
The process of cleansing or purification by which the individual is freed from obstacles to spiritual growth and development.

Catholic
An adjective which is used both to refer to the universality of the church in space and time,
and also to a particular church body (sometime also known as the Roman Catholic Church)
which lays emphasis upon this point.

Chalcedonian definition
The formal declaration at the Council of Chalcedon that Jesus Christ was to be regarded as
having two natures, one human and one divine.

Charisma, charismatic
A set of terms especially associated with the gifts of the Holy Spirit. In medieval theology, the
term "charisma" is used to designate a spiritual gift, conferred upon individuals by the grace
of God. Since the early twentieth century, the term "charismatic" has come to refer to styles
of theology and worship which place particular emphasis upon the immediate presence and
experience of the Holy Spirit.

Charismatic Movement
A form of Christianity which places particular emphasis upon the personal experience of the
Holy Spirit in the life of the individual and community, often associated with various "charis-
matic" phenomena, such as speaking in tongues.

Christology
The section of Christian theology dealing with the identity of Jesus Christ, particularly the
question of the relation of his human and divine natures.

Circumincession
See Perichoresis.

Conciliarism
An understanding of ecclesiastical or theological authority which places an emphasis on the
role of ecumenical councils.

Confession
Although the term refers primarily to the admission to sin, it acquired a rather different technical sense in the sixteenth century – that of a document which embodies the principles of
faith of a Protestant church, such as the Lutheran Augsburg Confession (1530) embodies the
ideas of early Lutheranism, and the Reformed First Helvetic Confession (1536).

Consubstantial
A Latin term, deriving from the Greek term *homoousios*, literally meaning "of the same substance." The term is used to affirm the full divinity of Jesus Christ, particularly in opposition to Arianism.

Consubstantiation
A term used to refer to the theory of the real presence, especially associated with Martin Luther, which holds that the substance of the eucharistic bread and wine are given together with the substance of the body and blood of Christ.

Contemplation
A form of prayer, distinguished from meditation, in which the individual avoids or minimizes the use of words or images in order to experience the presence of God directly.

Creed
A formal definition or summary of the Christian faith, held in common by all Christians. The most important are those generally known as the "Apostles' Creed" and the "Nicene Creed."

Dark Night of the Soul
A phrase especially associated with John of the Cross, referring to the manner in which the soul is drawn closer to God. John distinguishes an "active" night (in which the believer actively works to draw nearer to God) and a "passive" night, in which God is active and the believer passive (p. 106).

Deism
A term used to refer to the views of a group of English writers, especially during the seventeenth century, the rationalism of which anticipated many of the ideas of the Enlightenment. The term is often used to refer to a view of God which recognizes the divine creatorship, yet which rejects the notion of a continuing divine involvement with the world.

Detachment
The cultivation of a habit of mind in which the individual aims to abandon dependence upon worldly objects, passions, or concerns. This is not intended to imply that these worldly things are evil; rather, the point being made is that they have the ability to enslave individuals if they are not approached with the right attitude. Detachment is about fostering a sense of independence from the world, so that it may be enjoyed without becoming a barrier between the individual and God.

Devotio Moderna
A school of thought which developed in the Netherlands in the fourteenth century, and is especially associated with Geert Groote (1340–84) and Thomas à Kempis (1380–1471), which placed an emphasis on the imitation of the humanity of Christ. The *Imitation of Christ* is the best-known work emanating from this school.

Dialectical Theology
A term used to refer to the early views of the Swiss theologian Karl Barth (1886–1968), which emphasized the "dialectic" between God and humanity.

Docetism
An early Christological heresy, which treated Jesus Christ as a purely divine being who only had the "appearance" of being human.

Donatism
A movement, centering upon Roman North Africa in the fourth century, which developed a rigorist view of the church and sacraments.

Doxology
A form of praise, usually especially associated with formal Christian worship. A "doxological" approach to theology stresses the importance of praise and worship in theological reflection.

Ebionitism
An early Christological heresy, which treated Jesus Christ as a purely human figure, although recognizing that he was endowed with particular charismatic gifts which distinguished him from other humans.

Ecclesiology
The section of Christian theology dealing with the theory of the church.

Enlightenment, The
A term used since the nineteenth century to refer to the emphasis upon human reason and autonomy, characteristic of much of western European and North American thought during the eighteenth century.

Eschatology
The section of Christian theology dealing with the "end things," especially the ideas of resurrection, hell, and eternal life.

Eucharist
The term used in the present volume to refer to the sacrament variously known as "the mass," "the Lord's Supper," and "holy communion."

Evangelical
A term initially used to refer to reforming movements, especially in Germany and Switzerland, in the 1510s and 1520s, but now used of a movement, especially in English-language theology, which places especial emphasis upon the supreme authority of Scripture and the atoning death of Christ.

Exegesis
The science of textual interpretation, usually referring specifically to the Bible. The term "biblical exegesis" basically means "the process of interpreting the Bible." The specific techniques employed in the exegesis of Scripture are usually referred to as "hermeneutics."

Exemplarism
A particular approach to the atonement, which stresses the moral or religious example set to believers by Jesus Christ.

Fathers
An alternative term for "patristic writers."

Feminism
A movement in western theology since the 1960s, which lays particular emphasis upon the importance of "women's experience," and has directed criticism against the patriarchalism of Christianity.

Fideism
An understanding of Christian theology which refuses to accept the need for (or sometimes the possibility of) criticism or evaluation from sources outside the Christian faith itself.

Five Ways, The
A standard term for the five "arguments for the existence of God" associated with Thomas Aquinas.

Fourth Gospel
A term used to refer to the Gospel according to John. The term highlights the distinctive literary and theological character of this gospel, which sets it apart from the common structures of the first three gospels, usually known as the "Synoptic Gospels."

Fundamentalism
A form of American Protestant Christianity, which lays especial emphasis upon the authority of an inerrant Bible.

Hermeneutics
The principles underlying the interpretation, or exegesis, of a text, particularly of Scripture, particularly in relation to its present-day application.

Hesychasm
A tradition, especially associated with the eastern church, which places considerable emphasis upon the idea of "inner quietness" (Greek: *hesychia*) as a means of achieving a vision of God. It is particularly associated with writers such as Simeon the New Theologian and Gregory Palamas.

Historical Jesus
A term used, especially during the nineteenth century, to refer to the historical person of Jesus of Nazareth, as opposed to the Christian interpretation of that person, especially as presented in the New Testament and the creeds.

Historico-Critical Method
An approach to historical texts, including the Bible, which argues that only proper meaning must be determined on the basis of the specific historical conditions under which it was written.

History of Religions School
The approach to religious history, and Christian origins in particular, which treats Old and New Testament developments as responses to encounters with other religions, such as Gnosticism.

Homoousion
A Greek term, literally meaning "of the same substance," which came to be used extensively during the fourth century to designate the mainline Christological belief that Jesus Christ was

"of the same substance of God." The term was polemical, being directed against the Arian view that Christ was "of similar substance (*homoiousios*)" to God. *See also* "Consubstantial."

Humanism
In the strict sense of the word, an intellectual movement linked with the European Renaissance. At the heart of the movement lay, not (as the modern sense of the word might suggest) a set of secular or secularizing ideas, but a new interest in the cultural achievements of antiquity. These were seen as a major resource for the renewal of European culture and Christianity during the period of the Renaissance.

Hypostatic union
The doctrine of the union of divine and human natures in Jesus Christ, without confusion of their respective substances.

Icons
Sacred pictures, particularly of Jesus, which play a significant role in Orthodox spirituality as "windows for the divine" (p. 60).

Ideology
A group of beliefs and values, usually secular, which govern the actions and outlooks of a society or group of people.

Ignatian spirituality
A loose term used to refer to the approach to spirituality associated with Ignatius Loyola (1491–1556), based on his *Spiritual Exercises* (p. 160).

Incarnation
A term used to refer to the assumption of human nature by God, in the person of Jesus Christ. The term "incarnationalism" is often used to refer to theological approaches which lay especial emphasis upon God's becoming human.

Jesus Prayer
A prayer which has the basic form "Lord Jesus Christ, Son of God, have mercy on me." This can be seen as an adaptation of the words spoken to Jesus by the blind man outside Jericho (Luke 18:38). The prayer is widely used in Orthodox spirituality, often accompanied by certain physical postures, such as specific patterns of breathing.

Justification by Faith, Doctrine of
The section of Christian theology dealing with how the individual sinner is able to enter into fellowship with God. The doctrine was to prove to be of major significance at the time of the Reformation.

Kenoticism
A form of Christology which lays emphasis upon Christ's "laying aside" of certain divine attributes in the incarnation, or his "emptying himself" of at least some divine attributes, especially omniscience or omnipotence.

Kerygma
A term used, especially by Rudolf Bultmann (1884–1976) and his followers, to refer to the essential message or proclamation of the New Testament concerning the significance of Jesus Christ.

Liberal Protestantism
A movement, especially associated with nineteenth-century Germany, which stressed the continuity between religion and culture, flourishing between the time of F. D. E. Schleiermacher and Paul Tillich.

Liberation Theology
Although this term designates any theological movement laying emphasis upon the liberating impact of the gospel, the term has come to refer to a movement which developed in Latin America in the late 1960s, which stressed the role of political action and orientated itself towards the goal of political liberation from poverty and oppression.

Liturgy
The written text and set forms of public services, especially of the eucharist. In the Greek Orthodox church, the word "Liturgy" often means "the [liturgy of] the eucharist."

Logos
A Greek term meaning "word," which played a crucial role in the development of patristic Christology. Jesus Christ was recognized as the "word of God"; the question concerned the implications of this recognition, and especially the way in which the divine "logos" in Jesus Christ related to his human nature.

Lutheranism
The religious ideas associated with Martin Luther, particularly as expressed in the Lesser Catechism (1529) and the Augsburg Confession (1530).

Manicheism
A strongly fatalist position associated with the Manichees, to which Augustine of Hippo attached himself during his early period. A distinction is drawn between two different divinities, one of which is regarded as evil, and the other good. Evil is thus seen as the direct result of the influence of the evil god.

Meditation
A form of prayer, distinguished from contemplation, in which the mind uses images (such as those provided by Scripture) as a means for focusing on God.

Modalism
A Trinitarian heresy, which treats the three persons of the Trinity as different "modes" of the Godhead. A typical modalist approach is to regard God as active as Father in creation, as Son in redemption, and as Spirit in sanctification.

Monophysitism
The doctrine that there is only one nature in Christ, which is divine (from the Greek words *monos*, "only one," and *physis*, "nature"). This view differed from the orthodox view, upheld by the Council of Chalcedon (451), that Christ had two natures, one divine and one human.

Mysticism
A multifaceted term, which can bear a variety of meanings. In its most importance sense, the terms refers to the union with God which is seen as the ultimate goal of the Christian life. This union is not to be thought of in rational or intellectual terms, but more in terms of a direct consciousness or experience of God.

Neo-Orthodoxy
A term used to designate the general position of Karl Barth (1886–1968), especially the manner in which he drew upon the theological concerns of the period of Reformed Orthodoxy.

Ontological Argument
A term used to refer to the type of argument for the existence of God especially associated with the scholastic theologian Anselm of Canterbury.

Orthodoxy
A term used in a number of senses, of which the following are the most important: Orthodoxy in the sense of "right belief," as opposed to heresy; Orthodoxy in the sense of the forms of Christianity which are dominant in Russia and Greece; Orthodoxy in the sense of a movement within Protestantism, especially in the late sixteenth and early seventeenth century, which laid emphasis upon need for doctrinal definition.

Parousia
A Greek term, which literally means "coming" or "arrival," used to refer to the second coming of Christ. The notion of the *parousia* is an important aspect of Christian understandings of the "last things."

Patripassianism
A theological heresy, which arose during the third century, associated with writers such as Noetus, Praxeas and Sabellius, focusing on the belief that the Father suffered as the Son. In other words, the suffering of Christ on the cross is to be regarded as the suffering of the Father. According to these writers, the only distinction within the Godhead was a succession of modes or operations, so that Father, Son, and Spirit were just different modes of being, or expressions of the same basic divine entity.

Patristic
An adjective used to refer to the first centuries in the history of the church, following the writing of the New Testament (the "patristic period"), or thinkers writing during this period (the "patristic writers"). For many writers, the period thus designated seems to be *c.*100–451 (in other words, the period between the completion of the last of the New Testament writings and the landmark Council of Chalcedon).

Pelagianism
An understanding of how humans are able to merit their salvation which is diametrically opposed to that of Augustine of Hippo, placing considerable emphasis upon the role of human works and playing down the idea of divine grace.

Perichoresis
A term relating to the doctrine of the Trinity, often also referred to by the Latin term *circumincessio*. The basic notion is that all three persons of the Trinity mutually share in the life of the others, so that none is isolated or detached from the actions of the others.

Philokalia
A Greek term (literally meaning "a love of that which is beautiful"), which is generally used to refer to two anthologies of Greek spiritual works: extracts from the works of Origen, or the collection of writings assembled by Macarius of Corinth and Nicodemus of the Holy Mountain in the eighteenth century.

Pietism
An approach to Christianity, especially associated with German writers in the seventeenth century, which places an emphasis upon the personal appropriation of faith, and the need for holiness in Christian living. The movement is perhaps best known within the English-language world in the form of Methodism.

Postliberalism
A theological movement, especially associated with Duke University and Yale Divinity School in the 1980s, which criticized the liberal reliance upon human experience, and reclaimed the notion of community tradition as a controlling influence in theology.

Postmodernism
A general cultural development, especially in North America, which resulted from the general collapse in confidence of the universal rational principles of the Enlightenment.

Praxis
A Greek term, literally meaning "action," adopted by Karl Marx to emphasize the importance of action in relation to thinking. This emphasis on "praxis" has had considerable impact within Latin American liberation theology.

Protestantism
A term used in the aftermath of the Diet of Speyer (1529) to designate those who "protested" against the practices and beliefs of the Roman Catholic church. Prior to 1529, such individuals and groups had referred to themselves as "evangelicals."

Quadriga
The Latin term used to refer to the "four-fold" interpretation of Scripture according to its literal, allegorical, tropological moral, and analogical senses.

Radical Reformation
A term used with increasing frequency to refer to the Anabaptist movement – in other words, the wing of the Reformation which went beyond what Luther and Zwingli envisaged, particularly in relation to the doctrine of the church.

Reformed
A term used to refer to a tradition of theology which draws inspiration from the writings of John Calvin (1510–64) and his successors. The term is now generally used in preference to "Calvinist."

Sabellianism
An early trinitarian heresy, which treated the three persons of the Trinity as different historical manifestations of the one God. It is generally regarded as a form of modalism.

Sacrament

A church service or rite which was held to have been instituted by Jesus Christ himself. Although Roman Catholic theology and church practice recognize seven such sacraments (baptism, confirmation, eucharist, marriage, ordination, penance, and unction), Protestant theologians generally argue that only two (baptism and eucharist) are to be found in the New Testament itself.

Salesian

Relating to Francis de Sales (1567–1622), or organizations which aim to base themselves on his ideas and values. The most important Salesian group is the Society of St Francis de Sales, founded in 1859.

Schism

A deliberate break with the unity of the church, condemned vigorously by influential writers of the early church, such as Cyprian and Augustine.

Scholasticism

A particular approach to Christian theology, associated especially with the Middle Ages, which lays emphasis upon the rational justification and systematic presentation of Christian theology.

Scripture Principle

The theory, especially associated with Reformed theologians, that the practices and beliefs of the church should be grounded in Scripture. Nothing that could not be demonstrated to be grounded in Scripture could be regarded as binding upon the believer. The phrase *sola scriptura*, "by Scripture alone," summarizes this principle.

Soteriology

The section of Christian theology dealing with the doctrine of salvation (Greek: *soteria*).

Synoptic Gospels

A term used to refer to the first three gospels (Matthew, Mark, and Luke). The term (derived from the Greek word *synopsis*, "summary") refers to the way in which the three gospels can be seen as providing similar "summaries" of the life, death, and resurrection of Jesus Christ.

Synoptic Problem

The scholarly question of how the three Synoptic Gospels relate to each other. Perhaps the most common approach to the relation of the three Synoptic Gospels is the "Two Source" theory, which claims that Matthew and Luke used Mark as a source, while also drawing upon a second source (usually known as "Q"). Other possibilities exist: for example, the Grisebach hypothesis, which treats Matthew as having been written first, followed by Luke and then Mark.

Theodicy

A term coined by Leibnitz to refer to a theoretical justification of the goodness of God in the face of the presence of evil in the world.

Theopaschitism

A disputed teaching, regarded by some as a heresy, which arose during the sixth century, associated with writers such as John Maxentius and the slogan "one of the Trinity was crucified." The formula can be interpreted in a perfectly orthodox sense and was defended as such by

Leontius of Byzantium. However, it was regarded as potentially misleading and confusing by more cautious writers, including Pope Hormisdas (died 523), and the formula gradually fell into disuse.

Theotokos

Literally, "the bearer of God." A Greek term used to refer to Mary, the mother of Jesus Christ, with the intention of reinforcing the central insight of the doctrine of the incarnation – that is, that Jesus Christ is none other than God. The term was extensively used by writers of the eastern church, especially around the time of the Nestorian controversy, to articulate both the divinity of Christ and the reality of the incarnation.

Transubstantiation

The doctrine according to which the bread and the wine are transformed into the body and blood of Christ in the eucharist, while retaining their outward appearance.

Trinity

The distinctively Christian doctrine of God, which reflects the complexity of the Christian experience of God. The doctrine is usually summarized in maxims such as "three persons, one God."

Two Natures, Doctrine of

A term generally used to refer to the doctrine of the two natures, human and divine, of Jesus Christ. Related terms include "Chalcedonian definition" and "hypostatic union."

Vulgate

The Latin translation of the Bible, largely deriving from Jerome, upon which medieval theology was largely based.

Zwinglianism

The term is used generally to refer to the thought of Huldrych Zwingli, but is often used to refer specifically to his views on the sacraments, especially on the "real presence" (which for Zwingli was more of a "real absence").

SOURCES OF CITATIONS

CHAPTER 1

p. 5
W. Paul Jones, "My Days with the Trappist Monks," *International Christian Digest* 1, no. 7 (September 1987), 24.

CHAPTER 2

p. 21
Philip of Harvengt, *de institutione clericorum*, 99; *Migne Patrologia Latina* 203.802A–B.

CHAPTER 3

p. 30
Thomas Aquinas, *Summa contra Gentiles*, II.2.2–4.

p. 31
Thomas à Kempis, *de imitatione Christi*, I, 1–2; in *De imitatione Christi libri quatuor*, ed. T. Lupo. Vatican City: Libreria Editrice Vaticana, 1982, 4.7–8.8.

p. 32
Thomas Merton, *Seeds of Contemplation*. Wheathampstead, Herts.: Anthony Clarke, 1972, 197–8.

p. 33
James I. Packer, "An Introduction to Systematic Spirituality," *Crux* 26, no. 1 (March 1990), 2–8, quote at p. 6.

CHAPTER 4

p. 40
Jean Bodin, *Universae naturae theatrum.* Frankfurt: Wechel, 1597, 10.

p. 40
Jonathan Edwards, *The Images of Divine Things*, ed. P. Millar. New Haven: Yale University Press, 1948, 61, 69, 109, 134.

p. 43
Pelagius, *Letter to Demetrias*, 16; in *Migne Patrologia Latina* 33:1110A–B.

p. 44
Augustine, *de natura et gratia* iii, 3 – iv, 4; in *Corpus Scriptorum Ecclesiasticorum Latinorum*, vol. 60, ed. C. F. Urba and J. Zycha (Vienna: Tempsky, 1913), 235–6.

p. 46
Alan of Lille, *contra hereticos*, I, 51. *Migne Patrologia Latina* 210.356B.

p. 47
Jean-Pierre de Caussade, *Self-Abandonment to the Divine Providence* I, 5; in Jean Pierre de Caussade, *L'abandon à la providence divine.* Paris: Desclée de Brouwer, 1966, 23.

p. 49
Irenaeus, *Demonstration of the Apostolic Preaching*, 6; in *Sources Chrétiennes*, vol. 62, ed. L. M. Froidevaux. Paris: Cerf, 1965, 39–40.

p. 52
Leonardo Boff, *Trinity and Society.* London: Burns & Oates, 1988, 159.

pp. 53–4
St Patrick's Breastplate, in *Hymns Ancient and Modern Revised.* London: Clowes, 1922, 129–31.

p. 54
"Hark the Herald Angels Sing," in *Hymns Ancient and Modem Revised.* London: Clowes, 1922, 42.

p. 56
Athanasius, *contra Arianos* I, 5.

p. 58
H. Denzinger (ed.), *Enchiridion Symbolorum* 24–25 edn. Barcelona: Herder, 1948, 70–1.

p. 58
Maurice F. Wiles, *The Making of Christian Doctrine.* Cambridge: Cambridge University Press, 1967, 106.

p. 60
Origen, *Homily on Ezekiel* VI, 6; in *Sources Chrétiennes*, vol. 352, ed. Marcel Borret. Paris: Editions du Cerf, 1989, 228.35–230.49.

p. 61
John of Damascus, *contra imaginum calumniatores* I, 16; in *Patristische Texte und Studien* vol. 17, ed. P. Bonifatius Kotter O.S.B. Berlin/New York: de Gruyter, 1979, 89.1–4; 92.90–91.

p. 63
Fulbert of Chartres, "Chorus novae Jerusalem," in *Hymns Ancient and Modern Revised*. London: Clowes, 1922, 100.

p. 65
Karl Barth, *Church Dogmatics*. 14 vols. Edinburgh: T. & T. Clark, 1936–75, IV/1, 222–3.

p. 68
Isaac Watts, "When I survey the wondrous cross," in *Hymns Ancient and Modern Revised*. London: Clowes, 1922, 85.

p. 68
Ignatius Loyola, *Spiritual Exercises*, 53; in *Obras Completas*. 2nd edn. Madrid: Biblioteca de autores cristianos, 1963, 211.

p. 71
"Lyra Davidica," in *Hymns Ancient and Modern Revised*. London: Clowes, 1922, 105–6.

p. 72
George Herbert, "Easter," in *Works*, ed. F. E. Hutchinson. Oxford: Clarendon Press, 1941, 41.

p. 73
"At the Burial of the Dead," *Book of Common Prayer*. London: Oxford University Press, 1969, 388–98.

p. 73
John Donne, "Divine Meditations, 10," in *John Donne: The Complete English Poems*, ed. A. J. Smith. Harmondsworth: Penguin, 1973, 313.

p. 78
Martin Luther King, "I see the Promised Land"; in *Martin Luther King: A Documentary*, ed. Flip Schulke. New York: Norton, 1976, 223.

p. 79
Bernard of Cluny, "Brief life is here our portion," in *Hymns Ancient and Modern Revised*. London: Clowes, 1922, 219.

p. 79
Bernard of Cluny, "Jerusalem the Golden," in *Hymns Ancient and Modern Revised*. London: Clowes, 1922, 222–3.

CHAPTER 5

p. 83
Augustine, *de utilitate credendi* III, 9; in *Oeuvres de Saint Augustin*, vol. 8, ed. J. Pegon. Paris: Desclée, 1951, 226–8.

p. 85
Guigo II, *Scala claustralium* xii, 13; *Migne Patrologia Latina* 184.482D.

p. 85
Gerard of Zutphen [= Geert Zerbott van Zutphen], *The Spiritual Ascent*. Translated by J. P. Arthur. London: Burns & Oates, 1908, 26. Translation slightly altered.

p. 86
Ignatius Loyola, *Spiritual Exercises*, 47–8; in *Obras Completas*. 2nd edn. Madrid: Biblioteca de autores cristianos, 1963, 209–10.

p. 87
Martin Luther, "A Simple Way to Pray," in *D. Martin Luthers Werke: Kritisch Gesamtausgabe*, vol. 38. Weimar: Böhlau, 1938, 358–75.

p. 88
For this, and other relevant citations from Charles Haddon Spurgeon, see Lewis A. Drummond, "Charles Haddon Spurgeon," in T. George and D. S. Dockery (eds), *Baptist Theologians*. Nashville, TN: Broadman, 1990, 267–88.

p. 89
Theodore of Mopsuestia, *Catechetical Homily* 15.20; in *Katechetische Homilien*, ed. Peter Bruns. 2 vols. Freiburg: Herder, 1994–5, vol. 1, 404.

p. 90
Blaise Pascal, *Pensées*, 148; in *Pensées*. Ed. Louis Lafuma. Paris: Editions du Seuil, 1962, 86.

p. 90
C. S. Lewis, "The Weight of Glory," in *Screwtape Proposes A Toast*. London: Collins, 1965, 97–8.

p. 92
Jonathan Edwards, "The Christian Pilgrim," in *Basic Writings*. Ed. O. E. Winslow. New York: New American Library, 1966, 136–7.

p. 94
Peter Abelard, "O what their joy and their glory must be," in *Hymns Ancient and Modern Revised*. London: Clowes, 1922, 226.

p. 94
Anselm of Canterbury, *Prayers and Meditations*. Harmondsworth: Penguin, 1973, 95.

p. 96
John Owen, "On the Mortification of Sin in Believers," in John Owen, *Works*, ed. W. H. Goold. 23 vols. Edinburgh: Johnstone & Hunter, 1850–5, vol. 3, 17.

p. 98
Origen, *Homily on Leviticus*, 12; in *Sources Chrétiennes*, vol. 287, ed. M. Borret. Paris: Cerf, 1981, 178.5–21.

p. 100
Anselm of Canterbury, *Liber Anselmi de humanis moribus*, 92–6; in R. W.

Southern and F. S. Schmitt (eds), *Memorials of St Anselm*. London: British Academy, 1969, 78–9.

p. 100
Angelus Silesius, *Der cherubinischer Wandersmann*, I.61–3; in *Sämtliche poetische Werke*. 3 vols. Munich: Allgemeine Verlagsanstalt, 1924, vol. 3, 19–20. Scheffler's verse is difficult to translate while retaining its rhyme and rhythm; a prose translation is offered here, which conveys the main religious themes.

p. 101
Nicolas Ludwig von Zinzendorf, *Nine Public Lectures On Important Subjects in Religion*. Iowa City: University of Iowa Press, 1973, 40.

p. 102
Cassian, *Institutes* viii, 18; in *Institutiones cénobitiques*. Ed. Jean-Claude Guy. Sources chrétiennes 109. Paris: Editions du Cerf, 1965, 358.

p. 102
Origen, *Homilies on Joshua*, 12; *Migne Patrologia Graeca* 12.786B–C.

p. 103
Rupert of Deutz, *de trinitate et operibus eius*, in *Migne Patrologia Latina* 167.1017.

p. 105
M. Walshe (ed.), *Meister Eckhart: German Sermons and Treatises*. 2 vols. London: Watkins, 1979–81, vol. 1, 17.

p. 107
Arthur Michael Ramsey, *Be Still and Know*. London: Collins, 1982, 83–4.

p. 108
Gregory of Sinai, *Instructions to Hesychasts*, 1–2.

CHAPTER 6

p. 111
Paul Elmer More, *Pages from an Oxford Diary*. Princeton: Princeton University Press, 1937, 18.

p. 112
Heidelberg Catechism, Questions 96–98; in E. F. K. Müller (ed.), *Die Bekenntnisschriften der reformierten Kirche*. Leipzig: Böhme, 1903, 710.8–27.

p. 114
Hugh of St Victor, *de tribus diebus* 4; in J. P. Migne, *Patrologia Latina* 125.814B–C.

p. 114
Confessio Gallicana, 1559, article 2; in E. F. K. Müller (ed.), *Die Bekenntnisschriften der reformierten Kirche*. Leipzig: Böhme, 1903, 221–2.

p. 114
Confessio Belgica, 1561, articles 2; in E. F. K. Müller (ed.), *Die Bekenntnisschriften der reformierten Kirche*. Leipzig: Böhme, 1903, 233.

p. 115
Macrobius, *Commentary on the Dream of Scipio*. New York: Columbia University Press, 1952, 142.

p. 116
Mary T. Clark (ed.), *An Aquinas Reader.* London: Hodder & Stoughton, 1972, 540–1.

p. 118
John Chrysostom, *On the Incomprehensibility of God*, 3.

p. 120
Cyril of Jerusalem, *First Address on the Mysteries*, 1–3; in *Sources Chrétiennes*, vol. 126, ed. A. Piédagnel and P. Paris. Paris: Cerf, 1966, 82.1–86.13.

p. 122
Huldrych Zwingli, *On Baptism*; in *Corpus Reformatorum: Huldreich Zwinglis sämtliche Werke*, vol. 91. Leipzig: Heinsius, 1927, 217.14–218.24.

p. 125
Susanna Wesley, "Devotional Journal," in Michael D. McMullen (ed.), *Hearts Aflame: Prayers of Susanna, John and Charles Wesley*. London: Triangle Books, 1995.

p. 131
Karl Barth, *The Göttingen Dogmatics*. Grand Rapids: Eerdmans, 1990, vol. 1, 31–2.

CHAPTER 7

p. 139
Francis de Sales, *Introduction à la vie dévoté*, ii, 7; Paris: Mame-Tours, 1939, 89.

p. 141
Gregory of Nyssa, *Commentary on the Beatitudes*, 3; Migne Patrologia Graeca 44. 1225C–1227B.

p. 144
Augustine, *Confessions* X.xxi.31–xxii.32; in Saint Augustine, *Confessions*, translated by Henry Chadwick. Oxford: Oxford University Press, 1991, 198–9.

p. 146
The Prayers and Meditations of St. Anselm, translated by Benedicta Ward. Harmondsworth: Penguin Books, 1973, 94–5. Copyright © Benedicta Ward 1973. Reproduced by permission of Penguin Books Ltd.

p. 149
Francis of Assisi, *Canticle of the Sun*, in H. Goad, *Greyfriars: The Story of St Francis and His Followers*. London: John Westhouse, 1947, 137–8.

p. 151
Hugh of Balma, *The Roads to Zion*, prologue, 5–7; in Francis Ruello and Jeanne Barbet, *Theologia Mystica*. 2 vols. Paris: Editions du Cerf, 1995, vol. 1, 130–2.

p. 154

Ludolf of Saxony, *Vita Jesu Christi Domini ac salvatoris nostri*. Paris: U. Gering and B. Rembolt, 1502, praefatio. Note that this edition uses a variant title: the more common title is *Vita Jesu Christi redemptoris nostri*.

p. 156

Julian of Norwich, *Revelations of Divine Love*, translated by Clifton Wolters. Harmondsworth: Penguin, 1966, 63–4. Copyright © Clifton Wolters 1958. Reproduced by permission of Penguin Books Ltd.

p. 158

Martin Luther, *The Freedom of a Christian*; in *D. Martin Luthers Werke: Kritische Gesamtausgabe*, vol. 7. Weimar: Böhlaus, 1897, 25–6.

p. 161

Ignatius Loyola, *Spiritual Exercises*, 55–61; in *Obras Completas*. 2nd edn. Madrid: Biblioteca de autores cristianos, 1963, 211–12.

p. 163

Teresa of Ávila, *Life*, 11; in *Obras de Santa Teresa de Jésus*, edited by P. Silvero de Santa Teresa. 12 vols. Burgos: Editorial Monte Carmelo, 1915–24, vol. 1, 77–8.

p. 166

John Wesley and Charles Wesley, *Hymns and Sacred Poems*. London: William Strahan, 1739, 117–19.

p. 169

John Henry Newman, "The Self-Wise Inquirer," in *Selection from the Parochial and Plain Sermons*. London: Rivingtons, 1878, 293–301.

p. 172

J. I. Packer, *Knowing God*. London: Hodder & Stoughton, 1973, 41.

The kindness of copyright holders in granting permission to use material is gratefully acknowledged by both author and publisher. Every effort has been made to ensure that copyright material has been properly sourced and acknowledged. Where specific forms of wording are required, these have been followed precisely. Any omissions or errors will be corrected in subsequent printings of this work.

FOR FURTHER READING

ANTHOLOGIES

Robin Baird-Smith, *Living Water: An Anthology of Letters of Direction*. Grand Rapids, MI: Eerdmans, 1988.

Fiona Bowie, *Beguine Spirituality: An Anthology*. London: SPCK, 1989.

Tony Castle, *The Perfection of Love: An Anthology from the Spiritual Writers*. London: Collins, 1986.

Oliver Davies and Fiona Bowie, *Celtic Christian Spirituality: An Anthology of Medieval and Modern Sources*. New York: Continuum, 1995.

Séan Dunne, *Something Understood: A Spiritual Anthology*. Dublin: Marino Books, 1995.

Louis Dupré and James Wiseman, *Light from Light: An Anthology of Christian Mysticism*. New York: Paulist, 1988.

David Fleming (ed.), *The Fire and the Cloud: An Anthology of Catholic Spirituality*. New York: Paulist, 1976.

Richard J. Foster and James Bryan Smith (eds), *Devotional Classics: Selected Readings for Individuals and Groups*. San Francisco: HarperCollins, 1990.

John Garvey (ed.), *Modern Spirituality: An Anthology*. Springfield, IL: Templegate, 1985.

Paul Harris, *The Fire of Silence and Stillness: An Anthology of Quotations for the Spiritual Journey*. Springfield, IL: Templegate Publishers, 1996.

Paul de Jaegher (ed.), *An Anthology of Christian Mysticism*. Springfield, IL: Templegate, 1977.

John R. Tyson, *Invitation to Christian Spirituality: An Ecumenical Anthology*. New York: Oxford University Press, 1999.

Robert Van de Weyer, *Roots of Faith: An Anthology of Early Christian Spirituality to Contemplate and Treasure*. Grand Rapids, MI: Eerdmans, 1997.

GENERAL WORKS ON SPIRITUALITY

Jordan Aumann, *Spiritual Theology*. London: Sheed & Ward, 1980.

Michael Cox, *A Handbook of Christian Spirituality*. San Francisco: Harper & Row, 1985.

Lawrence S. Cunningham and Keith J. Egan, *Christian Spirituality: Themes from the Tradition*. New York: Paulist, 1996.

Michael Downey (ed.), *The New Dictionary of Christian Spirituality*. Collegeville, MN: Liturgical Press, 1993.

Louis Dupré and Don E. Saliers in collaboration with John Meyndorff (eds), *Christian Spirituality: Post-Reformation and Modern*. New York: Crossroad, 1989.

Bradley Hanson (ed.), *Modern Christian Spirituality: Methodological and Historical Essays*. Atlanta, GA: Scholars Press, 1990.

Urban T. Holmes, *A History of Christian Spirituality*. New York: Seabury Press, 1981.

Bradley C. Holt, *Thirsty for God: A Brief History of Christian Spirituality*. Minneapolis: Augsburg, 1993.

Grace M. Jantzen, *Power, Gender and Christian Mysticism*. Cambridge: Cambridge University Press, 1995.

Cheslyn Jones, Geoffrey Wainwright and Edward Yarnold (eds), *The Study of Spirituality*. London: SPCK, 1986.

John Macquarrie, *Paths in Spirituality*, 2nd edn. Harrisburg: Morehouse, 1992.

Bernard McGinn, *The Presence of God*, 4 vols. New York: Crossroads, 1991– .

Bernard McGinn and John Meyendorff (eds), *Christian Spirituality: Origins to the Twelfth Century*. New York: Crossroad, 1985.

Jill Raitt with Bernard McGinn and John Meyendorff (eds), *Christian Spirituality: High Middle Ages and Reformation*. New York: Crossroad, 1987.

William Reiser, *Looking for a God to Pray To: Christian Spirituality in Transition*. New York: Paulist, 1994.

Philip Sheldrake, *Images of Holiness: Explorations in Contemporary Spirituality*. Notre Dame, IN: Ave Maria, 1988.

Philip Sheldrake, *Spirituality and History: Questions of Interpretation and Method*. London: SPCK, 1995.

William Stringfellow, *The Politics of Spirituality*. Philadelphia: Westminster Press, 1984.

Gordon Wakefield (ed.), *A Dictionary of Christian Spirituality*. London: SCM Press, 1983.

Rowan Williams, *The Wound of Knowledge: Christian Spirituality from the New Testament to St John of the Cross*. London: DLT, 1991.

Richard Woods, *Christian Spirituality: God's Presence through the Ages*. Allen, TX: Christian Classics, 1996.

MAJOR STUDIES OF INDIVIDUAL WRITERS OR SCHOOLS

Benedict Ashley, *Spiritual Direction in the Dominican Tradition*. New York: Paulist Press, 1995.

Clarissa Atkinson, *Mystic and Pilgrim: The Book and World of Margery Kempe*. Ithaca, NY: Cornell University Press, 1983.

Francis Beer, *Women and Religious Experience in the Middle Ages*. Rochester, NY: Boydell Press, 1992.

Louis Bouyer, *Women Mystics*. San Francisco: Ignatius Press, 1993.

Douglas Burton-Christie, *The Word in the Desert: Scripture and the Quest for Holiness in Early Christian Monasticism*. New York: Oxford University Press, 1993.

Richard A. Cashen, *Solitude in the Thought of Thomas Merton*. Kalamazoo: Cistercian Publications, 1981.

P. Franklin Chambers, *Juliana of Norwich*. New York: Harper, 1955.

Oliver Davies, *God Within: The Mystical Tradition of Northern Europe*. New York: Paulist Press, 1988.

Joann Wolski Conn, *Spirituality and Christian Maturity*. New York: Paulist Press, 1989.

Daniel Dombroski, *St John of the Cross: An Appreciation*. Albany, NY: SUNY Press, 1992.

Elizabeth A. Dreyer, *Earth Crammed with Heaven: A Spirituality of Everyday Life*. New York: Paulist Press, 1994.

Sabina Flanagan, *Hildegard of Bingen: A Visionary Life*, 2nd edn. London: Routledge, 1998.

Richard J. Foster, *A Celebration of Discipline*. New York: Harper & Row, 1978.

Mary Frohlich, *The Intersubjectivity of the Mystic: A Study of Theresa of Avila's Interior Castle*. Atlanta, GA: Scholars Press, 1993.

Thomas M. Gannon and George W. Traub, *The Desert and the City: An Interpretation of the History of Christian Spirituality*. Chicago: Loyola University Press, 1984.

George Ganss, *Ignatius of Loyola: Exercises and Selected Works*. New York: Paulist, 1991.

David K. Gillett, *Trust and Obey: Explorations in Evangelical Spirituality*. London: Darton, Longman and Todd, 1993.

James M. Gordon, *Evangelical Spirituality from the Wesleys to John Stott*. London: SPCK, 1991.

Francis L. Gross and Toni Prior Gross, *The Making of a Mystic: Seasons in the Life of Teresa of Ávila*, Albany, NY: SUNY Press, 1993.

Ann Hamlin, *Celtic Monasticism*. New York: Seabury, 1981.

Ursula King, *Spirit and Fire: The Life and Vision of Teilhard de Chardin*. Maryknoll, NY: Orbis, 1996.

Gerard W. Hughes, *God of Surprises*. London: DLT, 1987.

H. Trevor Hughes, *The Piety of Jeremy Taylor*. London: Macmillan, 1960.

Thomas Keating, *Intimacy with God*. New York: Crossroad, 1994.

Ian Ker, *Healing the Wound of Humanity: The Spirituality of John Henry Newman*. London: DLT, 1993.

David Knowles, *The English Mystical Tradition*. New York: Harper, 1961.

Ernest Kurtz and Katherine Ketcham, *The Spirituality of Imperfection*. New York: Bantam, 1992.

Thomas A. Langford, *Practical Divinity: Theology in the Wesleyan Tradition*. Nashville, TN: Abingdon Press, 1983.

Jean Leclerc, *Bernard of Clairvaux and the Cistercian Spirit*. Kalamazoo: Cisterian Publications, 1976.

Jean Leclerc, *The Love of Learning and the Desire for God: A Study of Monastic Culture*, 3rd edn. New York: Fordham University Press, 1978.

Robin Bruce Lockhart, *Halfway to Heaven: The Hidden Life of the Sublime Carthusians*. New York: Vanguard, 1985.

Andrew Louth, *The Christian Mystical Tradition from Plato to Denys*. Oxford: Oxford University Press, 1981.

Andrew Louth, *Discerning the Mystery: An Essay on the Nature of Theology*. Oxford: Clarendon Press, 1983.

Andrew Louth, *The Wilderness of God*. London: DLT, 1992.

Robin Maas and Gabriel O'Donnell (eds), *Spiritual Traditions for the Contemporary Church*. Nashville, TN: Abingdon, 1990.

Margeret R. Miles, *Practicing Christianity: Critical Perspectives for an Embodied Spirituality*. New York: Crossroad, 1988.

John R. H. Moorman, *The Anglican Spiritual Tradition*. London: DLT, 1983.

Saskia Murk-Jansen, *Brides in the Desert: The Spirituality of the Beguines*. London: DLT, 1998.

Nelson Pike, *Mystic Union: An Essay in the Phenomenology of Mysticism*. Ithaca, NY: Cornell University Press, 1992.

R. R. Post, *The Modern Devotion: Confrontation with Reformation and Humanism*. Leiden: E. J. Brill, 1968.

Walter Principe, *Thomas Aquinas' Spirituality*. Toronto: Pontifical Institute, 1984.

Lucien Richard, *The Spirituality of John Calvin*. Atlanta: John Knox Press, 1974.

Frank Senn (ed.), *Protestant Spiritual Traditions*. New York: Paulist, 1986.

Jon Sobrino, *Spirituality of Liberation: Toward Political Holiness*. Maryknoll, NY: Orbis, 1987.

Tomas Spidlik, *The Spirituality of the Christian East*. Kalamazoo: Cistercian Publications, 1986.

Aelred Squire, *Asking the Fathers*. London: SPCK, 1973.

Columba Stewart, OSB, *Prayer and Community: The Benedictine Tradition*. London: DLT, 1998.

Dennis E. Tamburello, *Union with Christ: John Calvin and the Mysticism of St. Bernard*. St Louis, KY: Westminster John Knox Press, 1994.

Martin Thornton, *English Spirituality: An Outline of Ascetical Theology according to the English Pastoral Tradition*. London: SPCK, 1963.

Esther de Waal, *The Way of Simplicity: The Cistercian Tradition*. London: DLT, 1998.

Helen Waddell, *The Desert Fathers*. London: Constable, 1936.

Jared Wicks, *Luther and his Spiritual Legacy*. Wilmington, DL: Michael Glazier, 1983.

Richard Woods, OP, *Mysticism and Prophecy: The Dominican Tradition*. London: DLT, 1998.

INDEX